Praise for WOBBLIES & Zapatistas

"There's no doubt that we've lost much of our history. It's also very clear that those in power in this country like it that way. Here's a book that shows us why. It demonstrates not only that another world is possible, but that it already exists, has existed, and shows an endless potential to burst through the artificial walls and divisions that currently imprison us. An exquisite contribution to the literature of human freedom, and coming not a moment too soon."

—**DAVID GRAEBER**, Author of *Fragments of an Anarchist Anthropology* and *Direct Action: an Ethnography*

"With the patient and intelligent prodding of Andrej Grubacic, Staughton Lynd, preeminent historian/scholar/revolutionary, takes us on a calm, leisurely walk through the annals of history and shows us what it means to be a human being. From the Zapatista movement in San Cristóbal, Chiapas to the steel mills of rural Ohio, he reminds us that when it's all over, said and done, what truly matters the most is our willingness to reach out and love somebody."

—**BOMANI SHAKUR A.K.A. KEITH LAMAR**, Death Row, Ohio State Penitentiary

"In these desperate, often tragic, times, we look backward, forward, even to our dreams to be able to keep imagining a world in which justice may be part of more people's lives. We look to lives lived before ours, to stories and their meanings, to strategies culled from the worlds of politics or ancient wisdoms. We look in Africa,

Asia, Latin America, Europe, and here in the United States. We are willing to entertain any new idea or revamped strategy.

Staughton Lynd's life and work put him in a unique position to seek out someone like Grubacic, ask the pertinent questions, and tell the meaningful stories. Grubacic's experience perfectly compliments Lynd's. Here we have the best of a non-dogmatic Marxism listening to a most creative and humane anarchism. But this book is never weighted down by unforgiving theory. Just the opposite: it is a series of conversations where the reader feels fully present. It provides a marvelous framework for enriching the conversation that's never really stopped: about how we may make this world a better place.

Wobblies and Zapatistas: Marxism, Anarchism and Radical History is an absolute must read for anyone battered by the 1989-1990 defeat of what many called 'real socialism.' Here is a new and vibrant starting point for thought and action—and a great read as well."

—**MARGARET RANDALL**, Author of *Sandino's Daughters*, *When I Look Into the Mirror and See You*, and *Narrative of Power*, among other books.

"It is rare that words in a conversation approach the likeness of something truly new—such is the case of the friendly and productive dance of anarchist and socialist ideas in Andrej Grubačić's new book: Wobblies and Zapatistas, book of conversations between Andrej Grubačić and Staughton Lynd. It is a rich piece of literature, clearly benefiting from the lives and experiences of these two extraordinary human beings, and an important contribution to the continuing synthesis of revolutionary ideas. Exploring questions of participatory experiments, worker democracy, solidarity unionism, civil disobedience, organizing, and the role of theory and organic intellectuals, Wobblies and Zapatistas delves into the political questions of the twenty-first century with the utmost clarity, reflection, and insight. I'd recommend Conversations to all young people interested in building a movement towards a better, more democratic world."

—**BRIAN KELLY**, Students for a Democratic Society & Student Environmental Action Coalition

"Young organizers today are faced with a rapidly changing, complex world. Many of us are building new political compasses with which to navigate such a turbulent landscape. Conversations between Lynd and Grubacic are a perfect medium to weave a narrative of social movements that roots us in history. Through rich storytelling, debate, and political analysis, this book is about more than Wobblies and Zapatistas. It is a window into wildcat strikes in Youngstown OH, the civil war in Spain, the streets of Seattle, mountains of Nicaragua, Israel and Palestine, and that's just the start. This is no romanticized history or mindless celebration of confrontation; this is a reflection on the lessons organizers can learn and carry with them to build a new world. It contains portraits of Ella Baker and Thomas Paine, thoughts on informal leadership from Saul Alinsky, and descriptions of the education of Myles Horton. The reader is treated to historical examples of interracial solidarity and movement building. We learn of songs sung in SNCC, of liberation theology and Anabaptists. We read stories of consensus decision-making in a Supermax prison, and Rosa Luxemburg's feelings on internationalism. Lynd calls for organizers who are 'long distance runners, not sprinters.' This book is a tool to help us go the distance."

—**JOSHUA KAHN RUSSELL**, Climate Activist, Author, and National Organizer with Energy Action Coalition, Rainforest Action Network, and the new Students for a Democratic Society

"Here, Staughton Lynd is a story teller, drawing from critical moments of popular movements over centuries and continents, as well as his own experiences as historian and activist. Together, he and Andrej Grubacic reflect on such key issues of perennial interest to those of us working to build a just, sustainable future as: Archbishop Romero's idea of accompaniment, evolving anarchist solutions to the challenges of democracy, the implications of global citizenship and the Zapatistas' changing views of economic and political power, with the goal of 'helping us to prioritize…to abandon unsuccessful experiments without condemning persons who undertook them on behalf of us all.' I missed more than one subway stop whilst transported to Chiapas, the Youngstown steel *mills, the fight for the 8-hour day in Chicago of the 1880's, the Freedom Schools in Mississippi and Norman Morrison's power-ful protest against the Vietnam war."*

Wobblies &Zapatistas

CONVERSATIONS ON ANARCHISM,
MARXISM AND RADICAL HISTORY

PM PRESS

Wobblies

Zapatistas

CONVERSATIONS ON ANARCHISM, MARXISM AND RADICAL HISTORY

STAUGHTON LYND & ANDREJ GRUBACIC

INTRODUCTION BY DENIS O'HEARN

WOBBLIES & Zapatistas:
CONVERSATIONS ON ANARCHISM, MARXISM AND RADICAL HISTORY
By Staughton Lynd & Andrej Grubacic

Copyright © 2008 Staughton Lynd & Andrej Grubacic
This edition copyright © 2008 PM Press
All Rights Reserved

Cover illustration by Roderick Constance © 2008 www.shadowshapes.com
Designed by Courtney Utt
Special thanks to Alice Lynd

Published by:
PM Press
PO Box 23912
Oakland, CA 94623
www.pmpress.org

ISBN: 978-1-60486-041-2
Library Of Congress Control Number: 2008931839

10 9 8 7 6 5 4 3

Printed in the USA on recycled paper, by the Employee Owners of Thomson-Shore
in Dexter, Michigan.
www.thomsonshore.com

TABLE OF CONTENTS

Acknowledgments

WE BOTH EXPRESS our thanks to Alice Lynd, who was given questions and responses in a variety of formats and somehow made out of them a single, internally-consistent manuscript.

Andrej Grubacic additionally thanks Kathy Wallerstein for advice and help with the text; and Michael Albert, Noam Chomsky, David Graeber, and Immanuel Wallerstein, who brought him to the United States and thus made it possible for us to meet each other.

Finally, we acknowledge our connection with one who went before: Paul Goodman, whose widow Sally Goodman kindly permitted us to quote from his *Collected Poems*.

ANDREJ GRUBACIC AND STAUGHTON LYND

Foreword, Forward!

WHEN MY COMPAÑERO Andrej Grubacic told me that he was having a conversation with Staughton Lynd it was one of those times I wanted to be the proverbial fly on the wall. Andrej is that anarchist who writes provocatively in *Zmag* and elsewhere. We've had our little spats about Marxism (he's not impressed) and Makhno (I'm not impressed). But he's generous and inquisitive and always on the lookout for interesting new ideas about how to live better in this world. I've been familiar with the name Staughton Lynd for many years, as has anyone with a fleeting knowledge of the U.S. left. His travels from SNCC organizer to war protestor to Yale Professor to ex-Yale Professor to community organizer to lawyer are the stuff of legend. I became personally acquainted with him after my own conversation with Andrej about my work with Irish political prisoners and my time living with the Zapatistas. Staughton read our interchange, contacted me, and very generously brought me into conversations he and Andrej were having with prisoners in the U.S.

Well, it turned out I didn't have to do a Gregor Samsa to listen in to Andrej's encuentro with Staughton, and neither do you, thanks to this wonderful book. The conversation is centered on the necessity of a dialogue between Marxism and anarchism but along the way we are treated to a veritable feast of stories and recollections about a remarkable life in struggle.

The conversation starts with Zapatismo, a good place for anyone to start these days if they are considering how a better world might be possible. I was delighted to see Staughton

Lynd thinking very similar things to myself after his time in Chiapas. This is not because I want some kind of glory by association but because Staughton is a man of good sense and if I read him saying things that I've been saying and thinking, then it gives me confidence that the old ticker is still working. A Zapatista told me that if I wanted to understand what they were doing I should read Mariategui, the Peruvian Marxist. When I picked up Mariategui's *Siete Ensayos de Interpretación de la Realidad Peruana*, it was right there, clear as could be: the problem of the Indian is the problem of land. A lot of trendy lefties including some famous academics had been flying into Chiapas and coming out to tell us that this was the first "cyber revolution" and that the Zapatistas were all about the new struggle for identity. It seemed to me like they weren't listening to Comandanta Ramona when she told us that she was a Zapatista because she wanted her friends to have food to eat and she didn't want so many of them to die of sickness or in childbirth and she wanted the children to have an education. Their immediate motivation for rising on January 1, 1994 was that NAFTA, which went into effect that day, had taken away the most important achievement of the Mexican revolution: rights of rural communities to communal lands (ejidos), which before NAFTA made up more than half of all Mexican land. The first thing the Zapatistas did after they occupied towns throughout Chiapas on that January day was not to set up cybernetworks (which they did) but to occupy lands that had been appropriated by the big ranchers and finqueros. Staughton picked up on this, too, and his friendly and respectful warnings to the current generation of global activists who have flown into Chiapas and flown back out talking about identity and rebellion are worth listening to. He worries about a "movement" that goes halfway around the world to the latest meeting of the WTO but fails to build a real movement in their own yard.

He worries, too, about a tendency he sees among some in the anarchist left to lash out reflexively against Marx and

Marxists. Staughton Lynd has always been a democrat…in the sense that we mean and not the electoral party sense… so we should listen to him when he says, "As a lifelong rebel against heavy-handed Marxist dogmatism I find myself defending Marx, and objecting to the so-called radicalism of one-weekend-a-year radicals who show up at a global confrontation and then talk about it for the rest of the year."

He reminds us that Subcomandante Marcos was originally a Marxist guerrillero (and professor) from the city. But in the end he was the right kind of Marxist guerrillero (and professor), because when he went into the jungle of Chiapas he kept his eyes and ears open. Instead of trying to teach Marxism-Leninism to the Mayans, he listened first. He learned that the best way to lead is by obeying. Many of us have been encouraged by the result of that openness, fragile as this experiment continues to be.

Staughton Lynd tells us that we need Marxism to understand the structure of society and anarchism to prefigure or anticipate a new society.

As he explains why he thinks so, you'll hear him tell wondrous stories about Wobblies, the Haymarket, union history, the Highlander Folk School, solidarity, SNCC and the Freedom Schools, Rosa Luxemburg, E. P. Thompson, Simone Weil, and Jean Gabin. And Norman Morrison. Some names we should never forget, and after you read this document you will know why we should all carry the name Norman Morrison in our hearts.

All of the stories are peppered with common sense. I won't note all of my favorites, as I don't want to steal Staughton's thunder, but one stood out for me. He describes accompaniment, a concept he got from Archbishop Romero of El Salvador, which means "to live amongst [the poor and marginalized] for a time, and to assist, if possible, in articulating and transmitting their collective experience." He tells how he grew up in an eighth floor apartment in the upper west side of New York City and it always "seemed a long way to the ground, to the world of ordinary people" (he exaggerates: clearly, his beloved nanny Mary Bohan brought that world up to him and I'd say she probably took him down into it, too). So, he insists, if he can succeed at accompaniment with such a background anyone can. He tells how easy it is.

"The key is to acquire a skill useful to poor and working persons. Armed with such a skill, just behave as a moderately decent human being and 'accompaniment' will be a piece of cake."

Staughton is right about how easy it is. I learned a bit about accompaniment in Chiapas, although I didn't know it was accompaniment at the time. I was attached to the Escuela Secundaria Rebelde Autónoma Zapatista "Primero de Enero" in Oventik. It is a sort of Zapatista teacher training college, although they don't have teachers and students, only promoters and alumni. There, I learned a tremendous amount about how to teach and why the things we have been doing in western universities fall seriously short of the real learning experiences they could be. Young Mayan teenagers—who had never been out of the mountains of southeastern Mexico, never flown in an airplane, whose Spanish language proficiencies were usually less than two or three years old—were able to discuss the international financial system with proficiency and understanding, and at a level far above anything I would attempt with my school-trained university students in Ireland or New York. The secret was that their knowledge was grounded in their own lives. If they set out to learn about poverty, they began by examining their own experiences of poverty. Then, they worked upward and outward to Chiapas, Mexico, and the global system. They spent more time outside of the classroom than in the classroom.

I spoke at length with the promotores about their philosophies of learning and sharing and I carry one particular lesson with me.

In a discussion about Zapatista education, a lot of things

sounded very familiar. They sounded like things I'd read about Paulo Freire and, more recently thanks to Staughton Lynd, about Myles Horton. I said to the promotor, "but this Zapatista education all sounds like what Freire did in Brazil, aren't you reinventing the wheel?" "No, you don't get the point," he responded, "this is Zapatista education not Freirean education. If we are inventing the wheel, at least it is our wheel!"

I was humbled by such wisdom…and patience.

The goal of the autonomous "primero de enero" school is to put a Zapatista school with Zapatista promotores in every town and village in Chiapas.

During my stay in Oventik, the promotores asked me to lead a discussion on the Irish struggle. We all talked about the IRA, the hunger strikes, the peace process, the dangers of electoral politics. We learned from each other and my favorite line in my cv reads:

"La lucha en Irlanda," presented to Escuela Secundaria Rebelde Autónoma Zapatista "Primero de Enero," Oventik, Chiapas, Mexico, April 16, 2004.

Nobody in any university ever asked me to discuss "La lucha en Irlanda." But people in working class communities did.

One other experience from Chiapas stands out. My dear friend Father Henry, a liberation theologist who has been accompanying Mayans in Chiapas ever since he had to flee El Salvador, invited me to go with him to bless the bread oven that a women's cooperative had just built in his parish. The ceremony was astonishing. The oven was in a hut strewn with pine needles for the occasion; it was proudly sitting in the back of the hut, adorned with a huge Zapatista star. There were candles all around and the ubiquitous copal incense filled the air. Henry said his few prayers and the women took over. They cried and wept and recounted all of the horrible things that had happened to their people over the years. They spoke about how this oven would enrich the community and help to drive out those memories. This went on for quite awhile. Then we ate tamales and drank atole, a Mayan corn drink.

A year later another friend of mine was traveling through the village and the women took her to show off their bread oven. She was astonished to see the picture that hung in pride of place on the wall of the cooperative. It was a picture of the women, Father Henry, and me. She had expected to see pictures of Henry because he was their parish priest. It was a bit of a shock. "What is this picture?" she asked. "Oh, that's father Henry and his Irish compañero. They helped us bless our oven."

Being remembered so fondly by such people makes me prouder than any academic award I've ever got.

I tell you these stories because I want to add something to Staughton's words. Accompaniment goes both directions. Sometimes, if not always, we find that when we take our expertise to someone, we learn from each other. The accompanist becomes the accompanied. That was what El Sup (Marcos) found out when he went into the jungle intending to accompany the Mayans. The Mayans accompanied him.

What Staughton Lynd learned from organizing all his life is that leadership comes from below, it is being someone to whom others turn for help. Personal loyalty is valued more than intellectual consistency. "You have to swim in the sea of the people."

It reminded me how a dear friend of Bobby Sands once told me how hard it was to walk with him across the working class Belfast estate where they both lived. It took forever, because people kept coming up to him to tell him about their troubles, to ask a favor, or just to share the latest events in the area. As I heard more and more of these stories about Bobby, it dawned on me that this was the secret of leadership, sometimes as simple as just being able to sing to your neighbors without worrying about being embarrassed. That empowers them to sing, too.

Of course, songs are the stuff of revolution and struggle, and there is no shortage of insight here into how songs and films and stories play their role in the formation of a Staughton Lynd…and then continue to play their role in deepening the consciousness. I've mentioned Mary Bohan already. One of the first things Staughton asked me when he first wrote to me was did I know the words to "My Old Fenian Gun," the song that his beloved nanny sang to him when he was a child! These are the things that make us who we are. I won't spoil Staughton's story of the "Minstrel Boy" by telling it here, but that song has been following me about, too, since I was a youngster. It was written by Thomas Moore to commemorate his Trinity College colleagues who left the comfy university life of Dublin to join the United Irishmen in the 1798 rebellion (no wonder Staughton takes to this song). Yet, in the contradiction and irony that haunts many of our favorite things in life, you'd be as likely to hear the song being sung by marching soldiers or, as I recently found on YouTube, played as background to a celebration of that "band of brothers" in Iraq. You might even remember the corrupt British soldier/adventurers singing it as they marched to their downfall in John Huston's version of Kipling's "The Man Who Would Be King." Staughton Lynd, to his credit, had a more sensible understanding of the lyrics to the "Minstrel Boy" and it led him to a decision that he's carried with him through a long life.

There's so much else here. Jean Renoir's *Grand Illusion*, Ignazio Silone's *Bread and Wine*. Moving stories of Lynd's mother, Helen. Good reasons to dust off your volume of the Marx-Engels Reader to re-read the *Critique of the Gotha Programme* and *The Civil War in France*. An invitation to become familiar with grassroots democracy during the U.S. Revolution. The history of the Anabaptists. Guerrilla history. And Lucasville, where courageous men like Bomani Shakur and George Skatzes showed that Aryan Brotherhood and Afro-American prisoners can work together…and got sent to death row at Ohio's "supermax" prison for not acting with hate like prisoners are supposed to act.

If I tell you that today Joe Hill is in "supermax," you'll know what I mean after you read this wonderful book. And then you might want to read Staughton Lynd's history of how the Lucasville Five were framed (*Lucasville: The Untold Story of a Prison Uprising*). And then let's do something to get these men off of death row. The Irish did it when we got six men freed after serving sixteen years for the Birmingham bombings, even though the state knew all along that they were innocent. On that occasion, one of Britain's top jurists, Thomas ("Lord") Denning, said that:

"If the six men win, it will mean that the police are guilty of perjury, that they are guilty of violence and threats, that the confessions were invented and improperly admitted in evidence and the convictions were erroneous.... This is such an appalling vista that every sensible person in the land would say that it cannot be right that these actions should go any further."

He also commented that, "We shouldn't have all these campaigns to get the Birmingham Six released. If they'd been hanged, they'd have been forgotten and the whole community would have been satisfied."

Well, police do lie, confessions are invented, and testimony is fabricated. And good people protested and campaigned and refused to give up until they cut through the lies and stopped it. Accompaniment was a crucial part of the campaign to free the Birmingham Six. A journalist called Chris Mullan investigated the case and made several programs of *World in Action*, the BBC's equivalent to *Sixty Minutes*, but better. In 1986, Mullan's book, *Error of Judgment—The Truth About the Birmingham Pub Bombings*, set out a detailed case supporting the men's innocence. A tireless human rights lawyer from London, Gareth Peirce, kept up the legal side of the public protest campaign and, more than anything, gave the men hope and accompaniment during their prison ordeal.

It all sounds familiar to Staughton's story of working with the Lucasville Five: "the most demanding, at times the most frustrating, and overall the most rewarding work" he has ever done. I suppose the difference is that the Birmingham Six had a built-in and active support community in the form of the Irish community in Britain and Ireland. Unlike so many in the U.S., the Irish do not revile prisoners. It was their unrelenting pressure that freed these men by ensuring that the truth was heard and acted upon. How much more work will it be to create an active support community for prisoners in the United States?

Before I let you go, I want to say a few more words about that Balkan pirate, Andrej Grubacic. After all, this is a conversation, even if Staughton Lynd does most of the talking in its final edited form! Andrej Grubacic takes an innovative approach to conversation. He has a knack for putting forth the right question or statement in the right form, leaving a natural space for his compañero to fill with a recollection or an analysis that challenges us to move forward our own way of thinking and acting. Maybe it's all those Serbian cops he's had to deal with that makes him so good at drawing people out. I don't know. Staughton Lynd's (always kind and gentle, but very powerful) criticism of the dark side of "summit hopping" and erratic "activism for activism sake," is precious, and anarchists disregard this at their own peril. Andrej advocates, and hopes to propagate, a new anarchism, one that is based on accompaniment, that would utilize guerrilla history as a facet of accompaniment and a method of militant research, that would recognize the possibility of interracial solidarity, and all of this in a context of a thoughtful exchange with Marxism. May he continue to develop the ideas of a new anarchism, pushing it forward in the direction that is sketched and offered in this book.

At one point in this conversation, Staughton Lynd says that all of the experiments in government from below, whether during the U.S. Revolution or recently in Oaxaca, were shortlived. They would be deemed to be failures by many but the very fact that they happened at all makes them small victories. Staughton warns that we must maintain the necessary humility to work out how to make these dreams more lasting, first of all by working together and combining what is best from the anarchist and Marxist traditions. Yet it is still important to remember the victories and the people who made them. The Metacomets. The Brian Willsons. The Staughton Lynds.

The Moving Finger writes; and, having writ, Moves on.

DENIS O'HEARN
HAUDENOSAUNEE TERRITORY
NEW YORK
2008

PART I

MARXISM, ANARCHISM AND ZAPATISMO

Zapatismo

STAUGHTON, LET ME BEGIN *by saying how exciting this conversation is for me. As you know, I am an unrepentant anarchist. I belong to that perpetually reinvented, and perpetually re-emerging, ethical tradition, premised on the principles of prefigurative politics, direct action and direct democracy, decentralization and grassroots federalism. I believe that the anarchist tradition was suppressed and crushed by the hegemonic ideologies of Marxism and Liberalism. I believe that today we are witnessing a large revival of left libertarian thinking all over the world, and I propose the term "new anarchism" to describe this process. You are, on the other hand, one of the most fascinating contemporary protagonists of the Marxist tradition. It is virtually impossible to write or read about American radicalism after the second world war without encountering the remarkable activist life of Staughton Lynd. So I propose for us to begin this conversation in what might, on first glance, appear to be a somewhat unusual place: not in 1964 Mississippi, but in 1994 Chiapas, where a rather remarkable movement emerged, one that invited the rebels of the world to participate in what you have called, in* Stepping Stones, *a "fresh synthesis of what is best in Marxist and anarchist traditions." Let us talk about Zapatismo, its novelty, and the way it places into an historical perspective those defining radical ideas of the 1960s you write about in* Living Inside Our Hope: *nonviolence, participatory democracy, an experiential approach to learning, accompaniment, anti-imperialism and anti-capitalism.*

Yes, let's talk about Zapatismo!

About ten years ago Alice and I were in San Cristóbal, Chiapas, where the Zapatista uprising went public on January 1, 1994.

We were there with our daughter Martha and a friend of hers from Chile, Roberto. Roberto and I talked about our experiences in the armies of our two countries. Roberto said that when he and his friends were sent to the scene of working-class demonstrations, they fired into the air. I said that during the time of Senator Joe McCarthy, I had been given an "undesirable discharge" from the United States Army.

Roberto asked, "Were you tortured?" The question made me realize, once again, that the consequences of being Left in the United States are much less than in Latin America.

Alice and I were able to visit the community of Chamula, about ten miles from San Cristóbal. What was interesting there was a church that seemed to combine elements from both Mayan and Christian traditions. There was no altar and, apparently, no priest. Pine needles were strewn on the floor. Families sat in circles on the floor around lighted candles. Against both walls were niches for the saints, including one saint to whom you could turn if the other saints did not respond to your requests for help. "Deacons" came by, to ask that visitors take off their hats, and to solicit contributions.

Alice and I also talked with a woman named Teresa Ortiz, who later published a collection of oral histories by Chiapan women. She had lived in the area a long time.

Ms. Ortiz told us that there are three sources of Zapatismo. The first is the craving for land, the heritage of Emiliano Zapata and the revolution that he led at the time of World War I. This longing for economic independence expressed itself in the massive migration of impoverished *campesinos* into the Lacandón jungle in eastern Chiapas. But in Chiapas pioneering was different from the movement of individual farmers to the frontier in the United States. The Mexican Revolution wrote into the national constitution the opportunity for a village to hold its land communally, in an *ejido*, so that no individual could alienate any portion of it. Chiapas pioneers fiercely defended these communal landholdings. When the United States insisted that, as a precondition for participation in the North Atlantic Free Trade Agreement (NAFTA), Mexico must delete this provision from its Constitution, it triggered the Zapatista uprising. The uprising began on the day that NAFTA went into effect.

A second source of Zapatismo, we were told, was liberation theology. Bishop Samuel Ruiz was the key figure. He sponsored what came to be called *tomar conciencia*, a phrase that means "taking conscience (or consciousness)," just as we speak of "taking thought." Taking conscience also produced countless grassroots functionaries with titles like "predeacon," "deacon," "catechist," or "delegate of the Word": the shop stewards of the popular Church who have been indispensable everywhere in Latin America.

The final and most intriguing component of Zapatismo, according to Teresa Ortiz, was the Mayan tradition of *mandar obediciendo*, "to lead by obeying." She explained what it meant at the village level. Imagine a village. To use her examples, we feel the need for a teacher and a storekeeper. But these two persons can be freed for those communal tasks only if we, as a community, undertake to cultivate their *milpas* (their corn fields). In the most literal sense their ability to take leadership roles depends on our willingness to provide their livelihoods.

When representatives thus chosen are asked to take part in regional gatherings, they will be instructed delegates. If new questions arise, the delegates will be obliged to return to their constituents. Thus, in the midst of the negotiations mediated by Bishop Ruiz early in 1994, the Zapatista delegates said they would have to interrupt the talks to consult the villages to which they were accountable, a process that took several weeks. The heart of the political process remains the gathered residents of each village, the *asamblea*.

An anthropologist named June Nash has written a book about a village in Chiapas. She says that village functionaries (like the teacher and the storekeeper) meet frequently with the entire local population. According to Nash, at these meetings the functionaries are expected, not to talk, but to listen.

Now I want to address two questions. First, what is globalization? Second, what is the Zapatista strategy for change?

WHAT IS GLOBALIZATION?

Everyone agrees that the Zapatista uprising was prompted by something called "globalization" and kicked off a worldwide anti-globalization movement. It would seem that to build such a movement over the long run we need to understand the causes of globalization.

I got a glimpse on visits to other parts of Mexico. For a time our daughter Martha taught English as a second language in a village called Tlahuitoltepec, in the mountains of the province of Oaxaca ("wah-hah-cah") which is just north of Chiapas. (Every village in that part of Oaxaca has its band. The school was for band members from all over the region.) One day a farmer explained to me that over many generations his family had grown corn for the local and regional market. They could no longer do so, he said, because of cheaper imports from abroad. Harvesting timber was becoming unprofitable for the same reason.

Some time later, while attending a school sponsored by the Mexican network of independent unions, I heard the same story from a farmer in central Mexico. His family owned land near the city of Puebla. When he took over the farm he could not grow corn because corn imported from Iowa sold for less. He had begun to grow feed for animals. "Ah," I said, "you are selling meat?" "No," he responded. Meat, too, could be imported and sold at a price with which he could not compete. "I am raising sheep and selling the wool!" I could only wonder how long it would be before fibers from the United States would close off this market for him, too.

But why was NAFTA so much desired by United States corporations? I think the best answer comes from Marx. Marx argues in *Capital* that as capitalist firms compete with one another, they invest in new machinery. This changes the "organic composition of capital": an increasing percentage of investment is in fixed capital, like machinery, and a decreasing percentage in labor from which profit can be extracted. The rate of profit accordingly falls. This began to happen during the 1970s. And at about that time firms headquartered in the United States began a serious push to invest in Third World economies. There, as in the *maquiladora* factories just south of the border between the United States and Mexico, workers could be paid far less than in the United States and the rate of profit would increase correspondingly.

A friend of mine works for one of the largest employers in the Youngstown area, Delphi Packard. Delphi makes automotive parts. It used to employ more than 10,000 workers in this part of Ohio. Now it employs only a few thousand locally but is the largest multinational employer in Mexico, with a reported Mexican labor force of 40,000. From time to time when Delphi workers in Youngstown open shipments from Mexico, they find scraps of paper on which Mexican workers have written how little they are paid.

WHAT IS THE ZAPATISTA STRATEGY FOR CHANGE?

At the time of the initial uprising, the Zapatistas seem to have entertained a traditional Marxist strategy of seizing national power by military means. The "First Declaration of the Lacandón Jungle," on January 2, 1994, gave the Zapatista military forces the order: "Advance to the capital of the country, conquering the Mexican federal army…."

But, in the words of Harvard historian John Womack, "In military terms the EZLN [Zapatista National Liberation Army] offensive was a wonderful success on the first day, a pitiful calamity on the second." Within a very short time, three things apparently happened: 1) the public opinion of Mexican civil society came down on the side of the Indians of Chiapas and demanded negotiation; 2) President Salinas declared a ceasefire, and sent an emissary to negotiate in the cathedral of San Cristóbal; 3) Subcomandante Marcos carried out a clandestine coup within the failed revolution, agreed to negotiations, and began to promulgate a dramatically new strategy.

Beginning early in 1994, Marcos said explicitly, over and over and over again: We don't see ourselves as a vanguard and we don't want to take power. Thus, at the first massive encuentro, the National Democratic Convention in the Lacandón jungle in August 1994, Marcos said that the Zapatistas had made a "decision not to impose our point of view"; that they rejected "the doubtful honor of being the historical vanguard of the multiple vanguards that plague us"; and finally:

> Yes, the moment has come to say to everyone that we neither want, nor are we able, to occupy the place that some hope we will occupy, the place from which all opinions will come, all the answers, all the routes, all the truth. We are not going to do that.

Marcos then took the Mexican flag and gave it to the delegates, in effect telling them: It's your flag. Use it to make a democratic Mexico. We Zapatistas hope we have created some space within which you can act.

What? A Left group that doesn't want to take state power? There must be some mistake. But no, he means it. And because it is a perspective so different from that traditional in Marxism, because it represents a fresh synthesis of what is best in the Marxist and anarchist traditions, I want to quote several more examples.

In the "Fourth Declaration from the Lacandón Jungle," on January 1, 1996, it is stated that the Zapatista Front of National Liberation will be a "political force that does not aspire to take power[,]…that can organize citizens' demands and proposals so that he who commands, commands in obedience to the popular will[,]…that does not struggle to take political power but for the democracy where those who command, command by obeying."

In September 1996, in an address to Mexican civil society, Marcos says that in responding to the earthquake of 1985 Mexican civil society proved to itself

> that you can participate without aspiring to public office, that you can organize politically without being in a political party, that you can keep an eye on the government and pressure it to "lead by obeying," that you can have an effect and remain yourself.…

Likewise in August 1997, in "Discussion Documents for the Founding Congress of the Zapatista Front of National Liberation," the Zapatistas declare that they represent "a new form of doing politics, without aspiring to take Power and without vanguardist positions." We "will not struggle to take Power," they continue. The Zapatista Front of National Liberation "does not aspire to take Power." Rather, "we are a political force that does not seek to take power, that does not pretend to be the vanguard of a specific class, or of society as a whole."

Especially memorable is a communication dated October 2, 1998, from the Zapatista National Liberation Army to "the Generation of Dignity of 1968," that is, to students who survived the massacre in Mexico City prior to the 1968 Olympics. Here Marcos speaks of "the politics of below," of the "Mexico of those who weren't then, are not now, and will never be leaders." This, he says, is the

Mexico of those who don't build ladders to climb above others, but who look beside them to find another and make him or her their *compañero* or *compañera*, brother, sister, mate, buddy, friend, colleague, or whatever word is used to describe that long, treacherous, collective path that is the struggle of: everything for everyone.

Finally, at the *zocalo* (the public square in the center of Mexico City) in March 2001, after the Zapatista march from Chiapas to Mexico City, Marcos once more declared: "We are not those who aspire to take power and then impose the way and the word."

DOES IT WORK?

Does it work? Can a society be fundamentally changed without taking over the state? I don't think we know yet. Many people felt that the "other campaign" undertaken by the Zapatistas during the Mexican presidential campaign of 2006 was counter-productive. By refusing to endorse Obrador, by focusing on local struggles and criticizing Obrador more than his opponent, the Zapatistas may have helped to elect the candidate of the business community, Calderon.

Likewise, we in the United States have not done very well in ending the Iraq war while President Bush remains in office.

Latin American liberation theology, and the Zapatistas most incisively, have given us a new hypothesis. It combines Marxist analysis of the dynamics of capitalism with a traditional spirituality, whether Native American or Christian, or a combination of the two. It rejects the goal of taking state power and sets forth the objective of building a horizontal network of centers of self-activity.

Above all the Zapatistas have encouraged young people all over the earth to affirm: We must have a qualitatively different society! Another world is possible! Let us begin to create it, here and now!

A Haymarket Synthesis

I LIKE WHAT *you say about the Zapatistas very much. Our attempt, with this conversation, at least the way I see it, is to offer a distinctive contribution to the possible synthesis between anarchism and Marxism. In my opinion, one of the most exciting, and, at the same time, most neglected examples of anarchist-Marxist syntheses historically comes from the United States. I am referring to the Haymarket anarchists and the so-called "Chicago idea," an idea that is not all that well known even among U.S. activists. I would even go so far to identify something that might be called a "Haymarket synthesis," an experience of struggle and accompaniment, an experience that brings together, in a generous way, our two respective traditions.*

By way of introduction: This question presents itself somewhat differently in Europe and in North America, I think.

In Europe, a long-standing feud between anarchism and Marxism was firmly established in the quarter century following the *Communist Manifesto* (1848). Viewed from afar it seems almost like the wars of Protestants and Catholics in the seventeenth century, or an hostility between extended families that is handed down from generation to generation. If I am not mistaken the First International was moved from Europe to the United States so as to avoid a "takeover" by anarchists.

This is, well, ridiculous. What is Marxism? It is an effort to understand the structure of the society in which we live so as to make informed predictions and to act with greater effect. What is anarchism? It is the attempt to imagine a better society and insofar as possible to "prefigure," to anticipate that society by beginning to live it out, on the ground, here and now.

Isn't it perfectly obvious that these two orientations are both needed, that they are like having two hands to accomplish the needed task of transformation?

At any rate it is clear that during the past century and a half neither Marxism or anarchism has been able to carry out the transformative task alone. Marxism has produced a series of fearsome dictatorships. Anarchism has offered a number of glorious anticipations, all of them short-lived and many of them drowned in blood.

Before turning to North America, with its quite different experience, I wish to note that in their best moments Marxists have acknowledged their comradeship with anarchists. Marx spent a great deal of energy denouncing efforts to imagine the future, but when his anarchist opponents in Paris created the Paris Commune he defended them and even declared that they had discovered the form of the future Communist state. Lenin, hiding out in Finland on the eve of the Bolshevik Revolution, described in *State and Revolution* a state that "every cook" would be capable of governing, anticipated in the Russian soviets.

ZAPATISMO AND HAYMARKET

Again and again in these conversations we come back to Zapatismo and here again they have been where we are going.

As I understand it, Subcomandante Marcos was a member of a Marxist-Leninist sect in Mexico City that somehow found the imagination to move to the Lacandón jungle in the 1980s and to stay there ever since.

In the jungle, these Marxists encountered Mayans who had been living a decentralized, communal, essentially anarchist way of life for hundreds if not thousands of years.

And this is not the first attempt of the kind in North America! Of particular interest are the so-called Haymarket anarchists: workers in Chicago who took the need for a fusion of anarchism and Marxism for granted and did their best to create it before their untimely deaths.

Read Chapter 6 ("The Flame That Makes the Kettle Boil") in James Green, *Death in the Haymarket* (2006). What do we learn there?

1. In 1877, Albert Parsons, a former Confederate soldier and Radical Republican in Texas, now working as a printer, ran for office in Cook County and received 8,000 votes.

2. In the spring of 1878, Parsons ran for Chicago city council on a program that called for (among other things) enactment of an eight-hour day, abolition of vagrancy laws used to punish the unemployed and of conspiracy laws used to persecute trade unionists, as well as an end to the practice of leasing convicts to labor for private employers. He came close to winning.

3. That same spring Chicago workers began to form a Lehr and Wehr Verein (association to learn and fight) in order to defend their public meetings with arms, if necessary.

4. By the fall of 1878 the Socialistic Labor Party in Chicago had established Scandinavian, Bohemian, French, English, and German branches.

5. In spring 1879 the Party ran a candidate for mayor. The campaign culminated in a meeting to celebrate the eighth anniversary of the Paris Commune attended by more than 40,000 persons. The platform called for city ownership of streetcars and utilities.

6. Disillusioned with electoral politics, Parsons, his wife Lucy Parsons, and his comrade August Spies created the Socialistic Publishing Company and then joined in forming the International Working People's Association in

London. Back in Chicago, they organized clubs of Social Revolutionaries, remaining convinced by Marx and Engels (according to Green) "that the road to socialism was a long one and that there were no shortcuts through individual acts of terror."

7. Parsons, seeking what Green calls "a unifying issue and a solidifying organization," then turned to a labor organization called the Knights of Labor and its demand for an eight-hour day. He helped to form the first Chicago assembly of the Knights. He and his friends believed that the eight-hour day could be achieved "only through direct action by workers."

8. The Knights proclaimed that an injury to one is an injury to all. In March 1882, skilled English-speaking "curriers" struck in support of German-speaking "tanners" who were demanding equal pay for all. Hundreds of immigrant workers in Chicago flooded into the Knights, forming so-called "mixed assemblies" that included unskilled workers of all kinds.

9. In October 1883 Parsons and Spies went to Pittsburgh and announced the creation of the International Working People's Association which rejected "all attempts…to reform this monstrous system by peaceable means, such as the ballot." By 1885 one-fifth of the members of the IWPA were in Chicago, enrolled in fifteen neighborhood groups or clubs and in the Central Labor Union, a "parallel central labor union" with a membership of 20,000.

10. They imagined militant trade unions as "the living germs of a new social order." It was called "the Chicago idea." They were executed as a result of encounters with the police growing out of a nationwide general strike for the eight-hour-day in May 1886.

Were they socialists or anarchists? According to James Green, in 1884 militant socialists in Chicago began calling themselves anarchists, but Spies insisted that he remained a follower of Marx, not Bakunin. "The Chicago militants thought of themselves as socialists of the anarchist type—that is, as revolutionaries who believed in liberating society from all state control, whether capitalist or socialist." Green, their historian, can only report that "they invented a peculiar... brand of revolutionary socialism they called anarchism."

The Wobbly Experience

LET US CONTINUE *to explore the history of this "peculiar brand of socialism." I maintain that the Haymarket synthesis was kept alive by the Industrial Workers of the World. Wobblies, whom both anarchists and Marxists recognized as their own, and whom respectable contemporaries called "timber beasts," brought the Haymarket synthesis back to life. What is so fascinating is that the IWW, unlike many other groups, and perhaps because of this synthesis, has persisted and continues to exist. Both of us are members or fellow travelers of the Wobblies. You are, if you would allow me to phrase it this way, something of a guru of the new IWW. How can we account for the resurrection of interest in the IWW? What is it in the Wobbly experience, and in this particular culture of solidarity, that makes the idealism of the One Big Union again, or rather, still, so attractive to the young people active in, among many other examples, the Starbucks campaign?*

All American radicals love the Industrial Workers of the World, or Wobblies. They were the Zapatistas of yesteryear.

The Wobblies came into existence in 1905 as a heterogeneous assemblage of radicals opposed to the craft unionism of the American Federation of Labor. The idea was that if there was more than one union under contract in the same shop, when one such craft union went on strike the others were prevented from striking in solidarity by the no-strike language in their contracts. Thus, the IWW declared, in practice the AFL was the "American Separation of Labor."

The preamble to the IWW Constitution, still reproduced in every issue of the monthly *Industrial Worker*, declares in part that the working class must "take possession of the means of production [and] abolish the wage system." These are traditional socialist objectives.

But the anarchist strain was just as strong, or even stronger. The working class must organize itself in such a way, according to the preamble, that whenever a strike or lockout is on, affecting one group of workers, "all its members in any one industry, or all industries if necessary" can strike together. Echoing the Haymarket anarchists, the preamble observed that thus workers could make "an injury to one an injury to all."

By organizing industrially, the manifesto concluded, "we are forming the structure of the new society within the shell of the old."

A CULTURE OF SOLIDARITY

The Wobblies included in their "one big union" enormously varied groups of workers. There were metal miners organized in the Western Federation of Miners. This was the largest trade union in the IWW and it soon withdrew, leaving behind the Wobblies' most famous organizer, "Big Bill" Haywood. There were immigrant laborers like the textile workers in Lawrence, Massachusetts who won the famous 1912 strike "for bread and roses." There were lumber workers in the Northwest who lived in isolated logging camps and were derisively termed "timber beasts" by respectable citizens. There were migratory agricultural workers who followed the harvests from South to North, illegally hopping aboard railroad cars for transportation. On the Philadelphia docks, and in the "piney woods" of the South where men cut softwood timber, blacks and whites labored together in an equality altogether extraordinary in that era of segregation and lynch mobs.

Not surprisingly, persons whose lives were in many ways so different found it difficult to make decisions together. There were battles over strategy, struggles over the appropriate role of a central office, differences about whether to support the Socialist Party, splits and defections.

Moreover, during and after World War I the organization was mercilessly repressed. Frank Little was castrated and lynched. Joe Hill was framed on a murder charge, and executed by a firing squad in Utah. Dozens of organizers were found guilty of sedition and imprisoned for long terms. The organization barely survived the early 1920s.

What is all the more miraculous, therefore, is the flamboyant, innovative, and solid culture of solidarity this band of rebels created and left behind for us.

Again as with the Haymarket anarchists, the central principle was direct action. Lumber workers anxious to limit their backbreaking work simply walked off the job after eight hours. (In her pamphlet about the 1905 Revolution, Rosa Luxemburg describes Russian workers who did exactly the same thing.) In a metal shop in Schenectady, New York, metal workers invented the idea that instead of leaving the plant, and picketing, you should sit down next to your machine and occupy the workplace. (Hundreds of workers in the 1930s engaged in such sit-down strikes, most famously at the General Motors complex in Flint, Michigan in 1937.) Western towns and cities were notorious for prohibiting free speech. Wobblies thereupon would assemble from all over the region and fill the jails, to the point that their incarceration became so expensive that the town fathers, in disgust, would let them out of jail and permit them to mount their soapboxes in the public square.

Older readers will recall the style of the Student Nonviolent Coordinating Committee (SNCC, pronounced "Snick") in the 1960s. I cannot remember a SNCC staff person referring to the Wobblies but in truth it was a kind of Second Coming: the same blue overalls; the same indomitable readiness to sit in the front seats of the bus, or to "go down to the court house" to register to vote; the same sense of oneness with people all over the world struggling for their freedom.

Wobblies and SNCC were also alike in their singing. The idea was to take the church hymns omnipresent in American culture and give them new words. Wobbly Ralph Chaplin, jailed during World War I, took the tune of "John Brown's Body" and the "Battle Hymn of the Republic" from the era of the Civil War, and turned it into "Solidarity Forever." Joe Hill transformed the saccharine "Sweet Bye and Bye" into the promise by long-haired preachers that "You'll get pie in the sky when you die (that's a lie)." Just so, in the 1960s Michael rowed his boat ashore to "get my freedom on the other side," and "Go tell it on the Mountain" asked: "Who is that yonder dressed in red? Must be the children Bob Moses led."

But hierarchical leadership was precisely that which the Wobblies most fiercely contested. I first learned of the IWW from a book in my parents' living room. It was *The New Men of Power* by C. Wright Mills. To offset his sad tale of the bureaucratization of CIO union officials, Mills placed at the beginning of his narrative one of the eye witness accounts of what happened when the good ship Verona, full of Wobblies, approached the shore of Everett, Washington in 1916 to support protesting workers there. As the barge approached the dock,

> Sheriff McRae called out to them: "Who is your leader?" Immediate and unmistakable was the answer from every I.W.W.: "We are all leaders."

The sheriff and his men then opened fire, killing five.

THE NEW MOVEMENT

Crushed by government repression, burdened by the twin hierarchies of the Communist Party and a trade union movement dominated by the United Mine Workers, the IWW virtually disappeared as an organization between the early 1920s and recent times. Individual Wobblies played catalytic roles in the organization of local industrial unions in the first years of the 1930s. The critique of national CIO unionism as it emerged in the late 1930s and World War II, that Wobblies should have undertaken, fell to isolated worker intellectuals like Stan Weir and Marty Glaberman.

The IWW has been revived by a new generation of young activists. This phenomenon should no doubt be understood as part of a larger revival of libertarian socialist thinking all over the world. How those currents of thought and idealism survived or reached the United States from abroad is a story yet to be told.

One can identify certain components of the process. Murray Bookchin retrieved the idea of "affinity groups" from histories of the Spanish Civil War. At the occupation of the Seabrook nuclear facility, and in other environmental protests of the 1970s and 1980s, participants organized "spokes councils" to coordinate strategy. Nonetheless I for one perceive the emergence of a new movement as a great mystery for which we who went before can only be deeply grateful.

I reiterate, at the end of this long discussion, that "anarchism" is an inadequate term to describe what the new movement, or movements, affirm. Like the Haymarket anarchists, like the IWW, those who travel long distances to confront the capitalists of the world at their periodic gatherings, are not only opposed to "the state." They are equally opposed to capitalism, the wage system, and corporate imperialism.

I leave it to others to find the best labels for this confluence of intellectual traditions traditionally associated with Marxism on the one hand and anarchism on the other.

My plea is simply that we not replicate the fratricidal squabbles of the early pioneers of both traditions. We owe it to them, to ourselves, to those who will come after us, to do better.

Luxemburg, Weil, and E. P. Thompson

LET US MOVE *from the movement to individuals. Among a few people who "sought a fusion of Marxism and anarchism," a few names, and lives, come to mind and heart. You told me once, in a different conversation in my house in Brooklyn, that you and your friend, the late Daniel Singer, used to define yourselves as (among many other things) "Luxemburgists." You also mention Rosa in many of your essays as a revolutionary who offered a "working-class self-activity paradigm," and a revolutionary who might be "the most significant theorist of the twentieth century labor movement." Another libertarian critic of authoritarian Marxism whom we both admire is Simone Weil. Perhaps we can suggest to the attention of the new generation of libertarian revolutionaries, the life, work and ideas of this fascinating radical. A third person who constructively sought this particular fusion of traditions, a person who, in a different way, is a mentor-like figure to both of us, is E. P. Thompson. Both in his "Letter to Lesek Kolakowski" and in* The Poverty of Theory *he advocates "libertarian socialism."*

Luxemburg, Weil, and Thompson are discussed in my *Living Inside Our Hope*. I make the point that in each case a particular thinker emerged from a context, a setting in which the limitations of Marxism became apparent and thoughtful revolutionaries looked beyond its boundaries.

In the case of Luxemburg, the form of Marxism with which she contested was Social Democracy. Social Democracy is the idea of a mass political party based on the mass membership of trade unions with Left leadership. Germany was thought to be the leading exemplar although every European country had its version of Social Democracy.

The inadequacy of Social Democracy became apparent—once and for all—in August 1914 when each of the major parties instructed its parliamentary delegation to support war taxes for that particular government. (It is exactly what Congressional Democrats have done in 2006-2007.) Even Lenin was astonished, and went to the library to read Hegel on the dialectic and Hobson on imperialism.

Rosa Luxemburg was not astonished. Fifteen years earlier in her so-called Junius pamphlets she had counterposed the reformism inherent in Social Democracy with the possibility of revolution. Above all in her pamphlet on "The Mass Strike," written after her immersion in the 1905 Revolution, she pinpointed the fallacies of the mass trade union in language that still requires no translation: its servile press, which reports only alleged victories; its time-serving functionaries who believe all change is decreed from above and then merely implemented by followers in the streets and (especially) at the polls; its perpetual failure to confront the fundamentals of the system that oppresses working persons.

This diminutive female also took on Lenin. Ten years before the second Russian Revolution of 1917 she said that Lenin had the "soul of an overseer." Imprisoned for her opposition to World War I she grasped what was afoot in Russia, and wrote the immortal words: *"Freiheit ist immer Freiheit fuer den Andersdenkenden"* (Freedom is always freedom for the one who thinks differently).

This great, great woman was done in by a certain sacred naivete in her relationships with other human beings. When her comrade Karl Liebknecht acquiesced in a foolhardy attempt at insurrection (which caused them both to be killed), she said, "Karl, how could you?" When she was seized by rightwing thugs to be murdered she asked, "To what prison are you taking me?"

Simone Weil came on the scene after the great betrayal of Communism in making Social Democracy rather than fascism the main enemy, and so enabling Hitler to come to power. Weil dialogued with Trotsky but found his thinking inadequate. She forced her awkward body to confront what her brain discerned. She went to work in a factory, where she was hopelessly inept but lasted long enough to make her greatest single contribution: to comprehend why factory work does not make revolutionaries, rather it makes human beings desperate for the closing whistle and unable to think and feel beyond the next repetitive moment, unable to imagine a future. She went to Spain and stepped into a pan of boiling oil soldiers were using to cook their food at the front, and had to go home. And then she starved herself to death in solidarity with the impoverished citizenry of France during World War II.

Weil should be understood in conjunction with what I described in my essay on her as a "first New Left" that included the Italian novelist Ignazio Silone, a former member of the executive committee of the Third International, who in his book *Bread and Wine* anticipated liberation theology, and A.J. Muste, who after a career as a revolutionary Marxist and an unsatisfactory meeting with Trotsky, sat in a French cathedral and reaffirmed nonviolence.

Thompson was a Communist who shared the dream of Western European Communists during World War II that a Communism linked to the defense of democracy would emerge after 1945 as the vanguard of humankind. (Thompson's brother was killed in southeastern Europe. He parachuted behind enemy lines and, as I understand it, disappeared.) The Hungarian Revolution of 1956 was the turning point for Edward Thompson. First he wrote about William Morris. Then he wrote about the early nineteenth century

British working class. His thinking moved steadily backward in time, ending in village customs of the eighteenth century. After the mid-1960s he ceased actively to promote a contemporary revolution in England. But throughout, he was a great voice for the self-activity of ordinary people, subjected to the "enormous condescension" of historians and self-appointed political leaders.

So indeed, there is a thick tradition of fusing Marxist and anarchist insights by discontented Marxists, among whom I include myself.

But the problem we now face seems a little different. Anarchism is now the reigning orthodoxy, propounded by theorists whose writing is incomprehensible and who have no discernible relationship to practice. As a lifelong rebel against heavy-handed Marxist dogmatism I find myself defending Marx, and objecting to the so-called radicalism of one-weekend-a-year radicals who show up at a global confrontation and then talk about it for the rest of the year.

These are harsh words. But I consider them deserved. Anarchists, above all others, should be faithful to the injunction that a genuine radical, a revolutionary, must indeed swim in the sea of the people, and if he or she does not do so, is properly viewed as what the Germans called a "socialist of the chair," or in English, an "armchair intellectual."

It is a conspiracy of persons who make their living at academic institutions to induce others who do the same to take them seriously. I challenge it and reject it. Let them follow Marcos to the jungles of Chiapas in their own countries, and learn something new.

The Working Class

I BELIEVE WITH *my whole heart that the generation of new anarchists still has to and must learn how to "swim in the sea of the people." This "swimming lesson" might indeed be the most crucial challenge for the new anarchism. An intimately related problem is the tendency that I see in many new anarchists to a rather peculiar lack of class sensitivity and class analysis. A good number of new anarchists, and even some Marxists, have almost abandoned the working class, and any aspiration to a working-class movement. It seems that the movement has moved from one reductionism to another. What are your thoughts on this?*

Toward the end of the 1960s, radicals of all sorts in the United States focused their attention on "the working class."

As I have indicated elsewhere in these conversations, there were several reasons for this, some good, some not so good. In 1963 Students for a Democratic Society (SDS) formed an Economic Research and Action Project (ERAP), which projected the idea of an interracial movement of the poor. It was assumed that joblessness was increasing in the United States because of the increasing use of automation and other new technology.

Accordingly students dropped out of college or put training for professional careers on hold and went to live in urban ghettoes in hope of organizing a Northern equivalent of SNCC. The most successful projects were in the Appalachian community of Uptown in Chicago, and in Newark. The most successful organizers were women, because of the bond they were able to establish with low-income women on welfare.

In general, however, within three or four years it was clear that this organizing was not going anywhere. It seemed strange to people living in central Newark or the East Side of Cleveland that obviously well-to-do young white people, who didn't need to be doing it, would move into the neighborhood and live together in a "freedom house." The Vietnam war caused the economy to prosper (relatively speaking) in the late 1960s, so that unemployment decreased rather than growing. Moreover, the Vietnam war gave rise to an enormous resistance movement made up of students and ex-students subject to the draft. By the end of 1967 ERAP organizers, like Rennie Davis and Tom Hayden, were drifting away from ghetto organizing and into anti-war work.

Meantime, the Progressive Labor Party (PLP) had infil-trated SDS and was the most effective of several far Left groupings in pushing a turn toward the working class. The basic reasoning was simple. Students, it was said, were nei-ther numerous enough nor sufficiently strategically situated to be able to change American society alone. The same was true of African Americans. In order to amass a movement large enough and militant enough to change the structure of American capitalism, it was argued, a way had to be found to enlist the predominantly white working class.

Within SDS there was some consideration of the con-cept of a "new working class": white-collar workers subject to some of the same oppression and deprivation as workers in heavy industry. On the whole, though, it was felt that blue-collar workers were most truly workers and would-be organizers concentrated on reaching them. Accordingly, in the late 1960s and early 1970s many young people sought factory jobs in basic industries like steel and auto.

These young people sought out blue-collar employment in the same spirit as previous "colonists" on the Left, some of whom were still on the job, in places like Gary, Indiana or South Chicago. Typically, the colonists, whether old or young, found themselves writing union election leaflets for more genuine steelworkers or auto workers whose ideology was far more conservative.

Another variant of the turn toward the working class, well described by Cathy Wilkerson in her memoir, *Flying Close to the Sun*, assumed that white working-class youth would be attracted by street-fighting tactics on the part of former students turned revolutionaries.

The ideological warfare surrounding this new strategy was overwhelmingly dogmatic and heavy-handed. Students who had never read Marx confidently brandished the writings of Che Guevara, Regis Debray, Frantz Fanon, or Mao Tse-Tung.

ANOTHER PATH

At the time I, too, was seeking a way to become a full-time radical and to contribute more effectively to fundamental social change.

I had lost my career as an historian. (At five Chicago universities, the chairperson of the History Department offered me a job only to be overruled by the administration.) I needed a new way to make a living.

For a time I considered going to work in a steel mill. A friend who worked for U.S. Steel in Gary dissuaded me. "Staughton," he told me, "you could be in the mill twenty-five years and people would still say: Let's see what the Professor thinks." I remember saying to myself, "Well, if I am stuck with being a smart cookie, I had better find a way to use what's between my ears."

An important transitional experience was employment at Saul Alinsky's new school for organizers in Chicago, the Industrial Areas Foundation Training Institute. I was in the bathtub shortly after the Democratic Party convention protest in 1968 when Mr. Alinsky phoned to offer me a job. From his point of view, I believe I represented an opening to the young people of the New Left. From my standpoint, it seemed to me that despite many differences with Alinsky, we of the New Left might very well have much to learn from the nation's most successful community organizer.

We were an odd couple. I was a romantic idealist. Alinsky believed that human beings were motivated by money, sex and power. Nevertheless I learned from him. I learned that before projecting my own ideas of what needed to be done, I should listen and try to be sure that a given issue "was there" in the minds of people on the streets before trying to organize around it. I learned that the most important leaders were informal, the people to whom others turned for advice. I learned that in forming a leadership group, one should initially assemble informal community leaders as a "temporary steering committee" in order to discover, in practice, who could best give the group direction.

Another opportunity to learn presented itself when Marcus Raskin of the Institute for Policy Studies asked Alice and myself to try our hand at organizing around health and safety in the workplace with the help of the just-enacted Occupational Safety and Health Act. We formed the Calumet Environmental and Occupational Health Committee (or "choke"). We drew on this work years later when we helped to form Workers Against Toxic Chemical Hazards (WATCH) in Youngstown.

In the end, I decided to try to become a lawyer. There were at least three reasons for this decision.

Even after I was no longer able to teach, I continued to do oral history. My wife and I compiled a volume of oral histories entitled *Rank and File*. One evening in Gary I interviewed a steelworker named Frank Felix. Like most of those we interviewed for our book, he felt that the employer was oppressive and the union was not much help. When I turned off the tape recorder he said, "OK, I gave you what you wanted, right?" I said, "Yes." Frank continued, "Now it's your turn to help me." He disappeared into a nearby bedroom and returned with a shoebox full of letters to every imaginable government personality or agency. I had to confess that I was not a lawyer and could not assist him. But that evening helped me to resolve that I would go to law school with the particular mission of helping rank-and-file workers mistreated by the company and deserted by the union.

The law offered Alice and myself an opportunity to work together. She had shown in doing draft counseling, and then in training draft counselors, an enormous ability to relate to persons in vulnerable circumstances and to master a mass of administrative regulations. My talents were different but it seemed that we might make an effective team.

Most important, employment law appeared to offer the possibility that without disguising our class origins or our years of higher education, we could present ourselves as persons with professional training whom workers might find helpful. This is just what occurred. It was as if the unspoken question always hovered in the air, "Who is that guy?" (meaning myself), and the answer, spoken or unspoken, was, "He's our lawyer." That said, everyone could relax and we could get down to business.

Years later, in Central America, Alice and I came to view the mutual aid of worker and legal professional as a form of what Archbishop Romero called "accompaniment."

WHAT I LEARNED

I devoted almost a quarter century—first as a law student, then (briefly) as an attorney at Youngstown's leading union-side labor law firm, then (with immense satisfaction for almost twenty years) as a Legal Services lawyer—to the question posed by the movement of the late 1960s, What about the working class? I do not regret these years. What did I learn? I want to begin, not with grand theory, but with some of the particular things I learned, at ground level, over the years as a lawyer for the rank and file.

1. One should not expect a coherent ideology from workers, at least as a group. Growing up working-class is not an Ivy League sherry party. Personal loyalty is valued more highly than intellectual consistency.

2. Youngsters who grow up in working-class communities are constantly under the thumb of figures of authority. They encounter, first the father, then the priest and school teacher,

then (after high school) superiors in the armed forces, and finally, supervisors in the mill. These rites of passage make it difficult for a person to value his or her own thoughts and feelings.

3. However, there are individual, self-taught working-class intellectuals who develop a breathtakingly comprehensive and committed orientation to changing society. John Barbero was the son of an Italian steelworker discharged for union activity in the 1930s. John enlisted in World War II but emerged from the war a de facto pacifist: "I was lucky," he liked to say, "I didn't have to kill anybody." John learned some Japanese and Korean at language school and as a guard for prisoners of war. After the war ended, he married a Japanese wife, a gifted painter, whom he brought back to Niles, Ohio. While finishing college at Youngstown State University, John discovered a kindred spirit in Ed Mann. Together Barbero and Mann passed through the United Labor Party of Akron, a remarkable fusion of Trotskyists and persons belonging to the IWW. The two were civil libertarians, fought racial prejudice both in the mill and in the community (at a time when public swimming pools were segregated), opposed both the Korean and Vietnam wars, and were independent socialists with a lower case "s." Alice and I moved to Youngstown because of these two men. Meeting them in 1971, I had the reaction that I would never again meet persons who so fully embodied working-class radicalism. "On this rock let me build my church," I thought. I might add that John came to the house once a week to play Scrabble and regularly beat me.

4. In organizing among workers, it is essential that from the very first meeting workers are in the majority and create the atmosphere and tone of all occasions. Too often middle-class radicals sit around a table and ask each other, "How can we attract workers?" The result is that when one or two workers show up they are likely to feel uncomfortable, unsure whether they can hold their own in a room full of fast talkers from another social world. The key to the success of

the Workers' Solidarity Club of Youngstown was that college professors and lawyers were always in the minority.

5. When workers from different kinds of industries, workplaces, and unions (or lack thereof) sit together in a circle, addressing problems that anyone may bring to the group, class consciousness develops naturally. This was the experience of the Workers' Solidarity Club over more than twenty years.

6. Once you become known to workers as a trustworthy and helpful person, all kinds of radicalism may be acceptable because "we know him." During Gulf War I, I picketed every day in downtown Youngstown.

7. Despite the general absence of articulated world views, or perhaps because of it, working-class people can learn from experience and make big intellectual leaps. Steel mills closed in Youngstown in three successive years. When the first mill closed, 100,000 persons signed a petition blaming the government (not the company) for its environmental and trade policies, and carried it to Washington D.C. in chartered buses.

The next year, when a second mill closed, steelworkers concluded that their labor had created the capital that the industry was using to create new facilities elsewhere in the country and put them out of work. They distinguished the company's "greenfield" approach of throwing away a whole community and its experienced work force, like an orange peel, from a preferable "brownfield" strategy that would seek to retain existing assets, such as trained workers, infrastructure (often provided by the community free or at less than cost to induce the company to locate there), and the more up to date machinery, to rebuild their existing workplace. By the third mill closing Youngstown workers perceived that U.S. Steel was not committed to the steel industry but would put its money wherever the rate of profit was highest. They were prepared to smash down the door of U.S. Steel's Youngstown headquarters and occupy the building.

8. Although national unions are top down, hierarchical bureaucracies, workers need local unions and will create and recreate them regardless of what Left intellectuals may think or say. The problem comes when workers escape from the mill to become local union officers and instead of reaching out horizontally to other kinds of workers and local unions, set their sights on higher office within the national union.

9. A great deal of potential creativity and solidarity is locked up in persons who may rarely have had the opportunity to speak in public or to use their natural authority. We were privileged to work with one middle-aged steelworker's wife who, by telephoning radio talk show hosts, singlehandedly assembled LTV Steel retirees whose health insurance had been terminated when the company declared bankruptcy. Similarly we came to know four workers for General Motors, two white and two black, who with our help forced the company and the union to do an epidemiological study of cancer deaths among former Lordstown workers and in the community at large.

10. The particular virtue of the working class is that from time to time there comes into existence a solidarity that prefigures a better world. Race and gender differences can be overcome when confronting common oppression. Especially in the face of the layoffs that decimated the Midwestern "rust belt" at the end of the twentieth century, workers often spontaneously acted out the idea that an injury to one is an injury to all. I have experienced steelworkers and visiting nurses lay aside hard-won contractual provisions for seniority so as to make sure that there would be some work for everyone who worked together. Instead of putting the most recently hired worker on the street with nothing, while the rest of the work force works full-time and even accepts overtime, they would say, "We'll all take a little less." Indeed I experienced exactly this at the Youngstown Legal Services office. When President Reagan cut the national Legal Services budget in the early 1980s all the lawyers in the office, regardless of seniority,

volunteered to work four days a week. The secretarial staff was underpaid to begin with and was not asked to take less.

SOLIDARITY UNIONISM

About 1990, a network of groups and individuals concerned with "workers' democracy" held two national meetings, the first in St. Louis, the second in Minneapolis. My friend and mentor, Stan Weir, was to deliver the keynote address in Minneapolis. He was unable to do so for reasons of health and I was asked to substitute.

At the time I had spent roughly twenty years trying to figure out the historical role, if any, of the working class in highly-developed capitalist societies. In addition to the oral history and day-to-day experience as a lawyer sketched above, I had written analytical labor history and law review articles. I had come to believe that before the passage of a new federal labor law and the creation of the CIO, both in 1935, there had been a period of three or four years in which, without the help of national institutions, workers in particular locations turned to each other and organized from below. It was so not only in well-known local general strikes in Minneapolis, Toledo, and San Francisco, but in locations like Barberton, Ohio and the anthracite coal country of Pennsylvania, cotton textile communities in the South, and in a plant in St. Louis that extracted nuts from their shells. I had concluded that the problems with CIO unionism did not begin with class collaboration during World War II or the anti-Communist witch hunts after the war, but with the very first contracts in steel and auto, when trade union bureaucrats voluntarily gave up the right to strike.

So I resolved to "let it all hang out," to try to sum up everything I had learned. In a cavernous room on the top floor of a decaying old building in Minneapolis I stood in the midst of several dozen younger comrades and talked on and on. Afterwards it was suggested that I present my remarks in a small book. I did so, and at this point I refer the interested reader to *Solidarity Unionism: Rebuilding the Labor Movement from Below* (Charles H. Kerr, 1992), and to several kindred elaborations: my articles on solidarity unionism in *Living Inside Our Hope* (Cornell University Press, 1997), including *"The Possibility of Radicalism in the Early 1930s: The Case of Steel"*; my introduction to a volume of essays by like-minded labor historians, *"We Are All Leaders": The Alternative Unionism of the Early 1930s* (University of Illinois Press, 1996); and to a new edition of *Labor Law for the Rank and Filer*, with IWW organizer Daniel Gross (PM Press, 2008).

The core idea of solidarity unionism is simple. Workers should look primarily to each other to accomplish their objectives, rather than depending on laws, government agencies, or distant unions. Collective direct action is likely to resolve problems more rapidly than filing a grievance or bringing a complaint to the National Labor Relations Board. This doesn't mean that written resolutions of particular problems with the boss cannot be helpful or that Section 7 of the National Labor Relations Act is useless. It is a question of emphasis. So-called labor relations in the United States have drifted into a lockstep where it is expected that a union will seek to become the sole voice for workers in a given workplace, and will negotiate collective bargaining agreements that, first, surrender to the employer the "management prerogative" of making big decisions about the enterprise, and second, take away from the workers their only way to resist those decisions, namely, to take collective direct action whenever and however they so desire. Working people must step outside this lockstep.

There is a fierce joy that comes from successful collective action. I recall a situation at the Legal Services office where I worked. The executive director had taken steps that were felt to destroy the culture of work we had created together. Our weapons of choice were two petitions, one to the Board of Directors of the agency, the other to the National Labor

Relations Board seeking a union election. I remember how one by one every single person in a very heterogeneous work force approached me to sign the petitions. And we won.

AND SO?

And so, what is the historical mission of the working class? At the risk of seeming simple-minded, I believe it is a good deal like the historical mission of prisoners, students, farmers in the Third World, women, African Americans....

In other words, workers are a mighty force that can heave the world forward toward a new day, but they are only one such force. In Russia in 1904-1905 and Hungary in 1956, yes, students could not change the world alone, yet they played an indispensable role in setting the stage for workers to act.

We are all leaders, not just as a collection of individuals, but as persons embedded in different kinds of institutions and communities of struggle.

The framework within which all these aspirations must be lodged is the collective action, not of taking state power, but of building down below a horizontal network of groups and persons that is strong enough to command the attention of whoever is in government office. This is the concept of "*mandar obediciendo*," to lead in obedience, exemplified at this writing by Subcomandante Marcos in Chiapas from below and by Evo Morales, president of Bolivia, from above.

Direct Action and Accompaniment

YOU MENTION ACCOMPANIMENT, *and we have already touched upon direct action a few times in our conversation. I propose that we use these twin concepts to signal a possible path to an anarchist-Marxist synthesis. One of my favorite essays of yours is from 1963, on Henry Thoreau the Admirable Radical. Thoreau is yet another figure whom both anarchists and Marxists, for good reasons, see as belonging to their own tradition. In the essay I mention, you pointed out that what was central for Thoreau was not "growing beans" but the notion of direct action. Direct action, understood as an imperative that one practice what one preaches, or as a way of actively engaging with the world in order to bring about change in such a way that means and ends become indistinguishable, is a signature trait of the new anarchism. Let us broach the questions of the relation of direct action and theory, and of accompaniment, as a form of praxis and mutual aid.*

What direct action means is self-evident. It is well described in the quotation from my essay on Thoreau contained in your question. Here are three other versions of a definition. In Jewish tradition, the question is asked: If not now, then when? If not I, then who? Adam Michnik, the philosopher of Polish Solidarity, once said:

> Start doing the things you think should be done.
> Start being what you think society should become.
> Do you believe in free speech? Then speak freely.
> Do you love the truth? Then tell it.
> Do you believe in an open society?
>   Then act in the open.
> Do you believe in a decent and humane society?
> Then behave decently and humanely.

A final example comes from my granddaughter's essay on Burma.

> There are things that can be done other than marching in the streets. Hannah Beech reported

that in Yangon [Rangoon], residents joined in a raucous [protest] at 7:02, 8:01, and 9 PM every day in which everyone banged on pots, pans, and other things to express their distaste for the regime and its lucky number 9, which is the sum of each of the times [7 plus 2, 8 plus 1, 9]. Recently, those living in Yangon have plunged the city in a nightly blackout, turning off all lights [and] television at 8 PM, the time of the government's news broadcast.

The more interesting, and difficult, question is: What is the relationship between direct action thus understood, and theory?

LIBERATION MAGAZINE AND STUDIES ON THE LEFT

The contrasting approaches of New and Old Left may be illustrated by two magazines: *Liberation* and *Studies on the Left*.

From its creation in 1957 until 1967, when I left the East for Chicago, the editorial board of Liberation included at various times A.J. Muste, David Dellinger, Barbara Deming, Bayard Rustin, Paul Goodman, Sidney Lens, and myself.

I recall attending meetings in downtown New York City at the end of the 1950s. Neophytes like myself sat along the wall. Around a central table sat David McReynolds, later peripatetic organizer for the War Resisters League and at the time editorial assistant for the magazine, and the Big Three: Muste, Dellinger, and Rustin. We were supposed to be considering articles for potential publication but most of the time was consumed by the Big Three describing their recent travels and activities, and their reflections about same.

By way of contrast, the editors of *Studies on the Left* never met in person, at least while I was involved (roughly 1964-1966). There were two factions. Tom Hayden, Norm Fruchter, and I believed that the theory required by the New Left should grow out of its multifarious activities. Eugene

Genovese, James Weinstein, and Stanley Aronowitz believed that the New Left would flounder unless it had proper theory, and that the necessary theory had already been discovered: it was Marxism. Hayden, Fruchter, and I ultimately resigned.

Who was right? There is no doubt—and once again I refer the reader to Cathy Wilkerson's revealing memoir—that it would have been helpful to New Left activists had more mature and seasoned analysis been available to them. In its absence, they tended to gravitate to the latest pop Leftist: Regis Debray, with his theory of "*focos*" (liberated zones); Frantz Fanon, who argued that violence was therapeutic for the oppressed; Carl Oglesby (then and now my dear friend), brilliantly pasting together fragments of Left theory into a scenario to which none of us could live up.

The problem was that Marxism was not much help, either. Ever since I could remember various Left publications had been predicting an imminent collapse of United States capitalism. It didn't happen and hasn't happened yet. The most weighty of these publications was *Monthly Review*, initially edited by Harvard-trained economist Paul Sweezy and trade union educator Leo Huberman. But *Monthly Review* had almost no contact with the labor movement in the United States, and placed a series of mistaken bets on China *vis a vis* the Soviet Union, and other disappointments.

THEORY AND PRACTICE IN MARX

Marx himself, had we paused to look, exhibited a range of experiments in the relation of theory to practice. As a young man he wrote in his *Theses on Feuerbach*: "The philosophers have only interpreted the world, but the thing is, to change it." In middle age he said, I believe in his *Critique of the Gotha Program*: "Every step in the real movement is worth a dozen programs." A touching portrait of Marx's modus operandi as a man approaching old age was presented to me when I was a Harvard undergraduate by a visiting scholar who had access to Marx's unpublished papers, Karl Korsch.

Korsch recalled that Russian revolutionaries including Vera Figner had asked Marx whether it might be possible for Russian society to move directly from the village commune, or *mir*, to socialism, thereby bypassing the horrors of capitalism. In order to answer the question Marx learned Russian and immersed himself in Russian economic statistics. A brief letter to Comrade Figner finally emerged after several discarded drafts. Korsch said that the overwhelming impression from Marx's papers was that in the twilight of his powers Marx had become a passive recording and copying instrument, unable to turn theory into practice as in his youth.

IS THERE SUCH A THING AS THEORY ARISING FROM PRACTICE?

As humorous prologue to this immensely important question, let me seek to immortalize a comment of the late Marty Glaberman.

Glaberman, who spent many years working in automobile factories in the Detroit area, once tried to describe a wildcat strike. He said: You are working at your machine. You see a group of fellow workers coming down the aisle. There are too many of them to suppose that they are going to the tool room. It is too early for lunch. Only one possibility remains, so you shut off your machine and follow the line out to the parking lot. Once there you ask the nearest colleague: What the hell is this all about?

It was also Marty who said of the early 1970s, when wildcats in the plants were at their height: An optimist is a person who brings his lunch to work.

Someone out there may ask the question: What good is theory anyway? We know what our values are, why not just practice them and let everything else take care of itself?

I respect that attitude. I suspect it is an attitude of the young, who consider the amount of time available to them to be infinite. In response, I can only put on the table some inspirational examples of theory and some situations when it seemed to me that the absence of theory was a crippling handicap. Let's go back to the New Left, and to SNCC. There is a wonderful book by Charles Payne, entitled *I've Got the Light of Freedom*, in which he argues that SNCC did have access to theory and offers Myles Horton's theory of education and Ella Baker's theory of organizing.

During the 1930s, Myles Horton founded the Highlander Folk School in Tennessee. There are two stories about Myles which, along with a book of recorded conversations between Myles Horton and Paolo Freire entitled *We Make the Road by Walking*, provide an introduction to his theory of education.

Myles Horton came from a dirt-poor family in the Appalachian mountains. As a teenager during the Great Depression he found himself spending the summer in Ozone, a remote hamlet in the Tennessee mountains, teaching Bible studies for the YMCA. About halfway through the summer he decided that he couldn't stand just talking about the Gospel while people were starving in the here and now. He let it be known that on such-and-such an evening there would be a meeting to discuss, What is to be done?

People walked across the mountains barefoot to get to that meeting. And as the time to begin approached, young Myles realized he didn't have any solutions to offer. In panic and desperation, he said to the assembled crowd: "Let's just go around the circle and see what ideas people have brought with them." The group did as suggested. People built on each other's contributions, and solutions began to emerge. "Highlander education" was born.

Later, after the Center was founded, Myles would host gatherings of grassroots trade unionists confronting the difficult and dangerous task of organizing unions in the South. At a time when Jim Crow was still universal in that part of the country, he made no distinction between blacks and whites. Blacks and whites were assigned to cabins in the order that they appeared at the conference site. Everybody ate together.

Only at the end of their time together, after participants had shared an interracial experience, would Myles say: "Now, we all know that distinctions between blacks and whites are ridiculous and that the races have to work together if we're going to get anything done. How can we explain this to our fellow workers?"

Ella Baker's theory of organizing was that the organizer had to go out among the people, listen, and encourage the formation of small groups prepared to attempt whatever the people themselves had proposed. As I have already described, when my wife and I moved to Youngstown enough of Ms. Baker's wisdom had rubbed off on me that I insisted that there must be a majority of workers in the room when any activity for workers was discussed. Only in that way could an atmosphere be created such that when a new working-class person came into the room he or she would feel at home and able to offer ideas without fear of ridicule or criticism.

MORE THEORY?

These are examples of a homegrown, close-to-the-earth kind of theory that evolved directly from folks' experience in organizing.

I think there is another kind of theory that is needed, too. Recall that I made the point early in these conversations that in order to combat capitalist globalization one needed an explanation of why the export of capital was taking place. I found, first in SNCC, then in Youngstown, that in the absence of a theory to explain what is going on economically the best-intentioned, most grassroots and democratic sort of movement is likely to flounder.

I have explained that SNCC began in direct action to desegregate public accommodations and then moved on to obtaining the vote for African Americans (which, as has often been observed, also turned out to require direct action). After I was asked to be Freedom Schools coordinator, as Freedom Summer approached I hesitantly but persistently spoke as follows: It's no longer possible to speak of a significant "Black Belt" of Southern counties where African Americans are a majority, because the mechanical cotton picker is destroying their livelihoods and forcing them to move North. Doesn't the movement also need an economic program? What will be our answer, after people have the vote, to the problem of African American unemployment? I have a letter I wrote to Howard Zinn in June 1964 in which I named three SNCC staffers I had approached with this concern who reproved me for wanting SNCC to have an "ideology."

As I saw it then, and see it now, I only wanted SNCC to look beyond the next bend in the road. In fact after the traumatic experience at the Democratic Party convention in Atlantic City in August 1964, SNCC was unable to formulate a program for moving forward. Bayard Rustin wanted SNCC to enter into coalition with the trade union movement and the Democratic Party to seek economic justice for African Americans. But the trade union movement, in the person of Walter Reuther, and the Democratic Party, in the person of President Lyndon Johnson, had just finished deriding and subverting the efforts of black Mississippians to be seated as convention delegates. Moreover, these same so-called leaders were promoting an escalated war in Vietnam. As Bob Moses memorably described the dilemma to a SNCC conference in Waveland, Mississippi in November 1964, this was "the box" in which SNCC found itself. A program was needed to extricate the organization from the box, an economic analysis was needed in order to formulate that program, and neither analysis nor program was forthcoming.

Something similar presented itself throughout the Midwest ten or fifteen years later. Factories were closing as corporate directors sought to employ workers at lower wages in the South or in other countries. What should be labor's answer? I have explained that U.S. Steel was not committed to the steel industry at all but would put its money wherever the rate of profit was highest. Sure enough, in the early 1980s U.S.

Steel changed its name to USX and, rather than modernize its mills in Pittsburgh, bought the Marathon Oil Company.

I concluded that the only way to save manufacturing in the United States was to expropriate property without compensation, as the North did in the Civil War when (as I recall the figure) $2 billion in slave "property" was set free. This, of course, would be some variant of socialism. Rather than put forward such a politically controversial program, the trade union movement in the United States prefers to stumble from defeat to defeat, still without an answer, confronting each new plant closing with the same tired old words.

WHAT ABOUT ANARCHISM?

In all humility I offer one following observation. When our movement collapsed at the end of the 1960s, leaving some of us in a state of Post Traumatic Stress, naturally we looked with fear, trembling, and hope to the possibility of a new movement, a new upsurge. Tom Hayden wrote about the suicide of Abbie Hoffman that we were all waiting for a new movement, and he guessed Abbie came to the point where he couldn't wait any longer.

The new movement did arrive, first in the pentecostal appearance of the Zapatistas in 1994, then in 1999 and after at Seattle, Quebec, Genoa and Cancún. Moreover, *mirabile dictu*, it arrived not exactly with a theory, but at least with a rhetoric: the vocabulary of anarchism. I could only marvel that somehow, in an underground process no historian has explained, small fires kindled by writers like Paul Goodman and Murray Bookchin had emerged as a forest fire of belief that capitalism has had its day, that another world is possible.

Far be it from me, and I mean this, to tell these splendid and heroic young people that they need more and better theory. I will just say that I am worried that in the absence of theory, many of those who protest in the streets today may turn out to be sprinters rather than long-distance runners.

One of the things that has helped me to keep going through the years is the belief that history has a structure, that just as capitalism took the place of feudalism, so some form of socialism—no doubt after many tragedies, many false starts, in many different forms—will take the place of capitalism. Moreover, this structure of history really is dialectic. After the fall of the Berlin Wall and Iron Curtain, after the collapse of Soviet Communism, pundits opined that history had come to an end and capitalism had won. Fifteen or twenty years later (I am writing late in 2007) the whole of Latin America, in alliance with much of the developing world, has arisen to reject market capitalism, to safeguard the resources of developing countries, to say No to the United States. I am full of hope.

High and Low Theory

WHAT YOU SAY *about "theory that arises from practice" and the need for "more theory" reminds me of an essay on the new anarchism written by David Graeber and myself. In that essay, titled "Anarchism, or Revolutionary Movement for the Twenty-first Century," we distinguished "low theory" from "high theory." We tried to argue that new anarchism might not need High Theory, in the familiar sense of today. Anarchism does not need a single, anarchist High Theory, a notion completely inimical to its spirit. Much better, we think, would be to apply the spirit of anarchist decisionmaking processes to theory: this would mean accepting the need for a diversity of high theoretical perspectives, united only by certain shared understandings. Instead of being based on the need to prove others' fundamental assumptions wrong, it would seek to find particular projects in which different theories* *co-exist and reinforce each other. So, much more than High Theory, what new anarchism needs is low theory: a way of grappling with those real, immediate questions that emerge from a transformative project.*

LOW THEORY IN PRACTICE

I think I immediately understand what you and David Graeber are talking about because of the Workers' Solidarity Club of Youngstown. Let me review the Club's story.

The Club grew out of a strike by electric utility workers in Youngstown in 1980 or thereabouts. The strikers got almost no support from the official trade union movement, leaving behind among some members of Utility Workers Local 118 a desire for a better way to mobilize strike support for any group of workers in the Valley who "hit the bricks."

Meantime, members of the Local had twice asked me to lead classes on labor history and labor law. The second time I said to myself, "I'm not going to talk about how to process a grievance. I'm going to talk about why we are all so disappointed in the official trade union movement, why we are all, as I put it, broken-hearted lovers." We are persons who have devoted a good deal of our time and our dreams to the labor movement. Let's talk about what went wrong, and what might be done differently.

My favorite evening during that "class" was a discussion of an encyclical "*On Human Labor*" that had just been issued by the Pope. The Pope said there were two kinds of labor: for money and for the glory of God. Bob Schindler, a lineman, a member of Local 118 and along with Ed Mann the heart and soul of what became the Club, said that when he got up on the utility pole he did so for the glory of God. (These were not idle words. Years later I got a better idea what Bob was talking about when he described how he and fellow workers acted during the winter ice storms. If they encountered a customer who had lost electric power they were supposed to fix the line but then report the address to the company so that service could be resumed the next day. Bob and colleagues would hook things up then and there so that the customer, often an elderly woman living alone, would have power that night. It was also Bob who on his own initiative went to Nicaragua to try to complete the work Ben Linder had been doing on electric service in a remote village.)

When the so-called class ended we all wanted to continue. Alice, my wife, suggested the name Workers' Solidarity Club. For the next twenty-some years, workers anywhere in the Valley knew that on the second Wednesday of the month they could find friends willing to help at 4140 Southern Boulevard, the address of Local 118, at 7 p.m.

This brings me to the convergence of our practice with "low theory." Our regulars included a diversity of perspectives. A couple would periodically respond to Democratic Party election campaigns. At the other end of the spectrum, Ed Mann, after several terms as president of Local 1462, United Steelworkers of America, after he left office always introduced himself as "member of the IWW," and Tony Budak called himself an "aspiring anarchist."

1. We had no membership roster and no dues, but raised money when we needed to by passing the hat.

2. We had no chairman or other officers. If a member invited a speaker, that member would be chairperson for the evening.

3. We felt no need collectively to approve each action by an individual member.

When a member wanted to do something he or she did not ask the approval of the Club. Rather he or she would say, for example, "I stopped by the picket line of the so-and-so workers and they say they need firewood. I'm going to take a truckload in the morning. If anyone wants to go with me, let me know."

4. We hardly ever voted. Ed Mann would say, "Does anyone disagree?" and we would all burst into laughter.

5. At the end of the evening we stood in a circle and sang the first and last verses of "Solidarity Forever" (sometimes adding the verse about farmers in deference to Merlin Luce, who, before becoming a steelworker, grew up on a farm in western Ohio).

Club members took part in some lengthy and dramatic strikes. One was at a local hospital. Concerned members of the Club met in the Lynd basement one evening. As people told how they would explain refusing to cross a picket line, Alice wrote down the words. By the end of the evening we had our first leaflet, captioned: "Think Before You Cross A Picket Line. Think Before You Take Your Neighbor's Job." The media thought our little group was somehow connected with the official labor movement and gave us a lot of publicity. Wednesday afternoons folk would gather outside the main entrance to the struck hospital. When a local court enjoined mass picketing, we paid no attention but one day went to the homes of corporate members of the hospital board of directors where there were many arrests.

The Club ended after at least four key members, including Ed Mann, died. In its last few years it took the form of a monthly newsletter, and meetings became editorial gatherings at Bob Schindler's home. This, too, came to an end when Bob died.

ANARCHISTS NEED MARXISM

I also agree with you in wishing to distance myself from recent Left "high" theory. My objections are simple: 1. It is unintelligible; 2. It is produced by persons with no discernible relationship to practice.

Nevertheless, I am convinced that anarchists need Marxism. Let me try to explain.

I lived through a movement participants in which had no consensus strategy about how to reach the better world we all desired, mixed political gestures with alternative life styles, easily became discouraged when victory did not come quickly, and in their frustration, sometimes turned to senseless violence. It was the movement of the 1960s.

I perceive the new anarchism as a very similar movement. Well-intentioned individuals drift in a sea of vague idealism, but with little conception of how to get from Here to There. When people return to their homes from apocalyptic demonstrations they have no notion about how to turn their energy into day-by-day organizing until the next demonstration.

It seems to me that the critique of "utopian socialism" voiced by Marx and Engels applies with equal force to latter day anarchists. They want something better, something qualitatively different, but they do not know how to make it happen. Countless small prefigurative experiments are launched within the belly of the capitalist beast. Most fail. Those that survive tend to be transformed into replicas of that which initially they opposed.

I want to make it clear that I am not a believer in "scientific socialism" as a solution to all problems. I oppose Marxism Leninism as well as Stalinism. I am keenly aware of Marx's authoritarian personality and desire for control.

Nevertheless, the general theory of class conflict expressed in *The Communist Manifesto* and the theory of capitalist development presented in *Capital* seem to me fundamentally correct. Much as I share Luxemburg's critique of Leninism, I believe Lenin's analysis of imperialism is also basically true.

There is one other aspect to my insistence that anarchists need Marxism. I think we need to take seriously the fact that most of humanity is in a different situation than footloose students and intellectuals, and is necessarily preoccupied with economic survival.

This was brought home to me as a graduate student in history when I took a long look at tenant farmers and artisans during the period of the American Revolution. Most of my Left colleagues who sought to view history "from the bottom up" focused attention on the ideology of such groups. I found otherwise. Whether a tenant farmer was for or against the

Revolution in the Hudson Valley of New York depended on the politics of his landlord: whatever the landlord supported, the tenant opposed, in the hope that if the landlord's political party was defeated the tenant might come to own his farm. Similarly, artisans before and after the Revolutionary War favored whatever political party most effectively opposed the import of British manufactures: this meant the Sons of Liberty in 1763-1776 and Federalists including Alexander Hamilton, who wanted a national government with a strong tariff, in 1787-1788.

There was nothing ignoble about wanting to own the farm on which a tenant labored, or to preserve an artisan's livelihood in making shoes, or hats, or nails, or sails, or rope, or barrels. But it is necessary to recognize the concern for economic survival that drove these lower-class protagonists. And Marxism appeared to do this more understandingly than does anarchism.

Does anything require us to reject the project of combining what is best in anarchism and Marxism? Are we fated endlessly to repeat the squabbles within the First International? It should be remembered that when anarchists launched the Paris Commune, Marx defended them. Likewise, when anarchists and Social Revolutionaries in Russia wondered whether Russia could altogether bypass the capitalist stage of economic development, Marx took the question seriously. There is a good deal of truth to the notion, famously expressed by Marx himself, that Marx was more flexible than his followers and in this sense was "not a Marxist."

Burnham's Dilemma

THIS MIGHT BE *a good moment to ask you about the problem that "has nagged at and puzzled you all your adult life"—the problem of transition from capitalism to socialism. Let us talk about E. P. Thompson's "warrens" and the so-called Burnham's dilemma. In what sense are the temporary spokes councils of the new anarchists, as you recently stated, "very different from the kinds of institutions (guilds, banks, corporations, or free cities) whereby the bourgeoisie built up a base of power within feudal society," but "not so different from the radical Protestant congregations that were also part of the capitalist new society within the shell of the old"?*

If another world is possible, a student asked me once, should we want to begin to bring it "from the ashes of the old," or "within the shell of the old"? And, if we want to build it within the interstices of the hierarchical society, how shall we proceed? What institutions and intuitions can serve the new anarchist movement in "warrening" the present society with the emerging institutions of the new?

I have discussed this problem elsewhere. Briefly, an ex-Trotskyist named James Burnham wrote a book entitled *The Managerial Revolution* in which he argued that the institutions of a capitalist society—free cities, guilds, banks, corporations, Protestant congregations, courts, in the end parliaments—developed within feudalism long before the bourgeoisie seized state power. Socialist institutions could not develop within capitalism, he contended: notably, trade unions did not prefigure another world but were institutions that ameliorated capitalist excesses and thus stabilized capitalism.

I read this when I was fourteen or fifteen and only began to find an answer at age sixty-five. The answer, it now seems to me, is that the revolution to which we aspire need not and should not seek state power. Rather, its project should be to nurture an horizontal network of self-governing institutions down below, to which whoever holds state power will learn they have to be obedient and accountable.

Here I would like to stress a pedagogical reason for the importance of this problem. It is not just that poor and oppressed people are preoccupied with economic survival, as suggested above. Additionally, I believe passionately that it is unfair and unrealistic to expect poor and oppressed people, or, for that matter, anyone else, ardently to desire and sacrifice for something they have not experienced. We learn, as the poet John Keats once said, from what we experience "on our pulses." How can we expect people to hunger and thirst for something new and different if they have never had even a moment to experience it, to taste it, to live inside it?

Lately I have been wondering if this is why great leaps toward the new, post-capitalist world seem to spring from communities that are still in living contact with pre-capitalist folkways and institutions: in Chiapas, in Bolivia, in South Africa, to name a few.

Accompaniment

LET US MOVE *to the second concept that we have chosen to aid us in our travels through this contentious territory of synthesizing what is best in the anarchist and Marxist traditions. How do you define "accompaniment," a form of engagement that you have been advocating from the 1980s? And how would you define it today, in the light of the new anarchist and Zapatista critique of vanguardism, in the light of "mandar obediciendo"? My concern is for new anarchism to find its way from guilt, anti-*

intellectualism, and theoretical elitism of the likes of Holloway and Negri, to accompaniment.

"Accompaniment" is a word that Alice and I began to use in the 1980s to describe how we wished to relate to the poor, to draftees and soldiers, to African Americans and other marginalized groups, to workers, and to people resisting United States imperialism in other parts of the world. Later we sought to approach prisoners in that same spirit.

We encountered the term "accompaniment" during visits to Central America and in reading about liberation theology. But years before Alice and I encountered the word, we had made the acquaintance of the concept in a series of practical situations.

Two agents of the FBI came to see me in our tiny Chicago apartment after I applied for Conscientious Objector status in the early 1950s. I let them in, and explained that if there were ever a socialist revolution in the United States, I would expect to be a part of it but in a nonviolent capacity.

At Macedonia, the single person of working-class background was Jack Melancon. Jack told us, "Sometimes all you can do for another person is to stand in the rain with him."

At the end of the 1950s, when I decided to go to graduate school and study history, I wrote in an unpublished memorandum: "I feel the need for a trade. I feel the most natural way to relate to others is by unselfconsciously offering a service of unquestioned usefulness." Later, the law appeared to offer a more useful service of this kind than teaching history.

When at the end of my graduate studies Alice and I accepted Howard Zinn's invitation to move to Atlanta so that I could teach at Spelman College, Alice made it clear that she was uncomfortable with the idea of picketing or sit-ins, but was willing to take part in a "live-in": to live on the campus of an all-black Southern college.

Speaking just for myself, by far the single strongest push

in the direction of "accompaniment" came after my father's death in the early 1970s. His papers included a manilla envelope on which he had written, "Stau [one of his nicknames for me], save these." The envelope contained his first three published articles. The first, entitled "But Why Preach?" had to do with my father's decision to go to Union Theological Seminary. The other two articles concerned a preaching assignment he undertook during the summer between the first and second years of divinity school: he became the temporary pastor of a Rockefeller oil camp in Elk Basin, Wyoming.

My summary of my dad's experience that summer in *Living Inside Our Hope* went as follows:

> My father arrived by stagecoach. Necessarily, his first project was to find a house in which to spend the night (very much as with Mississippi Freedom School teachers when they got off the bus in the summer of 1964). Then came the most important decision of the summer. "I learned at the supper table," he writes, "that the men did not like the idea of my calling on their womenfolk while they were off in the field." After supper he made the rounds of the foremen and was hired as a roustabout by the Standard Oil subsidiary. He slept in a seven-by-nine foot cubicle in the company bunkhouse, ate at the company cook shack, and made $4.05 a day for a six-and-a-half-day week.

He preached in the schoolhouse on Sunday evenings.

ARCHBISHOP OSCAR ROMERO

The pastoral letters of Archbishop Oscar Romero in the years before his assassination in 1980 remain the richest description of accompaniment.

The "kingdom of heaven," Romero wrote, "is not something that comes only after death…. [I]t has already been inaugurated in history." Poor people, especially, have begun to "live together in such a way that they feel themselves to be brothers and sisters." It was therefore the poor to whom Jesus turned: "he united himself with, defended, and encouraged all those who, in his day, were on the margin of society… sinners, publicans, prostitutes, Samaritans, lepers."

Sin is everything that gets in the way of the coming of the kingdom. The church must denounce "structural sin" and "institutionalized violence," Romero wrote. Therefore the church should condemn the capitalist system. Many corporations base their ability to compete in international markets on starvation wages, and oppose trade unions.

The church should set up and encourage base communities of the poor, and should resist their manipulation by political organizations. Christians may belong to political organizations but should be urged to profess their faith openly. The church should favor "profound, urgent, but nonviolent changes."

FATHER URIEL MOLINA

Five trips to Nicaragua in 1985-1990 gave us a language of "accompaniment" to describe what we were aspiring to do in the United States. Repeatedly, Sandinista activists told us that they first became politically involved by working with priests and nuns who had been touched by the new teachings of Vatican II and liberation theology. When the Frente Sandinista de Liberación Nacional (FSLN) came to power in 1979, it declined to execute people who had carried out atrocities under the old regime.

On three of our visits to Nicaragua, we stayed in Managua with a family that spoke no English. Just around the corner was the Church of St. Mary of the Angels, where Father Uriel Molina, a Franciscan, was the parish priest. Outside the entrance to the church was a wrought iron statue of

St. Francis and the wolf whom he tamed. Inside, the walls were covered by murals of old and new examples of Nicaraguan popular resistance. A band of former soldiers using electric instruments played the Missa Campesina or Peasants' Mass written by Carlos Mejía Godoy. (His son, Camilo Mejía, was later the first well-publicized soldier to refuse further service in the second Iraq War.) Jesus is depicted as a sunburned farm laborer standing in line for his pay.

The liturgy included the civil rights anthem "We Shall Overcome," sung in English and Spanish. Another part of the service allowed congregants to circle the church floor, greeting one another in peace. Many of those present were diminutive, elderly women who, as they approached, would show you a picture of a son killed in the North. On one occasion during this so-called Peace of God a bearded man ran across the floor and embraced me. It was Abbie Hoffman, whom I had last seen in a Chicago jail cell in 1968, and who committed suicide not long after. At the Church of St. Mary of the Angels, for the first and last time in my life I took communion.

During our 1986 visit Alice and I joined other Americans in picketing against the contra war in front of the United States embassy in Managua. A tall man came up to us and asked if we were Staughton and Alice Lynd. He said he was Joe Mulligan, a Jesuit priest, who in the 1960s had come to our home in Chicago on Wednesday evenings to talk about the war, the draft, and what was to be done. He and I had been arrested together in August 1968. He was now living in Managua. There he served poor barrios where there was no priest, helped in the formation of base communities and cooperatives, and said mass for disabled soldiers, Sandinistas and contras alike. He became our arranger and guide for later visits to Nicaragua.

In August 1987, our friend Father Joe translated two conversations with Father Uriel, which we recorded. Following are excerpts from Father Uriel's responses to our questions.

I am just a person who has opted for the religious way. Religious experience presents itself, at least for me, as an enigma. I studied law before I became a religious person. At a certain point I realized that I wanted to turn myself over to something: I still did not know what it was.

There were different stages in my experience of God. I came to live in this community [Barrio Riguero] with university students who had Marxist concerns. For these young people there was no contradiction between the kinds of lessons I was getting from the Gospel and the kinds of Marxist concerns that these people had.

There is a letter from Comandante Borge to Ernesto Cardenal in which Borge says, "I feel that a God grows in me, but if I do not feed Him, He will die." I feel that I could have written that statement. There is a God that grows within us but if you don't feed it, it will die. The problem is, how do you feed this experience?

The path to God can be none other than the path to find humanity. If we take off from the words of the parable of the Good Samaritan, the important thing is the walking of that road.

The priest and the Levite when they went by probably were thinking about religious things that they had to do, so they couldn't attend to the wounded person, when the most important thing is to be thinking about the wounded person and how to take care of him. Attending to that wounded person is the real path to knowing God. The real path to God is to have a tender experience with humanity.

For me it is a clear fact that the Christian base communities in Nicaragua arose and flourished in a time of very hard repression under the dictatorship. The Christian base communities became the only space where people could protest and project a new future and organize towards that.

I believe this is a very creative moment for our pastoral work. It is a situation like that of the people of Israel in exile, in Babylon, when as a people they had nothing and they were losing their identity and in danger of being attracted to the gods and values and idols of Babylon.

The prophets like Ezekiel were there to try and remind them of their identity and try to keep them together as a people and to rebuild themselves as a people.

We should see the Christian identity not so much in terms of what goes on inside the church, the liturgy, as in relation to the lived experience of people in society.

We ourselves may not be the ones to discover our role but others may point us to it. For example, during the time of the insurrection against Somoza, we felt that we might lose, we might all be killed. One day I was talking with a young man who never came to church but was a very dedicated person. I said, "Things are looking very bad. Maybe we better pull out because it looks like it is all over and we are all going to be wiped out." And the young man, William, said, "If you do that then the whole community will lose their hope, because your presence here is during the day like an open door and at night, a light."

In the time of the New Testament, Christians were called atheists. They rejected the gods of the empire and the standard religious beliefs,

so they were called atheists. Now there is a new
need for a kind of atheist vision where the idols
need to be knocked over and the true God is to
be found, because the old conception of God
doesn't speak to people today. It may be time
for becoming atheists with regard to ideas about
God, and discovering the true God.

After our visits to Nicaragua, Father Molina's pastorate at
St. Mary of the Angels was taken away from him and he was
excluded from the Franciscans for being too radical.

Intellectuals and Accompaniment

WHAT IS THE *role, if any, of a radical intellectual in the project
of accompaniment?*

I have two responses, one straightforward and generally
applicable, the other somewhat more nebulous.

My basic response to this question is: Let "intellectuals"
become doctors, teachers and lawyers. When my wife and I
lost our initial professions, I as an academic historian and
she in early childhood education, we decided to become
lawyers.

Thirty-five years later I can report that I am the beloved
friend and comrade of many, many working people in
Youngstown and, to a lesser extent, Pittsburgh. Former steelworkers who are now employed as security personnel in stores
and banks call out to me, "Hi Staughton! Remember me? I
used to work at...U.S. Steel, or Commercial Shearing, or
Delphi Packard." Most often I do not remember that specific

individual. Sometimes the men who greet me in this way are now uniformed officers at one of Youngstown's prisons.

With a dozen or so men the relationship is closer. Jack Walsh used to work at Schwebel's Baking. In 1977, when I had just arrived in Youngstown and Jack was in his thirties, he was involved in a wildcat strike, and discharged. He saw a photograph of me in a local newspaper, leading an anti-war march in August 1965 with red paint all over my shirt. Instead of thinking, I want nothing to do with that Commie, Jack reacted: That's the lawyer I want.

Over the years a pattern developed. Wherever he worked Jack sought to organize a union and acquired the nickname "Union Jack." At some point he would be fired. I would get a mid-morning call at Legal Services where I worked. "Staughton, are you busy?" "What's up, Jack?' "Well, to tell you the truth, I've been fired again."

I represented Jack in unemployment compensation hearings and at the National Labor Relations Board. In one unemployment compensation hearing, the hearing started in bright afternoon sunshine and when we emerged it was dark, with snow falling.

Now Jack is entering old age, he is divorced, he is struggling with cancer. And he says: "Staughton, any time you want a quart of milk in the middle of the night, you know my phone number."

All this is the more extraordinary because my personal background is upper middle class. My parents were both tenured college professors. We were not inconvenienced during the Depression of the 1930s. We went to New Hampshire for the summer throughout those years. During the winter we lived on the eighth floor of an apartment house on Central Park West in New York City. Throughout my childhood it seemed a long way to the ground, to the world of ordinary people.

Accordingly I feel, If I could do it anyone can do it. Once again: The key is to acquire a skill useful to poor and working persons. Armed with such a skill, just behave as a moderately decent human being and "accompaniment" will be a piece of cake. People will need you, and over time, as you offer a useful service trust and friendship will emerge of themselves.

ON BEING AN INTELLECTUAL

There is, to be honest, a further residual meaning to being an "intellectual." It has to do with being very bright, with seeing through this or that posture or mannerism, with being consistent over time, with having the courage to stand alone in relationship to peers and political companions.

Being an intellectual in this sense has nothing to do with making one's living in a college or university. The person I have known who most qualifies as an "intellectual" is Lee Hosford, who lived with me after I dropped out of college in 1948-1949. My son is named for him.

Lee was the son of a suburban railway engineer in Pasadena. Before I came to know him, he had attended Reed College in Portland, Oregon. He seemed to have belonged to every possible radical political group and to have experienced every imaginable form of addiction. When I later spent time with him in Cambridge after I returned to Harvard, he pretended to go to college but in fact sat in the cafeteria at Boston University and gambled. Later still, in the late 1950s, he was imprisoned in San Quentin for armed robbery to get money for drugs. I hitch-hiked across the United States to visit him in prison.

Finally, while I was going to law school in the 1970s, Lee came to live with us in Chicago. He was a hollow shell of what he once had been. His last words to me, as he was boarding a bus for a treatment center (which he did not attend), were: "Staughton, I'm just a lost soul." Not long after I heard from his mother that Lee was dead. I wrote a long, long letter to my son about the man for whom he was named.

When I met Lee I was enveloped in middle-class optimism about life. Surely, properly understood things were getting better. One had only to put one's shoulder to the wheel and all would, in the end, be well. If asked, one always responded that one was "fine."

Lee changed all that. He maintained that in every twentieth century war the way in which prisoners were treated had deteriorated. He pointed out that Trotsky had said to the anarchist rebels at Kronstadt, "I will shoot you down like pheasants." He told me how Bukharin had abased himself when condemned by prosecutor Andrei Vishinsky in the 1930s. Vishinsky called him a "running dog" and "lackey" of the imperialists, to which Bukharin responded: "Citizen prosecutor, you have found the word." Whereas I was (and still am) inclined to books with happy endings, Lee favored deeply pessimistic authors like Celine. On the other hand, Lee also introduced me to Yeats. There is in my mind an image of following ever smaller stream beds up a steep hillside that I associate with Yeats, and with Lee.

So what is an intellectual? Two of my high school teachers helped me to become one. I wrote a paper in a history class taught by Katherine Wells about the fact that European Social Democratic parties supported their respective national governments in World War I, which still defines my fundamental skepticism about the trade union movement. In an English honors seminar taught by Elbert Lenrow I first encountered (in translation) the Greek tragedians, and Shakespeare. Othello's soliloquy about his love for Desdemona, beginning "Had it pleased heaven to try me with affliction," still seems to me the greatest love poem I know of in any language; and a challenge to historians, since these words of a black man to his white wife were staged in London at almost the same time that the first permanent British colony was established in Jamestown.

In college, the only subject that caught my imagination was anthropology. I remember reading Native American oral histories in the small anthropology library across from the Peabody Museum. In law school, the only teacher I admired was the late Harry Kalven who died at the beginning of my second year. He taught the First Amendment as a common law process whereby the law "worked itself pure." He considered the ultimate speech test to be that enunciated by the Supreme Court in a short, per curiam opinion of the late 1960s in a case involving a leader of the Ku Klux Klan, *Brandenburg v. Ohio*. *Brandenburg* held that speech is seditious only when it advocates imminent lawless action under circumstances that make such action likely. (Since Brandenburg made his heated remarks in a cow pasture to an audience of television cameras, his speech did not qualify as seditious.)

I AM AN OUTSIDER

Thus it came about that, despite my relatively sheltered and privileged background, I came to be an Outsider and a friend of other Outsiders.

Workers, African Americans, and others who are relatively unprivileged and deprived, feel this outsiderness about themselves. The ultimate question about "accompaniment," I suppose, is whether persons from upper- and lower-class backgrounds can come to feel this together.

I believe it is so with me. There is a very funny chapter in Howard Zinn's autobiography, *You Can't Be Neutral On A Moving Train*. Howard comes from an extremely poverty-stricken background: his father worked as a waiter, and the family moved from apartment to apartment to avoid the rent collector. Toward the end of his book, Howard talks about meeting me. He tells how we climbed a mountain in New Hampshire together with his children, Myla and Jeff. All the way up that mountain and all the way down it, Howard and I talked politics. We couldn't find anything about which we disagreed. As he observes, "class analysis" could not explain our relationship.

With one or two exceptions, all the close friends of my adult life have been working-class intellectuals. They include: Lee Hosford; Howard Zinn; Wally Smalakis, whom I met when we both worked as "stock boys" at the Hyde Park Coop in Chicago and who testified before my draft board at the hearing to determine whether I would be classified as a Conscientious Objector; Jack Melancon at the Macedonia Cooperative Community; Vincent Harding; Youngstown steelworkers Ed Mann and John Barbero (see their stories in *Rank and File* and *The New Rank and File*); Stan Weir and Marty Glaberman, lonely working-class critics of the trade union movement whom I was privileged to know in their last years (Stan's story is in *Rank and File* and "*We Are All Leaders*," and I edited Marty's writings in a book entitled *Punching Out*).

Radical Intellectuals

WHAT ABOUT RADICAL *intellectuals who choose to make a living in a college or university? At the 1968 New University Conference you said that none of the following put bread on the table by university teaching: not Marx, not Engels, not Plekhanov, not Lenin, not Trotsky, not Bukharin, not Rosa Luxemburg, not Antonio Gramsci, not Mao Tse Tung. You said that intellectuals should live amongst the poor and marginalized for a time, and assist, if possible, in articulating and transmitting their collective experience. Instead of being caught in the "upward scramble" of the university, a conditioning institution that is a marvelously effective instrument in making us middle class, you invited radical scholars to begin with the reality of the movement and "observe how an intellectual function crystallizes* *out from its activity." Our mutual friend, Jesse Lemisch, who was the first to use the later famous expression "history from the bottom up," responded with a critique. I do not think that the* Journal of American History *had ever before or will ever again publish an essay with a title like "Who Will Write a Left History of Art While We Are All Putting Our Balls on the Line?" Jesse argued that the movement should not define our scholarly goals, that we need people who know about everything and not just about the movements. He asked, what if " the movement is wrong," for instance, when it is sharing the larger society's sexism? Instead of intellectuals becoming captives of the current Left and reduced to a mere accompanying role, he argued for constructing a broadly ranging Left culture that "has no imme- diate or even apparent long-term usefulness to the movement." Lemisch emphasized the importance of doing history regardless of its relevance to current movements of resistance. This came to be known as the "Lynd Lemisch debate." Now, and this is the reason why I am introducing it, this is a question of tremendous importance for my generation of revolutionaries. A good number of my friends involved with the new anarchist movement are academics. AK Press has just published a book edited by two of them, and on the flip side of the book you can read "from the ivory tower to the barricades." Are universities not an important site of struggle? If we are all only on the barricades, who is going to write* The Making of the English Working Class, *or* Intellectual Origins of American Radicalism, *or* A People's History of the United States?

THE ROLE OF LEFT INTELLECTUALS IN ZAPATISMO

I believe that the history of the Zapatista movement offers enormous support to the position I advocated in 1968.

Let's recall that our conversations began, at your sugges- tion, with Zapatismo. No doubt that is so because both you and I, along with the rest of the international Left, consider Zapatismo as the beginning of a new movement, a movement against globalization, a movement affirming that another world is possible. You incorporate the word "zapatista" in your e-mail address. I consider that the Zapatistas helped me to begin to answer a dilemma concerning the seizure of state power that I had been unable to resolve for 60 years.

So what does Zapatismo tell us about the role of radical intellectuals? As I understand it, the man who has taken the name of "Marcos" and other members of a small Marxist sect gave up their academic affiliations in Mexico City and moved to the Lacandón jungle in Chiapas. There they "accompanied" indigenous Mayan communities for the next ten years, until, on January 1, 1994, all concerned were ready to make a public appearance. (Understand, I am not opposed to books. A book about those 10 years of accompaniment, by someone in a position to write it, would be immensely valuable.)

What we should learn from this experience goes beyond physical relocation. As Teresa Ortiz put it to my wife and myself, when we spoke with her in San Cristóbal several years ago, the Marxists from Mexico City learned more from the Mayans than the Mayans learned from the Marxists. There was in addition the demand for land by Emiliano Zapata and his followers during the Mexican Revolution which was still a live memory in Chiapas, where very little land had changed hands; and the influence of liberation theology, sponsored by the then-bishop of the diocese, Samuel Ruiz.

All these ideological elements had to be discussed and re-discussed, practiced and practiced again. The emerging synthesis could not have been created in a university library. It required the humility and persistence of students and professors prepared to live, and learn, in settings more primitive than they could have imagined.

We on the Left like to think of ourselves as scientific. Well, consider the Lemisch and Lynd positions as hypotheses, and Zapatismo as the experiment. Doesn't that experiment support what I advocated forty years ago in the most dramatic and sweeping way?

THOMPSON, ZINN AND LYND

At the end of your question, you ask, if we are only on the barricades who would write *The Making of the English Working Class*, *A People's History of the United States*, and *Intellectual Origins of American Radicalism*?

Thompson wrote his masterpiece not during his brief (and in the end, unhappy) sojourn at Warwick University, but during the 1950s when he was a tutor for the Department of Extra-Mural Studies at the University of Leeds. Each tutor taught four or five classes and had to travel long distances. A common pattern was that an initial recruitment of fourteen or fifteen lost six or seven during the autumn but gained two or three latecomers. Colleagues did not live near each other. Thompson drew emotional sustenance less from fellow professionals than from his students, with whom he often joined in political demonstrations.

Thus Thompson did his greatest scholarly work during the period of his fullest immersion in working-class life. He stressed how much he learned from his students. One assignment—thirty or forty years before this assignment became commonplace in the United States—was to find an older person to talk about his or her younger days. As Thompson came upon original sources, he shared them with his students and asked them to comment in class. Sheila Rowbotham recalls a class on the history of mining when one student finally told the instructor: "Give me the chalk, Mr. Thompson."

Dorothy Greenald—to whom, together with her husband, *The Making* is dedicated—came from a miner's home where there was only one book. Thompson, she later recalled, "brought it out that your background wasn't anything to be ashamed of…that changed me really."

Howard Zinn's trajectory was similar. Although he made his living as an academic, first at Spelman College and then at Boston University, he seemed entirely indifferent to academia. I recall that when he first recruited me to join him at Spelman College, I, fresh out of graduate school, asked Howard what papers he was working on to present at which conferences of historians. He looked at me as if I were speaking a foreign language. He was one of two adult advisers to the Student Nonviolent Coordinating Committee, and his head was into recording their experience and participating in their actions and emerging strategy.

I can share comparable patterns in my own journey. My graduate school instructors in history wanted me to go on to some pretentious program at another Ivy League school. I asked them instead to write letters of recommendation to "Negro colleges" in the South, where the student movement was beginning. I did better scholarship on the Constitution while I was teaching five courses at Spelman, and travelling across town to borrow books from the Emory University library, than when I came to Yale. I wrote *Intellectual Origins* not to obtain tenure—I knew from the beginning that it might cost me tenure—but with a sense of desperation that my beloved movement was losing its bearings as it turned toward pop Marxism and fantasies of violent insurrection. Later on, in law school, my favorite professor offered to help me get a summer job at a downtown public interest firm. I said No, I wanted to work for a personal injury lawyer in the working-class suburb of Hammond, Indiana. In public interest firms, I tried to explain, lawyers met on upper floors of skyscrapers, decided what law suits would be good for the world, and then went looking for clients. On the other hand in the Hammonds of this world, people who needed help would bring their problems through the door.

I believe I have also demonstrated that one need not be a college or university teacher in order to write a book. Since leaving academia I have written or co-edited more than half a dozen books, including three collections of oral histories, a revised documentary history of nonviolence in the United States, a history of the struggle against steel mill closings in Youngstown, a history of a 1993 prison rebellion in Lucasville,

Ohio, a collection of essays on unionism in the early 1930s, and a manual on labor law for the rank and filer.

Truly I think that for persons who consider the Zapatista experience exemplary and paradigmatic, that experience is dispositive with regard to the question of whether Left intellectuals should remain within the university, and the debate between Lynd and Lemisch should move to the "Closed" folder.

Dual Power

WITH THE CONCEPTS *of direct action and accompaniment in mind I would like us to go back to your article "Decentralization: a Road to Power?" published in* Liberation, *where you gave a definition of revolution that greatly influenced me, as it did many other anarchist writers. You wrote that "No real revolution has ever taken place—whether in America in 1776, France in 1789, Russia in 1917, China in 1949—without ad hoc popular institutions improvised from below simply beginning to administer power in place of the institutions previously recognized as legitimate. That is what a revolution is."*

Many other writers have described what I also described in the passage you quote. The last chapter of *On Revolution* by Hannah Arendt is one example. Another is Trotsky's *History of the Russian Revolution*, which coined the term "dual power" to characterize the historical moment when the two powers—on the one hand, the official, traditional state dominated by the possessing classes, and on the other hand, the new self-acting popular committees—confront one another.

But what are the circumstances that bring this moment about? This is what I have called Burnham's dilemma. The bourgeoisie went about their daily lives over a period of centuries in a manner that gave rise to a plethora of new institutions in which they expressed their own dual power. How do those at the bottom of capitalist society, or on the receiving end of United States imperialism, do likewise?

Peasant communities have such an institution: the village itself, with its necessary decisions about ploughland and commons, rotation of crops, and the like. I was fascinated in the Golan Heights when the remaining Arab villagers explained that they resisted Israelis' conception of absolute property boundaries. We prefer, they explained, to adjust the boundaries of family farms from generation to generation so as to take into account the changing size of different family units.

In the Southern civil rights movement, Baptist congregations were institutions of dual power in a very real way. That is where protest marches would originate, where discouraged demonstrators would gather to lick their wounds and repair their spirits.

I have not found such presently-functioning alternative institutions to the same extent in working-class Youngstown. There is an overlay of peasant culture because so many families are from Italy and Eastern Europe. Local unions sometimes function as centers of resistance to a factory shutdown but local unions are forever corrupted by the ambition of men who get out of the shop to become local union officers and wish to rise even higher in the union hierarchy.

In the Sixties, when I wrote the article you mention, there were many attempts to create what we called "parallel institutions," a term resembling "dual power." But what have survived? Only two national networks: Headstart, for pre-school children, and Legal Services, for persons too poor to afford an attorney in a civil (non-criminal) matter; as well as a scattering of NGOs, and colleges and universities still influenced by dreams of the Sixties, like The Evergreen State

College in Olympia, Washington.

I am inclined to think that Latin American societies, struggling to shake off the impositions of neo-liberalism and globalization, offer the most hope. True enough, someone else's grass always looks greener. But I see in the South a wonderful spectrum of varieties of "*mandar obediciendo*," governing in response to what Marcos calls "the below."

Nevertheless, and in spite of all the above, I am unrepentant in affirming the words you quote that I wrote forty years ago. Why is this? Because I have experienced the beginnings of the dual power process, first in Mississippi in 1964, then with Youngstown-area workers over the past quarter century. Let me explain.

THE FREEDOM SCHOOL CONVENTION

During the summer of 1964 I was coordinator of Mississippi "Freedom Schools." These were improvised summer high schools that usually met in church basements. They were hugely successful.

According to Sandra Adickes, a teacher from New York City who worked in the Hattiesburg, Mississippi Freedom Schools, it was I who suggested a "Freedom School convention." I have only a visual memory of a meeting in Jackson to which I had invited the coordinators of the twenty or thirty local Freedom Schools. It was at that meeting we made a decision. The idea was that each school would send two or three elected delegates to a gathering in one location to talk about their collective future.

We did it. Now remember, it was dangerous for African Americans—young or old, male or female—to travel around Mississippi by themselves. They came, mostly by bus. They came to Meridian, near Philadelphia, Mississippi where in June three young men had been murdered, including a young black Mississippian, James Chaney.

The Freedom School convention met at what appeared to be a seminary building on the outskirts of Meridian that was no longer in use. It was the end of the first week in August. During that week the bodies of the three young men who were murdered had been found in an earthen dam in Philadelphia, and a statewide convention of the Mississippi Freedom Democratic Party had been held in Jackson.

The first evening, Friday evening, there was a memorial service in downtown Meridian for the three young men. I remember young African American men, in their best black suits, walking along the sidewalks in silence to reach the meeting place.

At the convention there were many workshops, which ultimately reported to the delegates as a body and offered resolutions for approval. These resolutions included topics like the concentration of land ownership in Mississippi and relations with Cuba. (I cannot remember whether there was a workshop on the mechanical cotton picker, probably the single most important economic force shaping the lives of these young people.) There was also general discussion of the question: At the end of the Summer Project, should we try to create a statewide alternative school system? The delegates decided, No. I thought then and think now that it was the correct decision. We did not have the resources to pull it off, and many young African Americans already facing many difficulties would have had to go forward into adult life with inadequate credentials.

But the discussion, like the discussions at the Petrograd soviet reported by John Reed in *Ten Days That Shook the World*, stays in the mind. Professor Dittmer of Tougaloo College in Jackson, an African American institution, reports that he could always tell which of his students had been in the Freedom Schools: they thought for themselves, they asked questions.

And years later, as a law student, I learned what happened when black students in Philadelphia went back to their segregated schools that September. They wore buttons that said "SNCC" and "One Man, One Vote." They were sent home. They went to court. They won. And that victory, in a case called *Burnside v. Byars*, was the precedent later cited by the Supreme Court of the United States when it upheld the right of a young white woman named Tinker in Des Moines, Iowa, to wear a black arm band to school to protest the Vietnam war.

THE WORKERS' SOLIDARITY CLUB OF YOUNGSTOWN

And in fact, I have abundantly experienced the same thing here in Youngstown. As I indicated earlier, the Workers' Solidarity Club became embroiled in a very large hospital strike at Trumbull Memorial Hospital in Warren, Ohio. Ed Mann and Ken Porter visited their picket line. Most of those on the line were women, but the local union president and the union staff representative were male. Members of the Club met in the Lynds' basement to talk about what we might do. We decided to rally once a week in support of the strike and pass out a leaflet.

The weekly gatherings at the hospital entrance were a resounding success, and grew larger and larger. Established local unions, such as the UAW local at General Motors Lordstown, encouraged their members to turn out, and they did. Someone improvised the chant, "Warren is a union town, We won't let you tear it down." On one occasion there was a march from a park in downtown Warren to the hospital. The marchers were wall to wall: that is, they took over the main street of this medium-sized industrial city, with the front row of marchers stretching from the shop windows at one side of the main drag to the shop windows on the other side.

The hospital got an injunction. We paid no attention to it, and so the judge ordered a hearing as to whether we should all be held in contempt. Ed Mann was called to the stand. He was asked, Why did you violate the injunction? Ed replied, What injunction? I've never seen one. Nobody ever read an injunction to me.

The judge looked around the courtroom. There was a

standing-room only crowd: working-class men and women dressed cleanly but informally leaning against the walls, left, rear, and right. They all could vote when the judge next ran for office. Finally the judge said, Well, Mr. Mann, now that you know that there is an injunction: don't violate it again.

The next thing that happened passed into local mythology as the event at Country Club Lane. One Wednesday afternoon, on the street outside the hospital entrance, the crowd decided that blocking the entrance and giving speeches wasn't enough. They would go to the homes of the hospital trustees, many of them located on a nearby street named—believe it or not—Country Club Lane. There one of the strike supporters wrote a slogan with her lipstick on the glass front door of one of these big houses. She was arrested. The crowd surrounded the patrol car so that it couldn't move (exactly as at the University of California in Berkeley during the Free Speech movement eighteen years before). Finally the crowd returned to the hospital, where police officers seized Ed Mann and dragged him across the street. A photo in the local newspaper showed Ed clutching the top of his pants as the cops dragged him across the ground. We made a poster of it with the caption, "LABOR LEADER COOPERATES WITH WARREN POLICE."

There were other glorious battles. Workers at a Buick dealership in south Youngstown went on strike, and a particularly reactionary judge issued a sweeping injunction. He held a striker in contempt of court for bringing a cup of coffee to a picketer, thus momentarily placing two men at an entrance instead of the permitted one.

We foiled the judge by means of a weekly "honk-a-thon." The Buick store fronted a main street. Strike sympathizers formed a long cordon of cars, and drove slowly—oh, so slowly—past the Buick place at times of the week when it was especially busy, like Saturday afternoon. Were we marching? No. Were we picketing? No. We were just community residents going about our business, with signs fastened to our cars disparaging the ancestry and motivation of the owners of the dealership.

At Buick Youngstown, as at Trumbull Memorial Hospital, the intervention of the Workers' Solidarity Club saved the local union.

SOLIDARITY USA

All the steel mills in Youngstown closed over a three-year period, one each year, from 1977 to 1980. After the mills closed, the struggle was to hang on to the pension and health care benefits that the companies had promised to their workers in better days.

Several steel companies—Youngstown Sheet & Tube, Jones & Laughlin, Republic Steel—had been absorbed into a conglomerate known as LTV Steel. One day in the mid-1980s, as I walked past a local newsstand on the way to my Legal Services office, I noticed that LTV Steel had declared bankruptcy.

Not only had the company declared bankruptcy, it turned out. LTV Steel also stopped payment of health care benefits to retirees. People died as a result. A man named Roy St. Clair who had a heart condition had been released from a local hospital. He experienced a recurrence of symptoms, but, afraid that he had no way to pay for further medical care, did not return to the hospital. Instead he spent a day frantically calling local insurance providers in search of replacement coverage. Mr. St. Clair died the next day.

In the office building where Legal Services was located, there was an eye doctor on the floor below. The eye doctor's receptionist was a woman named Delores Hrycyk (pronounced "her-is-ik"). She was the wife of an LTV Steel retiree. She called local radio talk shows and said there would be a rally about LTV in the downtown square the next Saturday. A thousand people attended. It seemed that every local politician and union officer east of the Mississippi wanted to talk, but none of them had any idea what to do.

Ed Mann, himself an LTV retiree, stood at the back of the crowd with a megaphone calling out, "Bullshit!"

Ms. Hrycyk announced a follow-up meeting in a Youngstown church. There she posed the question, What shall we call ourselves? It was suggested from the floor that we were something like Polish Solidarity, which had recently been in the news. "All right," Delores pronounced. "We'll call ourselves Solidarity USA."

We met periodically in the Odd Fellows hall in nearby Hubbard. Our signature activity, however, was to charter a bus to go wherever we thought we might be heard. We went to city council meetings in Cleveland and Pittsburgh, to the headquarters of LTV Steel in Cleveland and of the United Steelworkers of America in Pittsburgh, to Congressional hearings in Washington D.C., and to the bankruptcy court in New York City. We would contact, for example, LTV Steel, but we never asked for an appointment. Instead we would say, "We're coming Tuesday morning." Our buses—sometimes half a dozen of them—would arrive, and we would set up a massive picket line. Without fail a representative of the beleaguered entity within would appear and invite "your lawyers" or "your leaders" to a meeting, sometimes specifying how many persons might take part. We always answered, No, we have a committee: we want you to hear from the people who have actually lost their benefits. Then Alice and the committee would go in, enter the elevator, and do their thing in some upstairs office, and I would stay on the sidewalk outside and walk up and down, up and down, with the elderly picketers.

As during the struggle against steel mill shutdowns, so in the struggle to preserve retiree benefits an analysis gradually emerged. We came to see that companies had promised retiree benefits when they took it for granted that the good times after World War II would go on forever. Now, though, there were more retired steelworkers than there were active employees, and the so-called "legacy costs" that the company had promised to retirees were increasingly burdensome. I shall never forget lunchtime in a New York City cafeteria while we waited for bankruptcy court to resume that afternoon. We had obtained a copy of the tentative collective bargaining agreement under consideration by the company and union. I made a rough calculation showing that active workers, who still produced surplus value for LTV, had been promised $7.00 in new compensation for every $1.00 envisioned for retirees.

We were successful. LTV resumed payment of health care benefits. The company tried to dump its pension obligations on the United States government, but a federal court found its action unlawful. (In any event the Pension Benefit Guaranty Corporation would have provided only pension payments owed after retirement. Most members of Solidarity USA had also lost so-called supplementary pension benefits that had been negotiated by the union to compensate members who were laid off before retirement age because of plant shutdowns.) Miraculously, but also because of many, many early morning and late night bus rides, when LTV Steel emerged from bankruptcy the retirement benefits promised to former steelworkers and their families were substantially intact.

WATCH

One day four men showed up at the Legal Services office. Two were white, two African American. They said they had been sent to me by our local state representative, a family friend. They said they were chemically poisoned automobile workers.

I responded, You are what? I'd heard about "black lung" among coal miners and "brown lung" as an affliction of textile workers. But automobile plants?

One of the four men, Chuck Reighard, invited Alice and me to go on a tour of their plant. At the end of the tour, he would be waiting for us on the stairs, and take us up to see the paint booth on the second floor.

The paint both turned out to be an enclosed space with a conveyor line down the middle of the room that carried each automobile chassis from one end to the other. On either side of the line stood men and women, wearing white cotton masks, who for ten hours a day sprayed paint toward the chassis as it moved slowly past. Inevitably the paint spray also went into one another's faces.

The four and I met at the office. I said I was convinced. We decided to set up a meeting with the local union officers, and to take along the state representative and the head of the Working-Class Studies program at the local university.

The meeting was a failure. We knew that the local union president had worked in the cushion room, and experienced respiratory difficulties. But he and the others were terrified that we might create a fuss that would cause General Motors to close their plant rather than a counterpart facility in Michigan or Ontario.

The four men and I met once again. One of them said, What about the obituaries? I said, What about the obituaries? They explained that they kept close track of obituaries in the two local newspapers, and the deceased identified as former GM employees seemed to die at very early ages. I asked that they xerox all the relevant obituaries during an 18-month period. They did it.

We met again. Now what? I inquired. One of the men said, What about the Vietnam Memorial? Their idea was to create a "Lordstown memorial" on which, using the information from the newspapers, the names of former GM employees and their ages at time of death would be inscribed in black Gothic lettering.

Using a very large sheet of plywood, painted white, they did it. We decided to hold a press conference. We picked an out of the way location that we could use for free, and an early afternoon time that apparently is the wrong time for an ordinary press conference that seeks media publicity.

But somehow, this was not an ordinary press conference.

That morning I got phone calls I had never gotten before, even at the height of our struggle to save the mills. "This is the Cleveland *Plain Dealer*. Where is this press conference?" When we arrived, there were people there from other plants we had not contacted. They said, for example, We're from the acid line at plant so-and-so. Too many people who work on that line are getting sick.

The plant manager and the local union president both showed up, made a nuisance of themselves, and were asked to leave. Chuck Reighard, standing in front of the Lordstown Memorial, chaired. For me the most dramatic moment in the meeting came when a woman stood up to describe how her husband, a Lordstown worker, had come home day after day with a mysterious black goo in his throat that he would cough up. Then he died. What was his name? Chuck asked. The woman called a name. Chuck said, I worked next to him. They fell into each other's arms.

We had a specific demand. Alice and I had done some work on health and safety before coming to Youngstown, and Alice found an old UAW booklet describing how workers could carry out a comparative "epidemiological study." The idea was to compare the rate of deaths from cancer among former employees of a plant with the death rate from cancer among the general population in the area from which the plant drew its workers. To do it properly, one needed the cooperation of the company, which had the best records, as well as of the union.

Our improvised press conference created such enormous publicity that within a matter of weeks the company and the union promised a study. WATCH (Workers Against Toxic Chemical Hazards), as we had named ourselves, kept track of its progress with the help of a "mole" in the health and safety department of the international union. When the results were announced, it turned out that 1.5 former employees died from cancer for every one person in the general population who died from the same cause.

Years later, Alice and I were driving down a street in Warren, Michigan, next to the Ford plant that makes its Suburban Utility Vehicles. With us was a friend who was at the time "shop chairman" of the large and powerful local union. He pointed to the exhaust stacks from the roof of the plant. They used to be shorter, he explained. "But you guys in Lordstown proved that toxic exhaust from the plant was being sucked back in through the pipes supposed to provide fresh air. We owe you."

Parallel Institutions during the American Revolution

WHAT ABOUT YOUR *work as an historian of American Revolution? Does this Revolution ("a kind of revolution," as Zinn calls it) offer examples of parallel institutions, dual power processes, self-activity and institutional creation? You mentioned Hannah Arendt. In her essay "The Revolutionary Tradition and its Lost Treasure," she writes about the emergence "of the germs, the first feeble beginnings, of a new type of political organization, of a system which would permit the people to become Jefferson's 'participators in government'." She also sees the "fateful failure" of the founders to "incorporate the township and the town-hall meeting into the Constitution," because it is precisely these institutions that have functioned as a breeding ground for revolution, that have served as springs of political activity and of lived experiences crucial to the founding of a new body of politics. According to Arendt, the founders, acting in this way, have in fact "taken the revolutionary spirit for granted," and "cheated" American people of their "proudest possession."*

You ask, Does the American Revolution offer examples of parallel institutions, dual power, self-activity and institutional self-creation?

The answer is, Yes of course. Sometimes such entities took names like "committee of correspondence" or "committee of safety." Sometimes they were almost nameless, as in the ad hoc assemblages that traditional historians describe with words like "the mob" or "the rioters." Sometimes they were extensions of previously-existing institutions: my understanding is that when the suffrage of the Boston town meeting was extended to let more persons attend, the resulting gathering was known as "the body." In general the American Revolution was a time when what were then called "the people out of doors" came to the front of the historical stage and made themselves heard.

According to Tom Paine these popular committees governed the states of the new nation from 1775 to 1777, and did so well. It would be good to know a great deal more about them, if sources exist and the scholarly energy can be found. The most important location to study is Philadelphia, located as it was in a Middle Colony where the town meeting in its New England form was not established.

A number of fundamental comments seem in order.

Self-acting popular committees appear not only in the American Revolution, but, as I said in *Liberation* in the 1960s, also in the French, Russian (both 1905 and 1917), and Chinese revolutions, and, I would now add, in the English revolution of the 1640s, in Italy in the early 1920s, in Spain in 1935-1937, in Hungary in 1956, in France in 1968, in Poland in 1980-1981, in Chiapas from 1994 to the present, in Bolivia…. The list goes on and on until one recognizes that as a general proposition, where traditional central authority breaks down, popular self-acting committees step up to take its place.

Each such upheaval has its own special characteristics and the American variety was neither deeper, wider, stronger, or in any overall way more impressive than counterpart phenomena in other societies during the past 250 years. Marty Glaberman liked to say that in Hungary in 1956 there was not an economic depression, the trade unions were captives of the state, and there was no popular press, yet committees appeared all over Hungary in a matter of days, if not hours.

An overview of the American events would emphasize:

New England and the colonies from Maryland and Virginia southward were two different worlds. The town meeting of which Jefferson and Arendt spoke did not exist outside New England. Local government in the South was administered by interlocking entities imported from Great Britain: county (not township) units of local government, the local Anglican Church vestry, and the Justice of the Peace. This was government by gentlemen and it did not change significantly during the years of the Revolution. A "committee of correspondence" in Virginia was composed of members of the provincial legislature, every one of them white and rich, meeting at a nearby tavern. A committee of correspondence in Massachusetts or even New York was likely to be a motley assemblage of middling landowners, merchants trading with the West Indies, sea captains, well-to-do artisans, and a fringe of less affluent hangers-on.

Furthermore, the policies of all the British colonies (with the partial exception of Pennsylvania) toward Native Americans and Africans cast a shadow over, poisoned, distorted—choose your metaphor—everything else undertaken by the settlers. My mother-in-law's father was commissioner of public health in Baltimore. In the early 1900s he purchased a waterfront property in Rhode Island on which he built a home called "Metacomet." On the dining room wall there hung an "Ode to Metacomet." It took me forty years to realize that Metacomet was the Native American leader also known as King Philip. When the Puritans finally captured him, they cut off his head and put it on a pole.

The ubiquity of horizontal networks of self-acting popular

committees in times of social change forces one to ask: What is a revolution?

From one point of view, the efflorescence of such a network in the new American states during the years 1775-1777 (according to Paine) was a revolution, and a largely non-violent one. Yes, many persons believed to be supporters of the King were tarred and feathered, a process both painful and humiliating. But it did not kill the victim. It was an insurrectionary version of putting a miscreant "in the stocks" on the village green. Yes, the lower orders broke into Governor Thomas Hutchinson's fine home, desecrated his library and drank his wine. But they did not kill him. Yes, in the late winter of 1770 unemployed seamen and apprentices accosted British soldiers at the custom house in Boston, and threw oyster shells and snowballs at them. But it was the British who opened fire and thus perpetrated the "Boston Massacre."

On the other hand, every single one of the ventures or experiments in government from below that we have been discussing existed for only a few months or years. In many societies they were drowned in blood. In most cases underlying economic institutions, that provided the matrix within which all political arrangements functioned, did not change. The leases on Hudson Valley manors after the Revolution did not differ dramatically from such leases before the Revolution. From this point of view what happened in these revolutionary moments did not amount to a revolution at all.

The so-called American Revolution may usefully be contrasted with the Civil War. Charles Beard called the Civil War the "Second American Revolution." It might be more accurate to say it was the first revolution. Millions of dollars in slave property was confiscated without compensation. The underlying economic institutions of the Southern states did change, notwithstanding the efforts of plantation owners to perpetuate slavery in the form of sharecropping and the convict lease system.

And this revolution was astonishingly bloody. When President Lincoln declared in his Second Inaugural Address that if it were necessary that every drop of blood drawn with the lash should be repaid with a drop of blood drawn by the sword, he described the situation as it was. There were about 500,000 slaves in the thirteen colonies at the time of the American Revolution; 750,000 Union and Confederate soldiers died in the Civil War. Before the Battle of Cold Harbor, Union soldiers pinned to their uniforms pieces of paper with their names and addresses, so that their bodies could be identified.

President Lincoln did not glorify violence. He wrote handwritten pardons for soldiers facing execution and in that same Address spoke of malice toward none and charity toward all. But the rhetoric to which the horrendous conflict gave rise is alarming. Julia Ward Howe wrote the words of "The Battle Hymn of the Republic" early in the war. Her carriage was immobilized by columns of Union soldiers marching through Washington, D.C. singing "John Brown's Body." As she waited in her carriage, Ms. Howe wrote new words to the tune, taking them from Revelations 14:18-20, 19:15. The "vintage where the grapes of wrath are stored" is not wine, but blood. God did indeed unleash a "terrible swift sword."

All this requires sober discussion as well as faithfulness to dreams. What I find annoying, indeed infuriating, are the following two attitudes:

On the one hand, I disagree with the belief that socialism has failed and we are at an "end to ideology." I believe that certain attempts to create socialism have failed, at terrible human cost, at least in the sense that regimes and economic institutions have collapsed. However, many persons in East Germany and the Soviet Union wish that certain aspects of the previous Communist society still existed. When Alice and I toured Eastern Europe with a choral group we found that our student guides had not imagined that they would lose free health care and free higher education when Communism was overthrown.

On the other hand, I object to the attitude of some anarchists that "we have the answer, now it's time for the world to listen to us." Surely one has to recognize that there has never been an anarchist revolution that lasted. Thus anarchist as well as socialist revolutions have failed.

This is not cause for despair. Capitalism took centuries to come into existence and it did so after a myriad of false starts, bastardized ventures, and outright failures. The good society that will come after capitalism should be expected to experience similar birth pangs.

However, there is abundant cause for humility. And from my point of view, the first expression of this desirable attitude should be an openness to combining or synthesizing what is best in the anarchist and Marxist traditions.

Oaxaca

DO YOU SEE *recent struggles in Oaxaca, and the short lived Oaxaca commune, as an illustration of the same " general proposition" of a failed venture in "government from below"?*

I feel sure you and I would answer this question similarly.

Throughout history, there have been moments when self-acting popular committees have taken control of local affairs for a brief period, only to be drowned in blood, to fall apart, or to be shoved to the side of the historical stage by resurgent central institutions.

One thinks of the Paris Commune, the Russian soviets,

the committees in Hungary and Poland.

Oaxaca is another case in point. The movement began as almost an annual occasion whereby teachers sought to be paid adequately. By mid-summer 2006 it had become a movement that reached out far beyond the ranks of teachers to demand the resignation of the provincial governor. After many deaths, including that of your friend and comrade, and ongoing imprisonment of many others, the provincial governor remains in power.

But of course, the moment of efflorescence is also an imperishable victory. So many things about Oaxaca were special: the role of women in taking over a hostile TV station, the deep support for the protest among the most ordinary householders, the fragile network that reached out to schools all over that large province (where our daughter Martha taught for a time in mountainous Tlahuitoltepec), a teachers' union that made one of its first demands: shoes for the children.

The tension between brief epiphanies and the hope for long-term institutionalization remains. Here is an anecdote. The former SDS member who has achieved most power and authority is Paul Booth, an early president of national SDS, who has for years been organizing director of AFSCME, one of the largest trade unions in the United States. At the third and last SDS reunion we formed a circle to articulate what we wished to pass on to our children. I was the facilitator. Paul approached me. He said in effect, "Staughton, I am shy about speaking. I will post my thoughts on the far wall. Please call them to the attention of others." When I read Paul's words, they emphasized his desire to contribute to lasting institutions as opposed to brief manifestations.

Spontaneity and Organization

ONE OF THE *central dilemmas in many of the discussions among the new anarchists is the tension between spontaneity and organization. How do you see this dilemma—if it really is a dilemma—and what is the best way to approach this question from the perspective of our proposed anarchist-Marxist synthesis?*

SDS and SNCC floundered in part because they never adjusted to the increased size of their organizations. SDS at the beginning was a couple of dozen friends. Years later there were literally hundreds of thousands of young people in the anti-war movement who identified with SDS. You can't operate democratically in a movement with thousands of participants as if you were still a roomful of friends. What happens is that a small clique makes backstage decisions without accountability to the membership.

Richard Rothstein of SDS used to say that another reason for formal democratic procedures is that consensus works best with people who share a culture. When you had middle-class "organizers" and working-class young people on the North Side of Chicago (where Rich worked in a project called JOIN) or blacks from Mississippi and northern whites who volunteered for the summer and then stayed (as in Mississippi after Freedom Summer), consensus decision-making is difficult even in small groups. There is a deference to the more articulate.

A certain integrity about losing is also required. Stokely Carmichael displaced John Lewis as chairperson of SNCC by the process usually associated with Communists: you wait until many people have left or gone to bed and then call for a new vote.

So, assuming that something more and other than

consensus is needed as an organization grows, what does that look like? Anarchists had some good ideas about "spokes" (representatives) and a "spokes council," but this can't be improvised in the midst of confrontation with the armed forces of the state, as happened at Seabrook. It is especially needed before and after such confrontations.

Representative democracy can be quite democratic if you try to make it democratic, rather than using large assemblages to impose preconceived ideas. The Zapatistas appear to be exemplary. In the first place, as it was explained to Alice and myself, the community (the local movement) needs to take responsibility for the livelihood of anyone it asks to serve as a representative. Second, the representative should be an instructed delegate. In the initial negotiations in San Cristóbal, when a problem arose as to which the delegates had not been instructed, they said: "Sorry, we'll have to go back to the village *asambleas* for instructions before we can respond." Third and fourth, rotation in office must be enforced and the salary of a representative can be no larger than that of ordinary people back home.

To the extent that there are caucuses prior to large assemblages, not only must they be transparent but unless caucus members are willing to approach the occasion with openness to what they may learn, they should be asked to leave. The attitude must be: "Hello. I am a member of Caucus X. We advocate So and So. But I want to be open to whatever other groups and individuals think. What do you think?"

I have other ideas but why don't I stop with these for the moment, and get your response. Would anarchists you know be willing to accept these ground rules?

Direct Democracy and Representation

WOULD NEW ANARCHISTS *accept the ground rules you mentioned? My answer would be a resounding yes. But allow me to disagree with recognizing the process you describe as a representative democracy. When you write that there should be "no separation between the Revolutionary people and decisionmakers" I understand this as emphasizing complex and multi-layered, but always direct relationships between people and their mandated, recallable delegates. This is, it seems to me, direct democracy of a kind that anarchists would always support.*

OK, good. I agree that I am not proposing a republic as opposed to a direct democracy, or a representative system as opposed to participatory democracy. But I am insisting that a movement of any size will require a process of representation and that this process has its own discipline, which must be respected. The attitude, "Nobody talks for me, I am a free spirit," will require restraint.

I have been thinking about the underlying dynamic. On the one hand folks who consider themselves part of the movement need the freedom to experiment, to try out organizing ideas. In the Sixties I compared it to (a) traveling without a map, (b) planting seeds to see, in the words of the New Testament, which seeds grow and which do not. On the other hand we need methods and moments of drawing the experiences together.

I know something about traveling without a map. I have done it both on foot and by canoe, in each case with my son. It is not so much traveling without a map. There is a map, at least there has been anywhere I have adventured. (One can compare Marxism to the map.) The question is, Where are we? I have climbed over a dangerous ridge because I somehow took the wrong fork at a juncture where the trail divided. I have recognized that we were mistakenly canoeing down an arm of water, exhausted but with the wind behind us, so that we had to turn around and paddle back against the wind.

The metaphor of sowing asks us not to be self-centered. If your organizing project prospers, while mine fails, it may not be a measure of our respective abilities: it may have to do with the soil.

But another way of describing the necessity of representation is that there has to be a way of drawing our experiences together, assessing them collectively, and adjusting the forward course. This is where we failed in the Sixties. At SDS reunions I used to say, "Wait a minute. Nobody sent me a letter saying the Movement was over. I am here to report on my experience." I spent 25 years exploring the Marxist and late-Sixties hypothesis that the working class was the key to revolutionary change. I felt that I had learned something about this. I wanted to be heard, and above all, to be part of collective decision-making about what came next.

And here comes a serious question to the new movement. I feel that participants have no idea how to organize locally so they wait for the next mega-confrontation in Seattle, Quebec, or Genoa, or now wherever last June took place, and then argue about their different symbolic actions there.

Here again I feel we in the Sixties gave you a bum steer, as they say in the United States. Everyone in the South went to the Democratic Party convention in August 1964, and almost no one was able to return to base and resume local organizing. The strategy had been to acquire the right to vote and the convention appeared to demonstrate that this achievement would be illusory, that one would continue to be manipulated from above but in a new way. The student movement in the North repeated the process in Chicago in August 1968. I opposed the idea of going to Chicago. Indeed, together with a young woman from Boston I carried a motion at a preparatory gathering that WE SHOULD NOT DO IT AGAIN! My friend Tom Hayden waited until some people had left, and then, in the classical manner of the Old Left, moved participation again and this time carried it.

Andrej, I need you to respond to this critique of periodic apocalyptic events. Paradoxically it is a caricature of representation. It is as if the anarchists were busy pursuing nothing but representation without the underlying experiences at the base that require representation to supplement themselves. Or to put it another way, in a concern to avoid representation one goes to the Big Event oneself, and ends with nothing: no local movements, no orderly decision-making at the center.

Are We Winning?

I HAVE TO *stress, though, that when we are organizing big actions against big summits, our intentions are really not so much related to the short term, not to stopping the meeting from occurring. Rather our decentralized direct actions are envisioned as learning experiences in prefigurative politics, as "intentional situations" where the very organization of the action is the example of the politics and of the world we wish to create. Global actions, or the organizing of them, are experiments in direct democracy, in building institutions of a new kind, which, as many have argued, is a "victory" in itself. It could also be argued that the new, anarchist-inspired global movement, has been rather victorious; that almost all the free trade treaties planned since 1998 have failed; that the WTO declared the Doha round dead; that the IMF is approaching bankruptcy. Some anarchists see this as a direct result of the worldwide mobilizations. I agree with you in your assessment that the crucial task for the new global movement is to find its way in organizing locally, at the base. But even more crucial is the need to integrate "summit hopping" and experiments in prefigurative organizing into a much broader movement of continuous local involvement. This brings me to a somewhat different question. I have here, in front of me, a new publication of the Turbulence collective, asking 14 groups, collectives and individuals, to confront "the essential question": Are we winning? What would—or could—it mean to "win?"*

Are we winning? Even the asking of the question has a delightful impudence. We—socialists, anarchists, rebels, insurgents, whoever—are supposed to have lost twenty years ago, once and for all. And yet, and yet, let's be honest with ourselves.

At least in the United States, the Sixties had an enormous simplicity. If you lived in the South, the movement had two phases. In the first phase the target was access to public facilities. There were sit-ins of all kinds: the would-be customer or client presented himself or herself at the department store lunch counter and endured, even if ketchup were thrown in one's face, even if one were called all manner of denigrating epithets, and of course, even if one were arrested. When the Lynds moved to Atlanta in the fall of 1961 there were perpetual picket lines outside major downtown department stores.

But quite early, actually also in 1961, the target became voter registration. This was decided at a conference of SNCC staff held at the Highlander Center in Tennessee. In the background was pressure from the Kennedy administration that, wishing to expand the number of black voters in Southern states, made money available through liberal foundations such as the Field and Taconic Foundations. But there is absolutely no question that this demand also came from below. When Bob Moses visited, first Amzie Moore, and then under Amzie's sponsorship, other local African American leaders in Mississippi, they said, We want the vote. At the time almost no black persons in Mississippi could vote.

The vote predictably turned out to be ambiguous. The campaign was "won" in 1964-1965 after SNCC brought off Freedom Summer in Mississippi and Dr. King led marchers across the bridge in Selma. A voting rights bill passed Congress. But it turned out that the ordinary black voter in the South did not want unity with African liberation movements or an end to United States imperialism, as did SNCC staff. The Mississippi Freedom Democratic Party and even the Black Panther Party in Lowndes County, Alabama within a few years became part of the local Democratic Parties.

Meantime, among white students in the North, the movement likewise settled for a winnable goal: an end to the Vietnam war. All kinds of direct action contributed to this objective, including draft resistance, trips to Hanoi, and of course in the end, the simple refusal of soldiers in Vietnam to go on fighting.

SDS was positioned similarly to SNCC. Its organizers saw quite clearly that Vietnam would be followed by other Vietnams—as it turned out, Lebanon, Grenada, Panama, Nicaragua, El Salvador, Haiti, Iraq—and therefore it was necessary to name and change the system (Potter speech April 1965) so as to be able to confront "the seventh war from now."

But like SNCC, SDS too was swept up in a surge from below. The so-called ERAP projects in Newark, Chicago, Cleveland and elsewhere, which sought to bring black and white poor people together to demand economic changes, floundered. The anti-war movement became a tidal wave. Nevertheless the anti-war movement, the largest anti-war movement in United States history, "won."

For worse and for better, the twenty-first century does not offer such "easy," discrete, achievable targets. Participants in the new movements delude themselves by serial attendance at the decision-making happenings of the Other Side. In 1999, in Seattle, capitalist decisionmakers were caught by surprise and demonstrators actually stopped the WTO from functioning. That has not happened since, and these summit encounters have accordingly become symbolic and ritualistic occasions at which both pacifists and anarchists fail in the only rationale for such occasions: the meetings are not prevented from occurring.

Herein the new movement repeats the fallacies of the old. At Democratic Party conventions in 1964 (Atlantic City) and 1968 (Chicago), local organizers streamed to central, apocalyptic encounters with the System, only to find that they did not know—intellectually, emotionally, politically— how to find their way back to organizing at the base.

In two ways the new movements appear to me to be on the road to…what is the best word? tangible, partial success, which lays the basis for longterm winning.

First I believe there has been a significant intellectual clarification. Whether one thinks of students at the summits, or *campesinos* and artisans in Bolivia, Venezuela, Argentina, and above all, Chiapas, there has occurred an emancipation from the hitherto self-evident objective of "taking state power." Speaking for myself, I would immediately add that we don't yet quite know what this means. But the historical record speaks for itself. No one has succeeded in taking state power without at the same time losing his way. Lenin danced in the snow outside the Kremlin when the Soviet Union had lasted one day longer than the Paris Commune. It might have been better had it not so lasted. I find it fascinating that both Marcos, who is out of power and does not want it, and Morales, a head of state, speak the same language of "*mandar obediciendo*": governing in obedience to what Marcos calls The Below.

Second, in the neo-colonial or "developing" world there is a huge global upheaval. It takes all kinds of forms but so what? The diversity proves that something is alive. Who would have thought that neo-liberal "globalization" would find itself so beleaguered as not only whole societies, but whole continents, slip from under its domination? We in the imperialist heartland need to be humble. Others are now on the front lines.

However, the dialectic appears to be alive and well even in the United States. There has been a double transformation. Only a few years ago it was thought that the Republican Party had taken over the government of the United States forever. Almost the reverse now seems to be the case. Also, and only in the last few months, war and terror have sufficiently receded that the candidates have turned to domestic economic issues, and candidates without foreign policy experience (Obama, Huckabee) surge forward. Obama was a community organizer in South Side Chicago, in exactly the kind of community where ERAP sought to organize more than forty years ago.

Finally, I believe that radicals in the United States need to become good gardeners, planting and nurturing seeds that will grow. There is no sell-out of longterm objectives in achieving what André Gorz envisioned as not merely quantitative but qualitative reforms, reforms that enhance the decisionmaking of participants. Since 1967 I have been part of efforts that achieved the following:

> ❧ Amid the general failure to find a way to stop capital flight and plant shutdowns, we managed to preserve promised benefits to retirees of LTV Steel.

> ❧ Confronting one of the largest capitalist corporations, General Motors, we forced first awareness of and then change in practices involving toxic chemicals in the workplace.

> ❧ For twenty years we maintained a "parallel central labor union" to which striking workers could turn for direct action in solidarity.

> ❧ Among historians, who in 1969 had dramatically failed to pass a resolution condemning

the war in Vietnam, we passed a resolution in 2007 condemning the war in Iraq.

❧ Conditions of confinement at the Ohio State Penitentiary in Youngstown, the state's supermaximum security prison, have been significantly improved.

❧ A movement has begun to be built in Ohio to end the death penalty and, more particularly, save the lives of five men who took part in an 11-day prison rebellion in 1993.

In every one of these instances, those at the receiving end of repression have been part of the action, and would express accord that the foregoing have been "wins."

Are we winning? Yes and No, of course. Enough Yes to repeat some old refrains: Take it easy but take it; We are a band of brothers and sisters standing in a circle of love; We shall overcome; Solidarity forever; My country is the world.

Old and New Movements: Similarities and Differences

ON A FEW *occasions in our conversation you remarked that the new movements tend to repeat the mistakes of the old ones. Can you outline—and I am fully aware of the enormity of this question—the most important similarities, and most strik-ing differences, between the contemporary movements and the movements of the 1960s? For instance, to mention only one of the many inherited conversations, we still suffer the dilemma of reform versus revolution.*

I am asked to comment on differences and similarities between the old (1960s) and new (1990s to now) movements. There is also a question about the difference between radical or revolutionary reforms, and reforms that are not radical or revolutionary.

I think the intellectual backgrounds of the old and new movements were somewhat different.

The early 1960s activists, both South and North, tended to be pragmatic and lifestyle-oriented rather than ideological. In this they are similar to the activists of the new movement, it seems to me.

As I have pointed out before, the political objectives of the 1960s were simple: in the South the vote, in the North to end the Vietnam war. Nonetheless there was an ideological background that I would describe as neo-Marxist. The writer who most influenced Tom Hayden, principal draftsperson of *The Port Huron Statement*, was C. Wright Mills. Mills differed with Marxists as to whether the working class was the principal agent of change and he posited a more complex process in ruling-class decisionmaking, involving the military and the government as somewhat independent actors along with the corporations. Still I think it is correct to call Mills neo-Marxist. When Paul Potter, president of SDS, stated in April 1965 that "we must name the system" responsible for Vietnam, he would probably have said it was "corporate liberalism," a fancy term for capitalism.

In the same way, SNCC staff persons (at least those from universities in the North) were influenced by DuBois and by African socialists like Nkrumah. Bob Moses left the United States for Tanzania. Stokely Carmichael went to live in West Africa.

The new movement is anarchist in background, surely, but as you point out here too there is a "neo": it is neo-anarchist in that it opposes not only the state but also, as at the various summits, capitalism and imperialism. Moreover Marcos, as I understand it, belonged to a Marxist grouplet at the time he went to live in the Lacandón jungle, and perhaps, even on January 1, 1994.

What all this tells us, I believe, is that there is ample background, good soil for a convergence of Marxism and anarchism. After all, had it not been for some of the personalities involved, would there ever have been the struggle for power in the First International? There are writings of both Marx (*The Civil War in France*) and Lenin (*State and Revolution*) that are very anarchist in orientation, in the sense that they celebrate local working-class assemblies that are self-acting and participatory. One more time I emphasize that the Chicago anarchists of the 1880s, and to some extent the IWW, sought a fusion of Marxism and anarchism. And did you know that when Kropotkin died, Russian anarchists whom the Bolsheviks had put in prison were released to attend his funeral when they promised to go back to jail after the funeral?

As to reforms, as I understand Gorz what he meant by a "revolutionary reform" was a reform that increased participation by the people in decision-making, as opposed to merely increasing quantitative benefits.

But you know, that distinction sounds more clear than it really is. I am thinking of the agitation Alice and I have undertaken for the past ten years concerning the supermaximum (twenty-three hour a day isolation) security prison in Youngstown, Ohio.

Our maximum program has always been, Shut it down. Our minimum program has been, Make it into a maximum security prison with a small supermaximum security section for prisoners who actually have committed serious acts of violence while in prison.

We have accomplished the latter. There is consensus among the prisoner body, which itself is only half of what it was initially, that the place is now "tolerable."

Presently we are taking up the demand for death-sentenced prisoners that they should have full contact visits throughout their time on Death Row. Ohio allows contact visiting only just before execution. But ten other states, including the Southern states Alabama, Arkansas, Georgia, Louisiana, Missouri and Virginia, allow regular contact visits. And at the supermax prison many of the prisoners who are not death-sentenced, and are supposedly greater security risks than the men on Death Row, have half a dozen contact visits a year.

This is a struggle we can win. We will conduct it both in the courtroom and on the streets, in the courtroom of public opinion. And if we do so effectively it will not only seek to achieve an immediate humane objective, but to make the public more aware of death-sentenced prisoners as fellow human beings: the perception that may lead, over time, to abolition of the death penalty.

Thus this "reform"—that a person sentenced to death be able to touch and hug members of his family—while it may not be revolutionary, will draw on the efforts of prisoners and their relatives as well as the effort of lawyers, and has a horizon, a penumbra that suggests that a different kind of world is possible.

Seeds and Soil

FROM LANDAUER TO *Ward, from Kropotkin to Goodman and Bookchin, anarchists were celebrating precisely those pre-capitalist and non-state lifeways, existing "like a seed beneath the snow," a seed that remains healthy at the very heart of hierarchical society. Paul Goodman wrote that "free society is the extension of spheres of free action until they make up most of social life"; Gustav Landauer said that anarchism is "actualization and reconstitution of something that has always been present, which exists alongside the State, albeit buried and laid waste"; Colin Ward maintains that "Anarchist society, which organizes itself without authority, is always in existence." George Woodcock has captured this "conservative" aspect of anarchism in his fine essay on Paul Goodman. As regards the role of theory, I feel that what the new anarchism needs, in addition to the things you have mentioned, is a coherent vision of a future society. I came to this conclusion first in the course of my work with the workers of "Jugoremedija," an occupied factory in Serbia. Our heated political discussions would always end with their impatient question "but what are you for?," Later on, I read Gaston Leval, a Spanish anarchist who had left an important document about the history of collectives in the Spanish Revolution. Leval recognized as one of the greatest problems of the revolution the fact that "the preparation of revolutionary construction" was not advanced enough. He wondered about the "inexplicable Marxist incomprehension" which always "combated all anticipation concerning the post-revolutionary society." His conclusion was that "without organic preparation no social and truly socialist revolution is possible… The chances of success depend on the extent of the pre-existing constructive capacity." These words, together with my own experience as an organizer, brought me to the conclusion that the most important thing for getting from Here to There is the collective development of a coherent, shared, participatible vision of the post-revolutionary society. This is how I became an advocate of participatory economics.*

Going back to our conversation about practice and ideas, and speaking of "seeds beneath the snow," can you tell me something about a metaphor that you often use in relation to ideas, the one of a sower and "precious seeds"?

MARXISM AND ANARCHISM

I think it is time for a partial summing up with regard to Marxism and anarchism (or, anarchism and Marxism).

At various times you have referred to me as "an anarchist historian" or as "a Marxist historian." I am neither. I am a person who believes that Marxism and anarchism each has indispensable strengths and dramatic weaknesses. I think the future of the Left literally depends on synthesizing these two traditions. I do not believe one should be privileged over the other. Nor do I consider it helpful to contrive terms such as "Anarcho-Marxist." It is much simpler than that. A century and a half ago, for reasons that have more to do with personalities than anything else, these two viewpoints were made to seem mutually exclusive alternatives. They are not. They are Hegelian moments that need to be synthesized.

Incidentally, the so-called "Chicago school" of anarchism, represented by Albert Parsons, August Spies, and the other Haymarket martyrs, described themselves as anarchists, socialists, and Marxists. So do I.

VISIONS AND SEEDS

I agree that there is needed a "vision," but I do not think ordinary persons bleed and die for a vision that they have not experienced. I think the vision must be rooted in daily life, and if it is not, nothing will happen. If the vision is the seed, daily life is the soil.

Jesus spoke of seeds and soil. Matthew 13, Luke 8. His idea was that seeds are planted in different kinds of soil.

> Some fell by the way side; and it was trodden down, and the fowls of the air devoured it.
> And some fell upon a rock; and as soon as it was sprung up, it withered away, because it lacked moisture.
> And some fell among thorns; and the thorns sprang up with it, and choked it.
> And other fell on good ground, and sprang up, and bare fruit an hundredfold....

Luke 8:5-8.

We (the organizers) were the seed and what we accomplished or failed to achieve depended not only on ourselves, but also on the soil in which we sought to take root. I felt that we should create a strategy, a political "line," not by abstract analysis but by assembling periodically to assess our different experiences.

SEEDS OF SOLIDARITY

I have gradually come to the conclusion that the labor movement gives lip service to the idea that "an injury to one is an injury to all," but in practice behaves otherwise. With rare exceptions, unions recruit members and advertise their accomplishments in the language of individual, short-term, economic benefit. But if there is to be any hope of creating a labor movement that prefigures the "other world" we all desire, it cannot be built on individualism. The seeds must be such that, given proper soil, what grows is solidarity. They must be seeds of solidarity.

Last weekend I attended a meeting of labor historians at which I learned more about an interesting instance of such "solidarity unionism."

Southern and central Illinois in the first part of the last century was coal-mining country. The miners were from Italy, Eastern Europe, and Great Britain. Despite their diverse origins, in these one-industry towns a strong ethic of solidarity and community asserted itself.

John L. Lewis, president of the United Mine Workers of America, believed that only if these mines mechanized would they be able to compete with mines in Kentucky and West Virginia where wages were lower. (Does this sound familiar? It is an early instance of the logic of "globalization.")

The miners and their families, on the other hand, favored what they called "equalization." They said, Share the work evenly among existing mines and existing miners. In doing so, they argued, disregard seniority (how long a particular person has been employed): the new hire pays the same amount for a loaf of bread as the man who has been there many years.

Lewis disagreed. In 1932 he negotiated a contract with the Peabody Coal Company that called for mechanization in the form of cutting machines that loosened the coal by making a cut at the base of the face; loading machines that took the place of pick and shovel labor by human beings; and conveying machines that carried the coal and slag to breakers at the entrance to the mine. This proposed mechanization, historian Carl Oblinger reports, would have thrown over half of the men out of work. When Lewis unilaterally imposed the contract he had negotiated, local unions all over Illinois withdrew from the United Mine Workers, created a network of local unions that they named the Progressive Miners of America, or PMA, and went on strike. At its height approximately 35,000 Illinois miners belonged to the PMA.

As I understand it, the miners were not necessarily opposed to mechanization. They wanted a voice in how it was done. For example, as I know from conversation with steelworkers, if mechanization is introduced at the same rate that workers retire it is possible to mechanize and to reduce a work force in step with natural attrition, without taking away anyone's job.

Equalization, or job sharing, was not an unthinkable idea in the Illinois coal fields. In 1921, for example,

> the Illinois Coal Association's contract with Illinois miners recognized that if a mine threw laborers out of work for thirty days, miners at another mine could, "at their option, share work with those thrown idle."

During the contract negotiations in 1932, every Illinois local of the United Mine Workers demanded a substantial reduction in the length of the work week. The miners refused to work overtime when any union member was laid off. The president of the UMW local in Mt. Olive, Illinois (where Mother Jones is buried) recalled that the Progressive Miners of America

> simply adopted the rule that no man is going to work overtime without showing cause why no one else was available to share the work. We enforced this in order to equalize employment and got the company to train all to operate the machines. We got the company to go along by getting the key men in our union to cut down the production. Men's lives, and bread and butter for the kids, are just as important as the production profits for coal companies. The better companies grudgingly accepted this.

The practice of solidarity at work reverberated in the communities. A "flourishing barter economy and a strong help ethic developed."

> "My dad needed to dig his basement," related Frank Borgognoni, a miner from Kincaid. "No one said anything. They just come and pitched in. The women didn't even ask the men where they were going. They put together food and prepared a good meal…."

Neighbors shared food with those temporarily in short supply. Residents picked up coal along the railroad tracks for the elderly and disabled. An investigation of the 1932 strike by the Adjutant General's office concluded: "Rank and file miners…can resist the coal company since they share their meager resources." Voluntary contributions of working PMA members helped striking brothers and their families.

The high school students in Kincaid went on strike because their school used Peabody coal.

A SEED BANK FOR SEEDS OF SOLIDARITY?

A bank for seeds from all over the world has been created in the Arctic. Scientists believe that in that way the basis of new life can be preserved even in the event of global warming or other natural catastrophes.

But the communal seeds for a new society are also in danger. It is not just the Amazon rain forest that is being destroyed. It is also the indigenous communities of the vast Amazon basin.

There does not seem any practical way to store a communal way of life underground, in a controlled temperature, for mechanical access in time to come. No, the only way to preserve the seeds of solidarity is to practice solidarity, here and now. Solidarity is a relay race in which the torch must continually be passed from one living runner to the next.

How Can We Rebuild Our Movement?

LET US NOW *try to put a few threads of our conversations together. We have tried to examine the historical journey of what we termed the Haymarket synthesis. We have talked about the Chicago school of anarchism, the IWW, and the Zapatistas. We have insisted on the usefulness of reviving a synthesis between anarchism and Marxism that should combine prefigurative direct action and coherent structural understanding. We talked about theory rising from practice; about accompaniment, as a*

*form of mutual aid and revolutionary practice; about revolu-
tion understood as a process and not a cataclysmic break; about
workers and prisoners. It has been almost ten years since the
Seattle protest. A new movement has exploded in the United
States, it is my impression, with an admirable, breathtaking
strength. But today, a few years after 9/11, we find ourselves
in a situation where, according to comrades from the Retort
collective, our "own powers are afflicted," and the movement is
in dire need of rebuilding. Drawing on our conversation, I think
that we should try to offer a possible answer, one among many, of
course, to the question that is on the lips of almost every activist
I have met since my arrival in the United States: how can we
rebuild our movement?*

You have asked me to set out my thoughts about, How
can we rebuild the movement today? I do so with humility.
The answers will be demonstrated in practice.

WHY THE 1960S HAD IT EASIER

Again I emphasize that the key to the effectiveness of "the
Movement" of the 1960s was the simplicity of its demands.

In the South it was, "One Man [that is, one adult human
being], One Vote."

In the North it was, "We Won't Go [to the Vietnam
war]."

Building a movement is a lot easier when you don't have
to haggle continuously about strategy. In the 1960s, there
was general consensus about what needed to be done, and
the major disagreements were about tactics, not strategy.

Early on, there was division within the Student Nonviolent
Coordinating Committee (SNCC) about tactics. Some
people wanted to continue direct action to integrate public
accommodations (such as department store lunch counters
or buses) undertaken in 1960 and 1961. Others wanted to
turn to voter registration. It was decided that each group
should proceed as desired. Then it was discovered that "going

down to the court house" in order to register to vote was itself a direct action that might result in beating or arrest. Thus SNCC remained a movement of direct action, whatever its immediate objectives.

It seems to me that the movement of the twenty-first century, the movement that began in San Cristóbal, Chiapas in 1994 and in Seattle in 1999, faces more complex problems. How do you stop corporations from shutting down their plants in the United States and investing overseas? The organized labor movement has faced this problem since the late 1970s and has not found an answer. When a corporation like General Motors operates facilities in both a relatively high-wage area (such as the United States) and a relatively low-wage area (such as Mexico), on behalf of what demands can workers of both countries strike together against that corporation? To the best of my knowledge there has not yet been such a strike anywhere in the world. Rural laborers in Mexico wish to come to the United States, driven by provisions of NAFTA that permit United States farmers to undersell Mexican farmers in the Mexican market. What should be the policy of the labor movement in this country toward such immigrants? Fear and disagreement dominate that debate.

Accordingly, we should be gentle with ourselves if solutions to such problems do not emerge overnight. A period of experimentation, of trial and error, seems to me inevitable.

A FALSE START AND AN INCOMPLETE APOCALYPSE

Not long after the Chiapas uprising began on January 1, 1994, John Sweeney became president of the AFL-CIO. Borrowing the rhetoric of Mississippi Freedom Summer, the new union leadership launched what it described as "Union Summer." Union Summer turned out to be a pale substitute for the Freedom Summer of 1964.

In Mississippi, the Freedom Schools that I coordinated necessarily operated in an extremely decentralized manner.

Each local situation was different. A white college student from the North who had been designated as Freedom School "principal" in, say, Ruleville, Mississippi, got off the bus at the Greyhound station with a slip of paper giving him or her (usually her) the name and address of a courageous black family prepared to provide lodging. In theory, a church had been found prepared to let its basement be used during weekdays as a Freedom School. (But sometimes the church had been burned or bombed because of that decision and a new site had to be found.) Beyond these basics, it was up to the summer volunteer to improvise a way forward.

The use that the trade union movement makes of youthful adherents is far different. I know a young student at a local university who told me, "I want to be an activist." A few years ago she went through a training seminar with a major union and, on its instructions, got a job as a "salt" in the local campus cafeteria. Almost every evening she had long telephone calls with a staff man in another city who directed her work. Unbeknownst to her fellow workers, she received a secret salary from the union over and above her pay at the cafeteria. She agonized as to how her fellow workers would regard her if they knew about this money. Her first step was to give up that supplemental salary, and soon after, she dropped out.

Whereas Mississippi volunteers came home politically energized, often for the rest of their lives, young people who take jobs with the new trade union movement in the United States are worked unconscionably long hours and given no voice in deciding anything, become disgusted with the authoritarianism of their union handlers, and often leave the movement to resume personal careers.

Seattle was something much more promising, as were the ensuing confrontations with global capitalism in Quebec, Genoa, and Cancún. Seattle was a success. The WTO had to cancel its meeting, and the only gathering that took place was called into session by a demonstrator, Medea Benjamin of Global Exchange. The Steelworkers sent members to Seattle in order to protest the import into the United States of steel manufactured in other countries. The Teamsters union likewise paid members to attend in order to prevent Mexican truck drivers from crossing the Rio Grande. In my view these are objectives incompatible with international working-class solidarity. Nonetheless, there was considerable fraternization between protesting rank-and-file workers and protesting students, to the mutual benefit of all.

But after Seattle, corporate sponsors of these occasions have become better able to insulate them from protest, and for the protesters, there is a problem about what to do when you get home again. Two young persons who had been in Seattle stayed overnight in our basement on their way to the next anti-globalization encounter in Quebec. They confessed that it had been difficult to know how to take hold in day-to-day organizing once they got back home.

I am keenly aware of the phenomenon of post-demonstration depression because of our experience in the 1960s after the Democratic Party conventions of 1964 and 1968.

In August 1964, the Mississippi Freedom Democratic Party brought the disfranchisement of African Americans into the homes of TV viewers all over the United States. But many of those who made the long journey from the Deep South to Atlantic City were unable effectively to resume their local organizing. The atmosphere, the tempo, everything about a huge confrontation at a climactic historical moment, whether in Atlantic City or Seattle, is different from the patient, often discouraging, long-distance running required of a local organizer.

The same thing happened after the even more dramatic "Battle of Chicago" at the 1968 Democratic Party convention. As I have narrated elsewhere, at that time Students for a Democratic Society was still seeking to develop an interracial movement of the poor in Northern ghettoes. Very little of that activity continued after August 1968.

SEEDS BENEATH THE SNOW

If there is a single outstanding virtue about the first decade of this new century, perhaps it is that underneath the surface of conventional politics a great deal of prefigurative civic activity is afoot. This is true even in the United States, where anti-globalization activity tended to collapse after the terrorist attack in September 2001.

Anarchist theorists write about networks of mutual aid that exist alongside the elections and the wars that seek to represent themselves as the whole of meaningful political activity. One thinks of forest ecology. Peel back the surface scatter of leaves or pine needles, and there will often be revealed dense tangles of interconnected roots from which new growth will eventually emerge. Even in societies subjected to the greatest violence—Guatemala in *la violencia* of the early 1980s or southeastern Europe in the 1990s—small projects present themselves in time, like bright green shoots emerging from a burned-over, blackened forest floor.

For such a society, brutalized and dismembered, an approach loosely described as anarchism may be singularly appropriate. For a time, anything beyond the small-scale is impractical and likewise, the need to begin again, even if on a small scale, is overwhelming.

Seeds beneath the snow is therefore just the right metaphor for organizing in such circumstances. The activist should concentrate on bringing together individuals who can be honest and direct with one another in cooperatively seeking common goals. Soon enough it will be time to bring to bear the analysis of "high theory" or to gather experimental results into a nationwide political platform. For the moment, though, an insistence on such theorizing or on such a platform might be disastrous. If, as we so often say, we advocate that which human beings truly want and need, then we must have the confidence to let prefigurative experiences grow organically.

We say we need to organize. But what is organizing, anyway?

Is it organizing when a person acts out his or her convictions, alone or in company with others of similar background and like mind? Or is it organizing when a person sets aside personal convictions and carefully persuades others whose life trajectories are quite different to take action prompted by the external situation?

The answer is, Organizing must be neither of these in isolation, but a combination of both.

In the 1960s taken as a whole, individuals typically "did their (own) thing," alone or in the company of friends. Obviously, when Rosa Parks refused to go to the back of the bus or four young men sat-in at a segregated lunch counter, their personal actions inspired many others to act likewise. But if organizing is personal expression alone, more often than not it will fail to give rise to mass action. The late Saul Alinsky used to insist that would-be organizers who sought to develop an issue must first ascertain that a concern about that issue was really "there" in the minds of the persons to be organized.

On the other hand, in the union organizing of the 1930s and in the community organizing of Mr. Alinsky (which was closely modeled on the organizing methods of the CIO), the emphasis was on numbers, on achieving power, on winning. But sometimes large groups will move into action and yet the action may have a certain hollowness and lack of integrity that will cripple its effectiveness in the long run. The union organizer who checks out of the motel the day after a lost NLRB election may leave behind workers who will be fired because they had the courage to make known their union sympathies, and now lack protection. Anti-war demonstrations that consist largely of speeches and become routine will ultimately turn people off, and do not really build a movement no matter how large at any given time. Organizing, then, must be a combination or synthesis of personal self-expression and thoughtful appeal to the interests of others.

We need to organize. We cannot be afraid of it. But we must do it with all our faculties in play. I want to examine organizing in three different constituencies with which I am familiar.

SOLDIERS

The best way to stop a war is for soldiers to refuse to fight. When I was growing up in the 1930s, a man named Carl Sandburg wrote a play that contained the line, "Sometime they'll give a war and nobody will come."

However, it makes a difference whether the army in question is made up of conscripts or volunteers.

In the 1960s most of the men and women in military service, especially in the Army, were drafted. A student, himself subject to conscription, could readily explain his own position to other potential draftees. This was one kind of fusion of personal self-expression with the objective situation of a constituency.

Precisely because of the successful anti-draft movement of the 1960s, since then the United States has had a volunteer military. The organizer can no longer say to a volunteer for military service, "I am in the same situation you are. Here's what I think. How about you?"

Nevertheless, volunteers like Camilo Mejía and Kevin Benderman in time came to conclusions very much like those of anti-war organizers of the 1960s. Instead of saying, "I won't go," they experienced one tour of duty in Iraq and said, "I won't go back."

In the end, then, the task of the anti-war organizer remains much as it has always been. If you are a college teacher or student, the first step is respectfully to make contact with any veterans in your classes or on campus. After the vets themselves, seek out family members of men and women who are or have been in military service. Finally, talk to young people wondering whether to enlist.

In all of the foregoing, the first task is to listen. There

are some organizers who believe that any vet who does not publicly condemn the war should himself or herself be denounced. That is madness, and shows a lack of the humility required of any organizer. Whoever has spent time with veterans knows that most of them did not enlist for ideological reasons. As Camilo Mejía said in his application for Conscientious Objector status, he wanted financial help to make it through college and most of his colleagues were similarly motivated.

Moreover, it is the veterans themselves who are going to be the organizers. I was part of a citizens' panel that in early 2007, in Tacoma, Washington, listened to the witnesses whom the officer presiding at the court martial of Lieutenant Ehren Watada would not permit to testify. There were some very distinguished experts, beginning with Daniel Ellsberg (the man who released the *Pentagon Papers*). But it was the vets who blew us all away.

One young man described the dilemma of the eighteen-year-old soldier who is asked to man a checkpoint. He does not speak the local language. A car speeds toward him. Is it a suicide bomber or a father on his way home from work? He has to make a split-second decision. In one such instance, the soldier guessed wrong and opened fire killing a family of four, including two young children. This soldier's unit discussed the incident. The discussion ended when the highest ranking officer present said, "If only these fucking hajis would learn to drive, we wouldn't have this problem."

The vets themselves are the best organizers. Their testimonies, from experience, are what people most need to hear. Our task is to find them, support them, and help them to connect with others.

WORKERS

Elsewhere in these conversations I share some of my experiences with "the working class."

When I began to do oral histories with rank-and-file

workers, and when I became a lawyer with the project of representing such folk, I had the question, "Is there a special language I need to learn in order to communicate with workers?" I could not believe that the ponderous vocabulary of Marxism Leninism would make sense to anyone. But I wondered whether terms like "participatory democracy" or "direct action" would get across to my new friends and clients.

I need not have worried. There is no group of human beings in the United States who have been more crudely shouldered away from meaningful decisionmaking, or more abruptly silenced when they try to act out their beliefs, than people who make their living with their hands. If a stranger approaches them with a modicum of respect, especially if that stranger has some useful skill to provide, communication will not be a problem and words are unlikely to be an obstacle.

My wife Alice for many years represented applicants for Social Security disability. Other lawyers would tell her that she spent too much time with clients but her attitude was, If only ten percent of what they tell me is useful to the case, those may be the facts that make all the difference. Alice said that as she listened to such a client she tried to glimpse, beneath the mask of pain, the person who had once not been disabled: how they cooked their meals, what they did with their children, how their life then differed from the way in which physical limitations compelled them to live now. She had phenomenal success.

PRISONERS

With prisoners as with soldiers, with workers, indeed with all potential comrades: first, listen; second, recognize that it is the person with whom you are talking (the soldier, the worker, the prisoner) who will be the organizer and that your role is to support and to accompany. In addition, I feel that I have learned from prisoners to glimpse how the racial divide among the poor and oppressed might be overcome.

As I perceive our situation, since the mid-1960s blacks and whites in the United States have been walking separate paths. First it was Black Power, and then a variety of successor ideologies that encouraged African Americans to hold themselves apart from common struggle.

I do not criticize these developments. I believe that they are altogether understandable. Yet the fact remains that blacks alone cannot change the system that oppresses them, and that only when blacks and whites learn how to work together again will there be hope of changing United States capitalism and its imperialist foreign policy.

What prisoners have done, what prisoners at the Southern Ohio Correctional Facility in Lucasville, Ohio did during eleven days of desperate rebellion in 1993, is to create a decisionmaking process in which each significant racial or ethnic group has what amounts to a veto while at the same time all recognize that only together can anything be accomplished. Thus in the Lucasville rebellion representatives of the Sunni Muslims, Aryan Brotherhood, and Black Gangster Disciples met every day in an improvised leadership council.

One might analogize the process to the way in which SNCC, during its best days, made important decisions. Decisions were made by consensus, that is, with the support of everyone in the room. I have heard Northern radicals mock such consensus decisionmaking as petty bourgeois, and inappropriate for serious revolutionaries. But the reason SNCC made decisions by consensus was precisely because their work was so much more dangerous than anything being done in the North: in such a setting, no one felt comfortable making a decision by majority rule that might cost somebody else's life.

In the same way prisoners, precisely because the common oppression that they face is so much more burdensome than that confronted by anyone outside the bars, have learned to love and respect each other without surrendering their very different identities. And we who are not in prison have much to learn from them.

DRAWING THE THREADS TOGETHER
AND BEHAVING LIKE COMRADES

I hope these fragmentary observations at least open a door to the perception that real organizing and small victories are possible. After the traumatic disintegration of both SNCC and SDS, I have worked with war resisters, with rank-and-file workers, and with prisoners. In each case I have helped to create significant struggles and at least partially succeeded in most of them. Especially, I have experienced the coming into being of trust across barriers of military experience, of class, of gender, and of race.

Two final observations seem necessary. As the new movement grows in dozens of scattered settings, so the anarchist mode of putting down roots in a variety of locations will need to be supplemented by structural analysis that helps us to prioritize, to concentrate resources, to abandon unsuccessful experiments without condemning persons who undertook them on behalf of us all.

I confess to a certain fear of national gatherings and large organizations. The kind of gathering I believe would be most helpful would, to begin with, focus on the exchange of experiences. Have you been working with soldiers? What has been successful and what has not worked so well? What might you suggest in a situation where such-and-such variables are present? And so on.

Lastly, something that neither Marxists or anarchists have been very good at: We need to proceed in a way that builds community. There must be certain ground rules. We should practice direct speaking: if something bothers you about another person, go speak to him or her and do not gossip to a third person. No one should be permitted to present themselves in caucuses that define a fixed position beforehand and are impervious to the exchange of experiences. We must allow spontaneity and experiment without fear of humiliation and disgrace. Not only our organizing but our conduct toward one another must be paradigmatic in engendering a sense of truly being brothers and sisters.

PART II

GUERRILLA HISTORY

What Is Guerrilla History?

THE ZAPATISTAS HAVE *recently issued a call for "other theory." I would like us to talk about "other history," or other possible ways of writing history, as a form of accompaniment. In your article in* Liberation *magazine, you proposed the term "guerrilla history" for the kind of history you were writing. I believe this to be one of the most provocative and innovative ways of thinking about, writing about, and making history that I have ever encountered. It is of interest for our discussion to note that the set of practices made famous by the Italian movements of the 70s, the so called "co-research," "militant investigation," or "militant research," have gained new currency among today's generation of radicals. The Argentine Colectivo Situaciones, the Spanish Precarias a la Deriva, and the Italian collective Derive Aprodi all promote a form of intervention that studies the practices, experiences and situations of people in struggle. I do feel, however, that guerrilla history is different. It stands apart from history "indoors," from a history conceived as a privileged profession of academic historians; but it also, as a history "out of doors," involves a very specific choice of perspectives. So, what is it you meant with "guerrilla history?"*

I wrote an article entitled *"Guerrilla History in Gary"* in *Liberation* magazine after interviewing two steelworkers, John Sargent and Jim Balanoff.

The point about guerrilla history is that one begins with the situation of the worker, the prisoner, or whoever the poor and oppressed person is in a particular situation, NOT with the existential dilemma of the radical intellectual.

People in struggle need to do history. The example I recall providing is this: We create a picket line. When the demonstration is over, we return to the local union hall and evaluate the action. How did it go? Why did more people not come? How did we react to the employer and the police? Was it a success? How can we do better next time?

This is history. People need to do it, and people will do it, whether we radical intellectuals show up or not. But if we do show up, we may be able to assist. Such "guerrilla history" will be, for the most part, oral history. But there is nothing sacred about oral as opposed to written sources. Indeed, if documents are available that can add to what we understand, so much the better. But we begin by talking together about what we have experienced. Interestingly, precisely this same choice of perspectives presents itself when one considers liberation theology. Initially, Gutierrez and others projected what they called "the preferential option for the poor." As with the exchange between Lynd and Lemisch, this phrase mistakenly takes as its starting point the middle-class religious person wondering how to respond to the injustice in the world, to the class struggle, to the project of creating the Kingdom of God on this earth. The correct starting point is the poor person himself or herself. What does he or she, what do they need from radical intellectuals or radical religious persons? I find that "accompaniment" transcends this deficiency. We—Left intellectual and prisoner, for example— need to walk together. Just as we need to do history together so as to act most effectively, so more generally, we need to journey side by side, confronting whatever comes.

History from the Bottom Up

IT IS MY *impression that younger activists, not to mention historians, are not entirely familiar with the history of militant historiography, and, particularly, with New Left history. Can you assist with a brief introduction to the work of British Marxist historians, history from below, total history, history from the bottom up, and people's history?*

When I was in high school (1942-1946), there was a book somewhat comparable to Howard Zinn's *People's History*: Charles and Mary Beard, *The Rise of American Civilization*. Therein, for example, the Civil War is characterized as the "second American Revolution."

There were other writers of "people's history." Philip Foner edited the writings of Thomas Paine and other radicals. Leo Huberman was, first, the educational director of the Left-leaning National Maritime Union, and then, co-founder with Paul Sweezy of the Marxist periodical *Monthly Review*. He wrote a popular history of the United States entitled *We, the People*.

Nonetheless, as of 1960 whatever history-writing in the United States might be considered "history from the bottom up" was very general, very vague. For example, Arthur Schlesinger, Jr.'s book *The Age of Jackson* was considered radical, yet its hero, Andrew Jackson, ardently supported slavery and was responsible for the "trail of tears" whereby the Cherokee Indians were deported from Georgia to Oklahoma.

BRITISH MARXIST HISTORIANS

The big influence on the historiography of younger historians such as Jesse Lemisch and myself in developing history from the bottom up was British, and especially *The Making of the English Working Class* by Edward Thompson. I have written about Thompson in my book *Living Inside Our Hope*. Here let me make the following summary comments.

1. Thompson was a member of the British Communist Party who broke with it after the Hungarian Revolution of 1956. Thereafter he published two very large books in which he sought the origins of a more humanistic socialism: first, his biography of William Morris, and then *The Making*. I can recall reading *The Making* while in graduate school (1959-1961).

2. Thompson wrote these two masterworks while serving as an adjunct lecturer for a workers' education program in the North of England. He did not hold a regular academic position until he went to the University of Warwick in the mid-1960s, and stayed there for only a few years.

3. In *The Making* Thompson deplored the "enormous condescension" of historians toward bygone working-class protagonists, and showed in unprecedented detail the effort of British workers between 1790 and 1850 to make a new world. However, in roughly the same period his main concern was to bring about a socialist revolution in Great Britain, which he felt sure would occur before the end of the twentieth century. He developed the concept of "warrening": that is, that beneath the surface of capitalist society the working class was developing new institutions, such as trade unions, consumer cooperatives, Methodist chapels, and local branches of the Independent Labor Party.

4. By the mid-1960s, Thompson felt politically defeated within British radicalism. Control of the *New Left Review* passed out of the hands of Thompson and his friends into the hands of a group of dogmatic Marxists led by Perry Anderson. When the New Left in the United States was just beginning to become a mass movement, in the Vietnam protests of 1965, Thompson was writing of the "former New Left" in Great Britain. Thereafter, his scholarly writing tended to move backward in time: his last books were on village customs in eighteenth century England and William Blake.

Beside Thompson there were British historians Christopher Hill and Eric Hobsbawm, who, like Thompson, came to history through the Communist Party. Hill focused on the seventeenth century English Revolution. Thompson and Hobsbawm divided the historiographical terrain in an unfortunate way, as suggested by the following anecdote. At a conference in the United States, Thompson was asked why his work was limited to rich description of the oppressed but did not challenge the structural interpretations of the whole of history offered by mainstream historians. "I leave that to Eric," Thompson is said to have replied. But a history that only tells the story of the "inarticulate" (that is, those who don't write much) is only half a history. We have also the obligation to make sense of history as a whole, and if we don't, interpretation remains in the hands of those who (as Jesse Lemisch put it) write biographies of "great white men."

There is one other important influence on at least my own version of history from the bottom up that must be mentioned: liberation theology. At a gathering in Medellin, Colombia in 1969, Peruvian theologian Gustavo Gutierrez proposed what he called "a preferential option for the poor." Religiously committed persons were urged to choose sides in the class struggle, to stand beside the poor and serve their needs as Jesus was said to have done in the first century.

I believe there is a parallelism between advocacy within academia of "history from the bottom up," and advocacy within the world of Christianity of "a preferential option for the poor." In each case, the message is addressed to middle-class individuals and to the role they should play in relation to an undifferentiated category of persons known as "the people" or "the poor." In each case, there has begun a painful transition, away from seeing this part of humanity as romanticized visionaries or objects of charity, and toward viewing the world through the eyes of the people and the poor themselves. In each case, the way forward appears to call for a kind of partnership between academics, or committed religious, on the one hand, and workers, peasants, or prisoners on the other, such that neither group denigrates itself or reflexively defers to the other, but both, together, develop a vision of a better world.

American Radical Historians

I THINK THAT *you would agree with the assertion that despite the apparent widespread acceptance of "history from the bottom up," an important part of American history is still written from above, even, interestingly, by fellow radical historians who have left the small matter of master narrative and interpretation to "indoor" or established historians. We still have to endure hagiographies of Founding Fathers or Funding Fathers (Great Union Leaders). But even when we read amazing works on the self-activity of the miners, or on the self-government of the pirates, we are still left with the feeling that the response from the Left was to write an ethnography of the poor. Valuable as this task is, we should not surrender the questions of interpretation to the "vertical" historians.*

A young historian named Thomas Humphrey has written: "[We] have succeeded only in pressing the authors of the master narrative to alter their stories slightly, or to add another box for 'the poor' on the side of the page." That is, the historical Establishment is happy to give us the franchise for chimney sweeps who get cancer, or textile workers who burn to death when the employer locks the door. We may talk to our heart's content about—I am quoting David Brion Davis' review of *The Many-Headed Hydra*—"romanticized pirates as well as prostitutes, religious zealots, bandits, highwaymen, and criminals of all sorts." But we must leave the overall interpretation of what it all means to historians who celebrate society as it is.

No change in the historiography of the Revolution is more important than that which has ever so slowly recognized the centrality of slavery. Yet we have recently watched a cinematic version of the abolition of the British slave trade in which slave revolts in Haiti and Jamaica go almost unmentioned and abolition happens because of the conscience-stricken efforts of aristocrat William Wilberforce. As Peter Linebaugh has said, it is an "Amazing Disgrace." Thankfully, others such as Adam Hochschild, Marcus Rediker in his history of the slave ship, and Simon Schama's brilliant *Rough Crossings*, have rediscovered the slave as protagonist and tragic hero.

When my attention as an historian shifted from the adoption of the Constitution to the formation of the CIO, I was taken aback to find that in the one field as in the other the major works appearing were biographies of Founding Fathers. The underlying mindset appears to be that the decline of the labor movement in the United States can only be set right again from above. In 1995, when John Sweeney became President of the AFL-CIO, the biographers of Sidney Hillman and Walter Reuther circulated an open letter to Sweeney. The letter hailed his elevation as "the most heartening development in our nation's political life since the heyday of the civil rights movement," assessed his election as "promis[ing] to once again make the house of labor a social movement around which we can rally," and pledged "to play our part in helping realize the promise of October." A decade later, when another labor bureaucrat denounced Sweeney and led several major unions into a new organization, Barbara Ehrenreich declared that "the future of the American dream" was now "in the hands of Andrew Stern," who possessed a "vital agenda for change" and a "bold vision for reform." This was presumably before Stern's coalition with Walmart.

Thus demythologizing of those whom Jesse Lemisch called "great white men" remains an essential task. In labor history, we need to look again at the paradigmatic figure of John L. Lewis and to move beyond the hagiography of Saul Alinsky, Melvyn Dubofsky, David Brody, and Robert Zieger.

Here the research of Jim Pope is the gateway to understanding. He writes:

> According to the standard story, section 7(a) of the National Industrial Recovery Act [made possible] a brilliant organizing campaign that reestablished the mine workers' union in the soft coalfields. The story begins in late May 1933, when UMW President John L. Lewis—anticipating the enactment of section 7(a)—commits the union's entire treasury…. One hundred organizers fan out into the coalfields… claiming "the President" wants the miners to join the union…. [W]ithin weeks of section 7(a)'s signing, the union enrolls the overwhelming majority of workers in the soft coalfields.

In this standard story, Pope observes, "coal miners rarely appear and strikes—if they enter the story at all—play a subsidiary role," and are said to have been masterminded by Lewis.

In reality, Pope finds, the self-activity of miners in southwestern Pennsylvania and West Virginia began before any initiative by Lewis and without his aid. When the NIRA was enacted the organizing upsurge in coal was already "in full swing."

From self-organization the miners moved on, according to Pope, to "enforcement from below." Strike activity in the summer of 1933 involved 100,000 miners spread out over 1,000 miles of mountainous terrain. When UMW Vice President Philip Murray entered into an agreement with the owners that banned all mass picketing, striking miners ignored him because they viewed picketing "not as a form of communication, but as an enforcement device." Organizing themselves through pit committees which superseded the official UMW apparatus, the miners stayed out despite wage cuts and promised wage increases because, Pope says, what they wanted was "structural change" and a "new industrial order." In summary:

> Throughout the struggle, John L. Lewis had been a step behind the local union activists. His celebrated organizing campaign was not launched until after rank-and-file miners had already rejuvenated the union. Once deployed, his organizers worked persistently to undermine the strike movement…. Thus, the sensational recovery of the UMW union—later touted by Lewis as a product of centralized discipline and federal government lawmaking—was in fact brought about by a democratic movement of local activists enforcing their own vision of the right to organize.

Economic Interest and Ideology

HOW DO YOU *explain the interaction of subordination, economic interest and ideology in the choices of the "weak"? Horizontal historians have tended to romanticize the so-called inarticulate, leaving many complexities and contradictions out of their historical explanations.*

As an aspiring graduate student in history, I set out to prove or disprove what other historians—especially Carl Becker and Charles Beard—had to say about the political choices made by poor and working people during the American Revolution. I studied farm tenants in Dutchess County and artisans in New York City.

What I learned about tenants was that in southern Dutchess County and neighboring Westchester County tenant farmers supported the Revolution. I held in my hands the petitions that they wrote to the revolutionary New York legislature in which they asked for confiscation of Loyalist estates.

Thus far, Becker's idea that the Revolution was a struggle over who should rule at home, as well as a struggle for home rule, worked well. While a coalition of classes struggled for independence, little people at the bottom demanded more: economic independence in the form of freehold ownership of the land that they tilled.

But in Columbia County, just to the north in the approximate present site of Bard College, tenant farmers were Loyalists. They made their way out into the Hudson River where the Continental Congress had strung nets to obstruct the junction of British forces from New York City and Albany, stole the lead used to weight the nets, and made bullets out of it. In 1777 they staged a tenant uprising on Livingston Manor.

So what is the explanation of this ideological diversity? Why were the tenants who rented from Beverly Robinson in southern Dutchess County ardent patriots, whereas the tenants on the land of Robert Livingston only a few miles away became Tories?

There is a simple answer, I suggested. It all depended on the politics of your landlord. If you rented from a Tory like Robinson, who sheltered Benedict Arnold when the latter fled across the Hudson, you supported the Revolution in the hope that if Robinson and his friends were defeated, you might get fee simple ownership of your farm.

But if you rented from Livingston, an ardent Whig, your calculus was just the opposite. You sought victory for the King of England because if he won, Livingston might be deprived of his lands, and in this way you too might realize the American dream and become the owner of the land that you cultivated.

So it was not ideology that determined the political choices of Hudson Valley tenant farmers. It was economic interest.

I believe that we can deal most fruitfully with ideology if, like Karl Marx, we recognize that ideas typically emerge from the economic settings in which historical actors are imbedded. It does not denigrate the lives of farm tenants to understand that they wished to own the farms on which they toiled.

No one has better articulated the interaction of economic subordination and ideology than anthropologist and political scientist James C. Scott. He considers situations ranging all the way from a free dialogue between equals "to the concentration camp in which most of the victims' transcript is driven underground, leaving only a virtual parody of stereotyped, stilted deference born of mortal fear…. Ranged in between these extremes are a host of more common conditions in which subordinate classes typically find themselves." In such situations the weaker party is unlikely to speak his or her mind, but will rather enact a performance in keeping with the expectations of those who are more powerful.

On the one hand, Scott rejects the concept of "hegemony" if that is understood to mean that what the peasant or worker ordinarily dares to express is all that the subordinate thinks or feels. At those rare historical moments when the weak openly confront their masters, it is not so much that "a new consciousness, a new anger, a new ideology" has come into being, but rather that what was there all along is fully displayed.

On the other hand, however, Scott insists that the cries of "bread" and "land" so often at the core of peasant resistance arise from "the basic material needs of the peasant household." More generally,

> [t]o require of lower-class resistance that it

> somehow be "principled" or "selfless" is not only utopian and a slander on the moral status of fundamental material needs; it is, more fundamentally, a misconstruction of the basis of class struggle…. "Bread-and-butter" issues are the essence of lower-class politics and resistance.

Of course, Scott concedes, it is impossible to divorce the material basis of resistance from resistance to the values and ideology which justify that which exists. But crucially, for Scott

> forms of resistance that are individual and unobtrusive are not only what a Marxist might expect from petty commodity producers and rural laborers, but have certain advantages. Unlike hierarchical formal organizations, there is no center, no leadership, no identifiable structure that can be co-opted or neutralized. What is lacking in terms of centralization may be compensated for by flexibility and persistence. These forms of resistance will win no set-piece battles, but they are admirably adapted to long-run campaigns of attrition.

Moreover, while the forms of resistance Scott studies may be individual,

> this is not to say that they are uncoordinated…. [A] concept of coordination derived from formal and bureaucratic settings is of little assistance in understanding actions in small communities with dense informal networks and rich, historically deep, cultures of resistance to outside claims.

Sons of Liberty

SO WE MIGHT *suggest that history from below is not enough unless it is a whole history from below. I remember reading Perry Anderson's remark that "a 'history from above'…is thus no less essential than a 'history from below': indeed, without it the latter in the end becomes one-sided (if the better side)."*

I shall briefly indicate what I mean by another example drawn from my dissertation research.

Whereas the politics of Hudson Valley tenant farmers may be little known, it is otherwise with city artisans. These are the Sons of Liberty. These are the folks who erected liberty poles, enforced non-importation agreements, dumped tea into Boston Harbor, and carried the news that the British were coming. These were Paul Revere and friends in Boston who met at the Green Dragon tavern, and comparable groups in New York City, Philadelphia and Charleston. Carl Becker said they were the heart and soul of both the struggle for home rule and the struggle over who should rule at home. And he was right. There is only one problem. As Charles Beard noted in passing but did not explain, these same artisans enthusiastically supported the Federalists' Constitution in 1787. They did so not only at the ballot box, but in elaborate parades in every major seacoast city.

I have a longtime friend in the profession who is entranced by the creativity of the floats and banners that the artisans contrived in these parades. I believe he sees these parades as the emergence of an autonomous artisanal culture.

But I insist on asking: Why did the artisans support what Beard considered a counter-revolutionary Constitution? Why did the artisan radicals of 1763-1776 become Hamiltonians in 1787? And what does this ideological transformation tell us about class relationships in the Revolutionary era?

Again, there is a simple answer. What preoccupied artisans before the Revolution was the danger that imported British manufactured goods might destroy their livelihoods. Hence they supported all things anti-British, especially non-importation agreements.

And what preoccupied them in the mid-1780s as British manufactures once again began to pour into American seaports was…exactly the same thing. Their situation was similar to that of Mexican farmers today, whose livelihood is threatened by the importation of duty-free corn from the United States thanks to NAFTA. Hence artisans supported the project of a strong national government that could impose an effective tariff on imported manufactured goods.

Artisans were altogether consistent. There only appears to have been an inconsistency because we have supposed the politics of artisans to be driven, not by economic interest, but by ideology, and have ignored why they supported the constitutional project of those who were, after as before 1787, their class enemies.

History by Participants in the Struggle

WHEN YOU SAY *that guerrilla history views history through the eyes of its "victims," are you not afraid that we might here be taking some of the agency away from the "poor" or from the "victims"? I sometimes wonder if this language is the most appropriate one. A related question in writing guerrilla history, a question which you have touched on before, is whether people need historians. People do tend to write history themselves. Are we, radical historians, then guerrillas who lost their way in the jungle? What is our contribution?*

What I have called "guerrilla history" is a subset or variant of history from the bottom up. It is history from the bottom up carried on by the working-class activists and intellectuals whom academics typically view, from above, as the subjects of their research.

Those directly involved may understand what happened much more profoundly than academic historians. I want to give an example.

I had the honor of coordinating Freedom Schools during the 1964 Mississippi Summer Project. I want to talk about the voter registration part of the Project: the effort to send Mississippi Freedom Democratic Party delegates to the national Democratic Party convention in Atlantic City in August 1964, in the hope that they might be seated in place of the so-called regular delegates from the all-white Mississippi Democratic Party.

Going to Atlantic City sought to assist Mississippi African Americans to become part of the national Democratic Party. And it relied on a trade union leader who was close to President Lyndon Johnson and who would, in years to come, support the Vietnam War: Walter Reuther.

Unlike historians who have narrated these events, SNCC staff expressed a deep uneasiness with the idea of seeking to be seated at Atlantic City. The following are desperately brief extracts from the minutes of the SNCC staff meeting on June 9-11, 1964.

Ruby Doris Smith opened a discussion on goals with the words: "We could begin with discussion of whether we're working to make basic changes within existing political and economic structure.... What would the seating of the delegation mean besides having Negroes in the National Democratic Party?" Here were some of the responses.

IVANHOE DONALDSON. Disagrees with just making more Democrats and more Republicans. Perhaps the way is to create a parallel structure.... Our problem is that our programs don't change basic factors of exploitation. Perhaps it's better to create a third stream.... [W]hat is the point of working within the Democratic Party? It is not a radical tool.

CHARLIE COBB. Feels there would be negligible value in merely being part of the Democratic Party structure.... There is a danger of Negroes being manipulated by the national parties.... It is bad if you make people part of a decadent structure.

JOHN LEWIS. He is not sure that we can get what we want within "liberal politics." The basic things we want to achieve are equality for Negro and white, liberate the poor white as well as the Negro.

JIM FORMAN. We should agitate for dignity.... Dignity is an umbrella concept. E.g., a man without a job has no dignity.

JIM JONES. SNCC's program is limited to desegregating facilities and voter registration.

LAWRENCE GUYOT. If our goal is just voter registration then we should stop. We have to organize around something.

Ten days later, of course, we all learned that three young men who had risked their lives for limited goals had in all probability been murdered. It became much more difficult to continue the discussion begun at the SNCC staff meeting in June. On the one hand, support for actually seating the MFDP delegates at the Democratic Party convention increased dramatically. On the other hand, a feeling grew that only if the delegates were seated would the sacrifice of

Schwerner, Chaney, and Goodman have been worthwhile.

This was the latent or suspended state of dialogue within the movement when African-American would-be delegates from Mississippi arrived in Atlantic City. Nelson Lichtenstein in his biography of Walter Reuther and Taylor Branch in his biography of Martin Luther King, Jr. tell the identical story.

At Johnson's request, Reuther broke off negotiations with General Motors and flew to Atlantic City by chartered plane. Arriving at 3 a.m. Reuther went into session with Hubert Humphrey and Walter Mondale. They agreed that the MFDP would be required to accept a so-called "compromise": the Mississippi regulars would continue to be the official delegation and the MFDP would have two "at large" delegates named by the President, who, so Humphrey made clear, would not include "that illiterate woman," Mrs. Fannie Lou Hamer.

The next day exhausted MFDP delegates instructed their attorney, Joseph Rauh, to hold out for at least the same number of seats allotted to the regulars. But Rauh was also the lawyer for the UAW. Reuther told Rauh: "Here's the decision. I am telling you to take this deal." If Rauh did not do what he was told, Reuther added, he would terminate Rauh's employment with the UAW.

Reuther sought to employ the same kind of strong arm tactics with Dr. King. Reuther told him: "Your funding is on the line. The kind of money you got from us in Birmingham is there again for Mississippi, but you've got to help us and we've got to help Johnson."

The rest is, sadly enough, "history." In retrospect, the young SNCC organizers saw more deeply into the ambiguities of seeking to be part of the Democratic Party than have academic historians.

At a conference in Waveland, Mississippi, in November 1964, SNCC tried to digest the summer's experiences. Academic histories have emphasized the tension between black staff and white volunteers, exacerbated by the fact that so many volunteers stayed on in Mississippi after the summer; or the conflict between Jim Forman's desire to transform SNCC into a Marxist-Leninist vanguard party and the aspiration of others that SNCC continue as a decentralized network in which those who did the work made the decisions.

Bob Moses suggested a third explanation for the difficulty experienced by SNCC in finding a way forward. Bayard Rustin and others were encouraging SNCC to look to its "coalition partners" for allies in confronting the economic and social structures that underpin racism in the United States. But precisely those allies—the national Democratic Party, and Walter Reuther, allegedly the most progressive trade union leader in the country—had just finished stabbing the MFDP delegates in the back at Atlantic City. Here is how Bob Moses put it at the Waveland conference:

> Let's sum up the box we're in:
> ❧ Labor unions are political organizations, now within the Establishment.
> ❧ When labor is organized, it can only discuss a narrow aspect of the problem: wages. Reuther sat in the meeting with King, Humphrey and others to urge the FDP to accept the compromise, talking anti-Goldwater, keep morality out of politics, etc....
> If we organize people, all should decide where to focus attention.

SNCC failed to find a way out of the box described by Bob Moses. We ought not be too hard on SNCC, however. We are still in that box.

History as Accompaniment

IN *VISIONS OF HISTORY you said that practicing law is like "history with dessert," I wonder what you meant by that. You also told me that your most profound and rewarding experience in doing guerrilla history was as a lawyer, accompanying steelworkers and prisoners. So, continuing with the logic of my previous question, is being a lawyer perhaps a more appropriate position in historical guerrilla warfare than the one of the professional historian?*

Ideally, guerrilla history would be produced by the guerrillas themselves. And through much of the experience of humankind it has been so.

There are two principal variants. The first is oral history. Alex Haley went to West Africa in search of particular words repeated by parent to infant child in generation after generation of his family in the United States. He found those roots in a village where designated elders recited a memorized oral history that at a certain miraculous moment included reference to a young man whose name contained the long-sought-for words, and who had gone into the jungle in search of wood to make a drum and never been seen again. In Tony Hillerman's most recent detective novel, *The Shape Shifters*, a retired Navaho policeman and a transplanted young man from Laos exchange accounts of the tragic history and surprisingly similar mythologies of their two peoples. In the process, a trust arises between them that in the end saves both their lives.

A second major variant of guerrilla history has been created by political protagonists forced into exile, retirement or imprisonment, and thus given leisure to reflect and write. Examples are Thucydides, Machiavelli, Trotsky, and in our own time, Mumia Abu Jamal. I consider Mumia's *We Want Freedom: A Life in the Black Panther Party* the best history of the movements of the 1960s that has yet been written. Its special virtue is a combination of criticism of movement personalities such as Huey Newton with deep compassion for those critiqued. Cathy Wilkerson's *Flying Close to the Sun* is a close second. Again there is an ability both to criticize incisively and to forgive—in this case, to forgive herself—that seems beyond what any academic historian could attempt.

However, most guerrilla history will not be created by guerrillas alone and unaided, but will involve the assistance of a second person, acting as sympathetic listener, transcriber, editor, and/or presenter-to-the-world. Remarkably, Haley again offers the prototype in the *Autobiography of Malcolm X* that he and Malcolm made together.

Although I have co-authored an account of movements in which I took part (*The Resistance*, with Michael Ferber), co-edited three volumes of oral histories, assisted in the creation of an activist's autobiographical memoir (by Brian Willson), and edited the writings of an activist friend (Marty Glaberman), my most profound experiences as a co-creator of guerrilla history have been as a lawyer. I describe them below.

First, though, I want once again to emphasize the centrality of a right relationship between working-class protagonist and professional associate. On the one hand, the professional—whether journalist, minister, doctor, lawyer, teacher, or whatever—must feel a profound respect for the insights and perspective of his or her collaborator. On the other hand, as Archbishop Romero stressed in his pastoral letters about "accompaniment," there can be no place for a false deference whereby the associate romanticizes and exempts from criticism the experience of the activist.

THE U.S. STEEL CASE

In September 1977, about a year after my wife and I arrived in Youngstown, the Youngstown Sheet & Tube Company announced the closing of its largest facility in the area at the cost of about 5,000 jobs. The announcement was completely unexpected. Steelworkers tried to explain to the media that they had assumed the mill would "always be there." Older residents said they had experienced nothing like it since Pearl Harbor.

The day before the announcement I had led a small discussion group at the local Presbyterian church on plant closings. I said that in a family, when hard times come every one takes in their belts a little and the family survives "as a community." So it should also be if a city experiences economic hard times, I suggested.

When the Youngstown *Vindicator* appeared the next day with headlines on page 1 about the shutdown, there was a story "below the fold" on that page about my little talk, which would otherwise have drawn no attention. Perhaps for that reason I was invited to the first meeting, for breakfast at the Catholic Diocese, of an assemblage of persons that became the Ecumenical Coalition of the Mahoning Valley. This gathering of religious personalities and selected experts came to advocate reopening of the mill under worker-community ownership.

There is a movie, "*Shout Youngstown,*" made by two young women who grew up there, and a book that I wrote, *The Fight Against Shutdowns*, which tell the story of the mill closings that followed in 1978 and 1979. They turned what had been the second or third largest steel-producing city in the nation into a community where no steel is produced. Here I will not try to tell that whole story but will focus on what happened after the third mill closing announcement in November 1979.

The shutdowns of 1977 and 1978 had involved the Youngstown Sheet & Tube Company, and its conglomerate owner, the Lykes Corporation. The remaining steel mills in the Mahoning Valley were owned by U.S. Steel, and it was U.S. Steel that announced the third and last round of closings.

This announcement too was unexpected because as late as the summer of 1979, David Roderick, Chairman of the Board, had gone on local television and declared that the mills were doing well and would remain open. The president of Local 1330, United Steelworkers of America, said after the shutdown announcement that he felt emasculated. Another local union officer recalled charging a machine gun nest with the visceral assumption that whoever else might be killed, he would not be among them.

What was to be done? I noticed a *Vindicator* story in which steelworkers who were interviewed said they felt betrayed because the company had promised them to keep the mills open. In law school I had been attracted to the legal theory of "promissory estoppel," which says that if A makes an oral promise to B, and B (with A's knowledge) acts on that promise "to his detriment," the promise is legally enforceable. But I assumed there would be no way to use that theory in this situation because the Basic Steel Contract, like almost all collective bargaining agreements in the United States, contained a "management prerogatives clause" that gave the employer the authority to make unilateral investment decisions, such as closing a plant.

However, a colleague of mine at Legal Services, Jim Callen, pointed out that if the company had made an additional, separate promise, over and above the collective bargaining agreement, perhaps that could still be enforced. We went to court on behalf of the local Congressman, six local unions, the Ecumenical Coalition, and dozens of individual steelworkers.

During the next six months we rode a highly dramatic roller coaster, before a federal appeals court finally ruled against us. Here I want to highlight the "guerrilla history" that made our struggle possible.

On the strength of my colleague's suggestion I set out up and down the Valley with a tape recorder. Initially we did not know the details of company negotiations with the local union, in which a promise turned out to have been clearly made. But we knew of Chairman of the Board Roderick's televised pronouncement. Illustrative of the guerrilla history that emerged was the following.

A worker for U.S. Steel saw and heard Mr. Roderick's declaration that the future of the mill was secure. He arranged to buy a new house. As he drove homewards after signing the purchase agreement, he was obliged to stop at one of the many railroad crossings in this industrial community. To pass the time he turned on the car radio and heard that the mill was to be closed.

A young in-house lawyer for U.S. Steel made the mistake of asking us to file a "more particular statement" of our claims in federal court. We used the opportunity to set out for the judge a series of stories about homes purchased, expensive college programs committed to, medical procedures elected, and the like, in reasonable reliance on U.S. Steel's public statements. This testimony was so persuasive that the Sixth Circuit Court of Appeals, when it finally ruled against us, began by reproducing the stories contained in our Amended Complaint and calling them "a cry for help from the Mahoning Valley."

Another moment of guerrilla history was the following. Ramsey Clark and I argued before the United States District Court in Cleveland that U.S. Steel should be ordered not to close its mills until trial could be held. To every one's astonishment, the judge granted our motion. Within hours the young in-house lawyer had been replaced by a senior corporate attorney. He told the judge that U.S. Steel's Youngstown facilities simply lacked the raw materials to continue production.

By the next day we were back in the judge's chambers with an inventory of raw materials that, as workers say, had "fallen off a truck." The document proved that sufficient iron ore, limestone, and the like was already on site to keep production going for another three or four months.

Bob Vasquez, president of Local 1330, remarked that the struggle had salvaged the "dignity" of the men he represented. My friend John Barbero, another steelworker, commented with a smile, "Youngstown sure died hard."

THE SUPERMAX PRISON AND THE LUCASVILLE REBELLION

By the summer of 1980 all the steel mills in Youngstown were closed. A total of about 10,000 steelworkers had been laid off, with the additional loss of perhaps 20-30,000 jobs in steel fabrication, trucking, and other auxiliary occupations.

Throughout the 1980s the local governing class appeared to search for a new corporation that could move into town and make all well again. The Congressman projected a commuter aircraft company that never materialized. An automobile plant opened that would take a vehicle chassis from the nearby GM Lordstown factory, put a luxury shell around it, and sell it for $50,000. Moreover the plant was to be non-union. It lasted only a year or two. Other, similar ventures never happened or soon closed.

Judging by their actions, sometime in the early 1990s the Powers That Be in Youngstown adopted a new strategy: prisons in place of steel mills. The Corrections Corporation of America, the largest private prison company in the United States, was induced to build Ohio's first private prison. The State of Ohio agreed to construct the first supermaximum security prison in Ohio, at which up to 504 prisoners would be housed in indefinite solitary confinement. Other prisons were solicited and opened in nearby communities.

My wife Alice and I are not criminal defense lawyers. We had no experience in advocacy for prisoners.

We are, however, Quakers, that is, members of the Society of Friends. Friends have a traditional concern with prisons. In the mid-1990s there began to be mention in the media that a supermaximum security prison was to be built on the East Side of town.

Alice asked, What is a supermaximum security prison? A meeting to consider the results of her research was convened by the Workers' Solidarity Club of Youngstown and the local peace action group.

It was decided to hold a community forum. The gathering took place at a small church adjacent to the site of the proposed penitentiary. Effort was made to hear testimony from persons who had experienced solitary confinement or had close relatives in that situation. One of those who spoke was Jackie Bowers, sister of George Skatzes (pronounced "skates"), who had just been sentenced to death for his alleged role in a 1993 prison uprising at the Lucasville prison in southern Ohio. Jackie was speaking in public for the first time in her life.

Responding to Jackie, Alice and I were added to George Skatzes' visiting list. We volunteered to do paralegal work in his case and were assigned to collect relevant evidence that had not been presented at trial. We read the trial transcript of more than 6000 pages. At one point Alice came running from another room in our house and asked me to look at the testimony of the investigator for the State of Ohio, Sergeant Howard Hudson. Sergeant Hudson was asked if, when his forces entered the cell block that the prisoners in rebellion had occupied for eleven days, they found graffiti on the walls. He answered, Yes. He was asked, What did the graffiti say? Hudson answered, Most of them said things like "Black and White Together"; "Convict Unity"; and, most intriguingly, "Convict Race."

At the end of the 1993 disturbance five men, one of them George Skatzes, were sentenced to death. There was a good deal of evidence that the Ohio State Penitentiary, the new Youngstown "supermax," was being built especially for these five. And indeed, when the supermax opened in May 1998, the Lucasville Five were among the first prisoners to be transferred there.

Alice and I paid the first visit to any prisoner in the supermax prison. We spoke with George for two or three hours.

Although he was in a locked cubicle, separated from us by a wall of transparent material, he was handcuffed behind his back for the entire period. I was so angry about this unnecessary and painful humiliation that I said to Alice as we left, Give me a teaspoon so I can start to tear this place down.

After that visit, almost ten years ago as I write, Alice and I plunged into two-track advocacy. On the one hand, we assembled a legal team to confront the conditions of confinement at the supermax. In those early days selected prisoners elsewhere in Ohio were awakened early in the morning, and told without notice or hearing that they were going to the supermax; once arrived, they were placed in single cells for an indefinite duration, and allowed to possess only two paperback books (one scripture and one devotional holy book). Because of the ingenuity of prisoners in sliding food, notes and other items from one cell to another along the floor (a process known as "fishing"), metal strips were placed at the bottom and along the sides of the solid metal doors.

Alice developed an enormous correspondence with prisoners at the supermax, soliciting descriptions of their conditions of confinement and encouraging prisoners to file grievances about their complaints, a prerequisite to legal action. In January 2001 the legal team filed a federal law suit on behalf of prisoners who had been, were being, or would in future be, confined at the supermax.

Meantime, as we came to know the Lucasville Five, I became a fact-gatherer for all of their defense counsel. About two dozen of the men convicted of various crimes during the 1993 uprising were housed at the supermax. Alice and I could visit all of them. Other Lucasville defendants, housed at other Ohio prisons, agreed to talk with us. We collected documents, affidavits, introductions to yet other possible witnesses.

Thus together with a broad spectrum of those considered by Ohio to be the "worst of the worst," we became guerrilla historians regarding a prison uprising and a situation of severe confinement. It was very much like doing any other history, except that with regard to what happened in 1993, how well we did the history might determine whether a person spent the rest of his life behind bars or was executed.

The law suit went well. It survived a trip to the United States Supreme Court and lasted for more than seven years. At an initial hearing I questioned thirteen consecutive prisoners in their handcuffs and orange jump suits. Alice had chosen them on the basis of the particular complaints each had administratively "exhausted" and the documents supportive of each man's testimony.

We were allowed one or two plaintiff representatives in the courtroom during hearings. Almost from the beginning one of the representatives was Jason Robb, a member of the Aryan Brotherhood. He insisted that African Americans needed their own spokesperson. For the last few years, that second person was another of the Lucasville Five, Keith LaMar, or as he calls himself, Bomani Shakur (Swahili for "thankful mighty warrior"). Together with Jason and Bomani, Alice and I reviewed draft pleadings and determined legal strategy. Jules Lobel, vice president of the Center for Constitutional Rights, and professor of Constitutional Law, Civil Rights Litigation, and International Law, was the third key member of our legal team.

Meantime it became more and more clear that the convictions of Lucasville defendants rested on perjured testimony. The prisoners who occupied L block in 1993 did their best to destroy it, and when they emerged after a negotiated surrender there was (so the State said) no usable physical evidence. Hence the evidence presented by prosecutors in the approximately fifty Lucasville indictments and trials consisted essentially of the testimony of other prisoners. These informants, or "snitches," offered their testimony in exchange for letters to the Parole Board, reduced charges, or other benefits. It was inherently unreliable evidence.

So I have devoted the last decade to painstaking sapping and mining of the judicial proceedings against the Lucasville defendants, especially those sentenced to death. I have made evidence available to defendants' counsel. I have written friend of the court briefs, articles in periodicals like *Monthly Review* and *The Catholic Worker*, a law review article and a book, *Lucasville: The Untold Story of a Prison Uprising* (Philadelphia: Temple University Press, 2004). I have also co-authored a play by the same name that was produced in seven Ohio cities in April 2007.

It is the most demanding, at times the most frustrating, and overall the most rewarding work I have ever undertaken as an historian.

Stan, Marty and Solidarity Unionism

I BELIEVE STAN WEIR *and Marty Glaberman deserve to be mentioned in a separate question. Their ideas deserve a more detailed treatment.*

If "guerrilla history" were only a matter of how professionals like myself can draw on the insights of workers and prisoners in finding historical truth, it would be interesting but hardly earth-shaking. What is critically important is that workers, prisoners and others similarly situated themselves become analysts of their own experience.

Similarly, "solidarity unionism" among any group of the oppressed requires that ordinary people act for themselves, but beyond that, that they interpret their action and on that basis project future actions. Unless this intellectual function is part of the process, the poor will always be at the mercy of persons who presume to tell them what their action means and what they should do next, whether those persons are members of a Leninist vanguard party, staff of a union like the Service Employees International Union, or anarchist theoreticians.

Let me illustrate what I mean by describing in greater detail the life and work of Stan Weir and Marty Glaberman.

STAN WEIR

Stan tells his life story up to the mid-1950s in *Rank and File* (pp. 172-193). In a concluding chapter to a book I edited entitled "*We Are All Leaders*" (pp. 294-334), he describes the collective self-activity of seamen on one particular voyage during World War II.

The marriage of Stan's parents lasted only five months and he never knew his father. His mother's mother "was a scrubwoman in office buildings in downtown Los Angeles." His mother "quit high school in the tenth grade and became an apprentice dressmaker."

When the war came, Stan became a seaman in the Merchant Marine for the same reasons that I later sought to be an unarmed medic in the Army. It was a way to avoid killing and the discipline of the Armed Forces, and yet live the social experience of his generation.

THE S.S. HANAPEPE

Stan says of the ordinary sailors on his first ship that they "were a highly conscious group of men from the strikes of the '30s, an experience which was still fresh in their minds. They were involved…in job actions from time to time. Several among them were ex-IWWs."

Stan had come on board wearing the uniform of a midshipman cadet and the deckhands "wanted to win me away from the 'topside' for good."

> So they pumped all this history into me. And then they would quiz me. "What happened on such-and-such a date?" "What's Bloody

Thursday?" "What were the big demands?" "What was the 1934 award?" "Why were we able to win victories before getting a collective bargaining contract?"

On that ship, Stan Weir relates, "I finally found a cause and a vehicle for pursuing it. These guys were involved, day to day, in establishing dignity...."

"Red" Weir became a leader of shipboard collective resistance. In September 1943 his Deck Gang was scheduled to sail on the freighter *S.S. Hanapepe*. Speaking for the group, Stan told the Captain that the ship would not leave port until the crew had fresh mattresses, fresh milk and good coffee, "vegetables besides cabbage," four new shower heads, some good bar soap, lye soap, Clorox and kerosene. They got them. And on that voyage, too, the leading "'34 men" (participants in the San Francisco general strike of 1934), undertook to communicate "union history and organization (both official and unofficial)" in "unposted but almost regularly scheduled gatherings" throughout the trip.

THE OAKLAND GENERAL STRIKE

Never again did Stan and his co-workers experience so dramatic a victory of worker control as on the *S.S. Hanapepe*. Nevertheless, they "helped to seed changes that improved the lives of crews." And in 1946 Stan experienced an even more complete prefigurative moment, the Oakland General Strike.

Stan was working in a Chevrolet plant in Oakland as an assembly line spray painter. "One Monday morning I arrived downtown on the streetcar" on the way to work. The motorman and conductor got off. Passengers followed them off the streetcar to figure out what was happening.

Retail clerks had been on strike for many weeks at two department stores in Oakland. Police had been escorting scabs and merchandise into the stores.

> The union drivers of streetcars, buses, and trucks refused to watch two strikes being broken. By stranding thousands of work-bound people in the heart of the city, they had called the Oakland general strike…. No officials had announced or were leading it.

Block by block, people who had been on their way to work began to organize for celebration. Selected hamburger stands and coffee shops were encouraged to stay open. Dancing began in the streets. "Anyone could leave town but a union card was required to get in."

The second evening of the general strike there was a mass meeting, but none of the union officials who spoke could say what to do next. As people left the meeting and walked back to downtown Oakland they exchanged ideas. "Some would spend the night, and others would relieve them the following morning."

The strike ended on its fourth day when union officials directed the people milling about downtown to go back to work. Looking back, Stan blamed himself that he failed to climb onto a parked car and say: "We can lead this strike ourselves. Let's send out a dozen committees from one block to the other blocks to say this."

Regardless, "It was that vision and the experiences in that strike…, the vision in actual life of people determining their own destinies that sustains one and makes one stand fast for a long, long time."

THE INFORMAL WORK GROUP

In the course of the experiences thus far recounted Stan Weir joined a Marxist grouplet, the Workers Party. Under its direction he took job after job, in automobile assembly plants, in trucking, in a grocery store. There then came a time in the 1950s when Stan found that his political group had somewhat disintegrated, that other members were interested only in surviving, and that there was no longer a movement telling him what to do. He was "just a worker."

> A whole new world opened up to me. [To approach any work situation] with a whole set of preconceived slogans was way off the beam. One first had simply to learn what the subculture was so that one's actions were understandable to everyone else....

Stan made friends. He became part of a "ride group" that would go to eat after the swing shift in the black community, or the Hispanic community, or the Italian part of town. Politics "came in the natural course of life."

Reflecting on this many-layered journey, Weir developed a searing critique of trade unionism. Natural authority among those who work together lodges in the men or women to whom others spontaneously turn for direction. Such informal work groups cannot be bureaucratized. Union organizations housed away from the workplace fail to recognize that a workplace "isn't a collection of individuals so much as a collection of informal groups." The work day is a continuous meeting within each one of these groups. If delegates from such shop committees "were to be pyramided into councils on an area level and finally into congresses on a national level," the representatives so chosen "would still come under some kind of disciplinary hold of people on the job."

MARTY GLABERMAN

Marty Glaberman worked for twenty years in automobile plants in and around Detroit. He too belonged to a Marxist grouplet, Facing Reality, associated with the West Indian Marxist C.L.R. James.

Facing Reality adopted a principle that its members termed, "The Full Fountain Pen." In those days before tape recorders and copying machines, this meant listening to workers and writing down what they said.

In a pamphlet entitled "Punching Out," published in 1952, Marty Glaberman argued that in a workplace where there is a collective bargaining agreement with a no-strike clause, local union representatives are obliged to enforce the contract and thus tend to become cops for the boss. Himself white, in the late 1960s Marty conducted classes on Marxism for members of the executive committee of the Detroit-based League of Revolutionary Black Workers.

A significant chunk of Marty's thinking was presented to a conference on workers' self-activity held in the hall of Teamsters Local 377 in Youngstown, Ohio in June 1997, at a time when I was "local education coordinator" for that union. See *The New Rank and File* (Ithaca and London: Cornell University Press, 2000), edited by Alice and myself as a sequel to our earlier collection, pp. 202-209.

Just as the Oakland general strike of 1946 helped Stan Weir to stand fast over the years, so, for Marty, the Hungarian Revolution of 1956 confirmed his belief in "the revolutionary capacity of the working class even though nothing was visible." The whole Hungarian working class made a revolution "without any prior organization whatsoever."

Similarly in France in 1968, as Marty perceived that event, "whatever organizations of the working class existed were opposed to what the workers were doing" but ten million French workers spontaneously occupied their factories.

FROM ACTION TO IDEAS

For Marty, action comes first, and ideas follow. He wrote an entire book entitled *Wartime Strikes* in which he sought to demonstrate this proposition from the experience of members of the United Automobile Workers during World War II.

The UAW along with other unions in the United States officially endorsed a policy of not striking during the war. As prices rose while wages remained frozen, a struggle developed within the union over the no-strike pledge. Marty found that UAW members, voting alone in their homes, recorded a majority for continuing the no-strike pledge. But on the job, acting in groups, a majority of the workers in Detroit automotive plants took part in unauthorized wildcat strikes. The workers' "real" consciousness was better revealed by how they acted than by how they voted.

Similarly, Marty argued, workers will not become socialists because radical organizers go door-to-door passing out leaflets.

> You've got to take workers as they are, with all their contradictions, with all their nonsense. But the fact that society forces them to struggle begins to transform the working class. If white workers realize they can't organize steel unless they organize black workers, that doesn't mean they're not racist. It means that they have to deal with their own reality, and that transforms them. Who were the workers who made the Russian Revolution? Sexists, nationalists, half of them illiterate. Who were the workers in Polish Solidarity? Anti-Semitic, whatever. That kind of struggle begins to transform people.

THE GRIEVANCE

Marty was also a poet, and at the end of a collection of his writings entitled *Punching Out & Other Writings* there appear a number of his poems.

There are three different poems that tell what it is like to live through a wildcat strike. By contrast, there is a long poem entitled "The Grievance." On a summer day when the temperature is 93 degrees, the shop becomes a sweatbox. The writer goes to see his foreman and asks him "could he open up/That nailed-down window pane"? The boss replies, "It's out of my hands."

The worker files a grievance that passes successively through the hands of the steward, the committeeman, the shop committee, and the arbitrator.

> Of the one hundred grievances
> We lost ninety-nine.
> But the one that was salvaged
> Turned out to be mine.
>
> The window was opened
> On a cold wintry day.
> I shivered and shook
> Till I thought I'd give way.
>
> I went to the foreman
> And called him by name.
> And asked him to shut
> That damned window pane.
> But he said, "It's out of my hands."

In "Factory Song," the writer reflects on "twenty years in the auto shops,"

> Illuminated by politics
> the way the brights illuminate
> a foggy stretch of the Pennsylvania Turnpike.
>
> The cold, gray grinding winter mornings…
> What is there to see inside
> Only the reflection of a thousand men
> who touched you
> with their own bit of steel.
> They are not you
> You are not them
> But the parts can no longer be told apart.

Was it worth freezing your ass off
coming home from the night shift?

The rain cleans the asphalt
And the street light adds a shine.

PART III

MY COUNTRY IS THE WORLD

Homeland without Nationality

I LIKE THE *way you formulate the "new hypothesis" of Zapatismo, as a combination of insights inspired by Marxist analysis, anarchist praxis, spirituality and indigenous traditions. I think that it is not only that the old divisions between anarchism and Marxism are being eroded, but that Zapatismo is an active process of disarticulation of inherited historical dilemmas (revolution/reform, identity/interest, violence/nonviolence, spontaneity/organization, among many others). When I first encountered Zapatismo, my impression was that it offered the most coherent contemporary manifestation of what I call anarchism. But much more than that, the Zapatistas have given an original impulse to the emerging global movement. Through numerous global or intergalactic meetings, which became meeting points between very different kinds of activists and revolutionaries, and which inspired later organizational developments, such as Peoples Global Action and the World Social Forum, they have defined a new solidarity, a revolutionary global solidarity, that goes beyond traditional "internationalism." As Marcos writes, "dignity…is that homeland without nationality, that rainbow that is also a bridge, that murmur of the heart no matter what blood lives in it, that rebel irreverence that mocks frontiers, customs officials and wars." Going back for a moment to my question about re-thinking the ideas of the New Left, do you share my sentiment that this new internationalism, this "new international space of hope," is somehow different from the internationalism and anti-imperialism of the sixties and seventies? Let us go even further into history. Would you agree with me that these words of the Zapatistas, "dignity, homeland without nationality," bear a strong similarity to the words from another time: "my country is the world"? Is this the same "rebel irreverence" that "mocks frontiers, customs, officials and wars" across the landscapes of history?*

These are splendid questions, which call for careful answers.

GOING TOO FAR TOWARD A FALSE INTERNATIONALISM

I agree in critiquing the "internationalism and anti-imperialism of the sixties and seventies." Actually, we might go back to the statement at the end of *The Communist Manifesto* that workers have no country. The same sentiment was evident in the 1960s when activists spelled "America" with a "k": "Amerika."

This way of thinking about internationalism strikes me as abstract and dogmatic. Rather than affirming the ability of human beings to find common ground despite their differences, it calls for rejection of experiences that all human beings share. Every one begins life as part of a family, learns one or more particular languages, belongs for a time to a specific community. Modern technology denies us so much in the way of tactile, flesh and blood moments of commonality, I believe we reject and ridicule such opportunities at our peril.

In my own case, one reason I decided to study American history was to discover whether there was some time in this country's past in which I could feel more at home than in the United States of the late 1950s. On the whole I did not find that "usable past" in the period of the American Revolution. As the anthropologist Gregory Bateson put it, everything was to be seen in the old American nickel. On one side was the head of a Native American and the word "Liberty." On the other side was a bison and the words "*E pluribus unum*," or as Bateson translated them, "There used to be a lot of us and now there's only one."

The conclusion that the American Revolution fails to offer what Thoreau called "hard bottom and rocks in place" becomes even stronger if one considers slavery. The American Revolution had the possibility of abolishing slavery. The Constitutional Convention assembled in Philadelphia in the same month (May 1787) that the British anti-slavery society held its first meeting in London. But in this country, "my country," the revolutionary leadership failed to act. Even George Washington, the single such leader who provided in his will for the freedom of his slaves, tried to use the United States Custom Service to kidnap Ona Judge, a favorite house slave of his wife who had escaped to New Hampshire.

And yet, many Americans whom I admire made something out of the ideas of the Revolution, especially Tom Paine.

And there are other persons and incidents in the history of this country with which I profoundly identify. I believe that among United States presidents Lincoln was in a class by himself, and that his Second Inaugural Address is the most praiseworthy public document in United States history. That's the speech in which Lincoln asserted that if every drop of blood drawn by the lash had to be repaid by a drop of blood drawn with the sword, still must it be said as it was said of old that the judgments of the Lord are true and righteous altogether.

So I don't hold with an internationalism that rejects everything American.

FINDING ONE'S WAY TOWARD AN INTERNATIONALISM OF THE HEART

The words of Marcos which you quote suggest an attractive, exciting new way to understand internationalism.

I have been thinking about glimpses of other societies and their histories that came my way as a child.

My parents were both teachers, and they hired a young immigrant from Ireland to care for my sister and myself during the workday. Mary Bohan taught me many Irish revolutionary songs. I have fully retrieved the words of two of them only in the last few years. "Michael Dwyer" was an Irish nationalist guerrilla in the 1790s. He hid out in the Wexford hills in southeastern Ireland. One day the Black and Tans (the British soldiers) flushed him from his hiding place, and Dwyer and his friends took refuge in a house. The British set it on fire. A man named McAllister was wounded in the first exchange of gunshots. He told Dwyer and the others that he would stand in the doorway, the soldiers would discharge their single-shot muskets, killing him, and Dwyer could escape before they reloaded. It worked. Dwyer, according to the song, "swam the river Slaney and left them all behind."

The second song is "My Old Fenian Gun." As I remembered the first lines, a father and son lived alone and above the fireplace hung a gun, "its barrel long and grim." The father never speaks of it. One day, though, he takes it down in response to the child's repeated questions. He explains that his wife, the boy's mother, died on a night when the little family fled through the winter cold to escape the British soldiers.

I also remember records on which German volunteers for the International Brigades that fought in the Spanish Civil War sang of their experience. A commissar named Hans Beimler was shot and killed by the forces of General Franco. The song (to the tune of "*Ich hat ein Kamerad*") tells how the bullet came from his German fatherland, the rifle was well-made in Germany, and so he died. Another song, "*Die Moorsoldaten*" (The Peatbog Soldiers), tells of prisoners of war who each day march to the bog to dig peat. The last verse exclaims:

> But for us there is no complaining,
> Winter can't last forever,
> Some day we will cry, rejoicing,
> "Homeland, you are mine again."

A SYNTHESIS

If I have to choose, I side with internationalism rather than any form of patriotism.

A friend thinks that we radicals don't dare reject the idea that the United States has a special mission to the world, that it is a "city on the hill" with the destiny of improving other countries. I disagree. I believe that we should be down on our knees, seeking forgiveness for the historical sins of genocide and slavery.

Another form of the same debate was a disagreement between Rosa Luxemburg (with whom I agree about almost everything) and Lenin. Lenin said that socialists should support the "self-determination" of colonized nations, and worry about socialism later on. Luxemburg said that once you started down the road of parochial nationalism there was no way to find your way back to international solidarity. At the time (the era of World War I) Lenin seemed so obviously correct that Luxemburg was ridiculed. After the Balkan wars of the 1990s that is by no means so clear.

The form of internationalism that I have identified and which I celebrate, mentioned in one of your questions, is the idea that "My country is the world."

It's an old idea. Somebody said "*Ubi libertas, ibi patria*" (Where there is liberty, there is my country). But I think of it as beginning with Paine. He was born in Great Britain and came to Philadelphia just before the American Revolution. His first two published articles condemned slavery. Then he published the booklet *Common Sense*, a bestseller that helped to bring about independence. After the Revolutionary War, he went back to Great Britain and wrote *The Rights of Man*. Threatened with trial and imprisonment for sedition Paine fled to revolutionary France, where he was imprisoned and very nearly guillotined for opposing the execution of the King. In a second volume of The Rights of Man, Paine declared that "My country is the world."

When William Lloyd Garrison began his anti-slavery

newspaper *The Liberator* in 1831 he placed on the masthead the words, "Our country is the world, our countrymen are mankind."

One reviewer alleged that this was a radical tradition I had invented. It meant a good deal to me when I recently read James Green's fine book on *Death in the Haymarket*, and came to his description of how Haymarket anarchist Albert Parsons addressed the judge and jury before he was sentenced to death. Parsons spoke all one evening and into the afternoon of the next day. He explained that socialism "took two forms—anarchism, an egalitarian society without a controlling authority, and state socialism, which meant governmental control of everything." After hours of speaking, "rallying his strength," Parsons

> declared himself "an Internationalist," one whose patriotism extended "beyond the boundary lines of a single state." Opening his arms wide, he declared, "The world is my country, all mankind my countrymen."

Surely this is the form of internationalism we should espouse. It makes it possible for us to say, "Yes, I love my country! I love the fields of New England and Ohio, and also the mist-covered mountains and ravines of Chiapas and Nicaragua. I love the clarity of Thoreau, the compassion of Eugene Debs and the heroism of Bartolomeo Vanzetti, the paintings of Rembrandt, the music of Bach. I admire the conductors of the Underground Railroad and the self-organizing peasants and artisans in revolutionary Spain. My country is the world."

Humanitarian Activism

I FEAR THAT *the old debate between Rosa Luxemburg and Lenin is far from being resolved. I am almost tempted to say that there is, in the history of American radicalism, an inverted tradition to the one we both espouse, wherein the whole world is my country. You call this phenomenon "false internationalism." Others call it "third worldism." I call it humanitarian activism. If humanitarian imperialism promotes democracy, then humanitarian activism, in a similarly paternalistic fashion, promotes an internationalism of guilt. It is a peculiar intellectual and political habit of identifying a "noble revolutionary savage," both at home and someplace else—and the word "community" seems to always signify "someplace else"—while abandoning common people at home, in search of a more exotic functional equivalent. A convenient illustration is a recent upsurge of interest in the Weather Underground. It is a sad and puzzling irony that contemporary American radicals would search for examples in the history of the Weather Underground and not in the memories of the Underground Railroad, or in the history of immigrant movements like the IWW. There seems to exist an unfortunate peculiarity of the American activist simultaneously to support guerrilla movements abroad and behave like a social worker, tending the communities from the outside, not as a fellow student or fellow worker with a particular understanding of a situation shared with others, but as a professional organizer, a force outside of society, organizing those "inside" on their own behalf. What are the historical origins of this curious tendency?*

It has long distressed me that the Frente Sandinista de Liberación Nacional (the FSLN) was founded at almost the same time as SNCC by three Nicaraguan students meeting in Honduras, but whereas the FSLN, despite internal splits, persevered and made a revolution in 1979, the Student Nonviolent Coordinating Committee (SNCC) and Students for a Democratic Society (SDS) disintegrated. We need to ask, Why?

I do not wish to overlook or minimize the efforts of the government to kill, imprison, harass, and demoralize movement activists. But I am convinced that we ourselves have the major responsibility. And surely the "internationalism of guilt" was one of the reasons that the major movement organizations of the 1960s—SNCC, SDS—did not make it out of the decade.

BLACKS AND WHITES ALMOST TOGETHER

SNCC and SDS were both organizations of students. The question before these organizations was always, How do we relate to those who are not students: African American farmers in the South, workers, the unemployed, and the oppressed in our own and other countries? It was understood that unless students found ways to make political common cause with the wretched of the earth who did not attend universities in the United States, fundamental social change was impossible. Students alone were not enough.

In the early 1960s, the student organizers in SNCC found a relatively fruitful solution. Initially they sat-in and went to jail with the objective of desegregating facilities such as department store lunch counters. Early on there was a decision to concentrate instead on the right to vote. Older African Americans, especially in Mississippi where almost no black persons could vote, convinced SNCC field staff like Bob Moses that they should organize to obtain the suffrage.

In those years the relation of blacks and whites within SNCC was, for the most part, healthy. There was never any question that the leadership must be African American. Jim Forman was Executive Secretary, Charles Sherrod and Bob Moses were lead organizers in southwest Georgia and Mississippi, a majority of decisionmakers was always black. But whites were on the scene from the beginning. Jane Stembridge was one of a handful of initial headquarters staff. Casey Hayden, Mary King, Betty Garman, and other whites played important roles in the Atlanta office. And Bob Zellner, a white male from a part of northern Alabama where many people opposed the Confederacy during the Civil War, was arrested and beaten as many times as any other SNCC organizer.

I experienced SNCC's interracial atmosphere personally during the summer of 1964 when I was Freedom Schools coordinator in Mississippi. I will mention three small incidents.

Early in the summer Ivanhoe Donaldson and I found ourselves in a pick-up truck driving from northern Mississippi to Memphis. Night was falling. We were completely lost. The three young men who were murdered (Mickey Schwerner, James Chaney and Andrew Goodman) had disappeared shortly before. Sitting in the passenger seat, my unspoken body language grew more and more tense until Ivanhoe finally said to me, "Staughton, where's your sense of adventure?"

Later that summer, I had a tiny apartment in Jackson, the state capital. One morning I got up early and headed toward the Summer Project headquarters. The movement was not noted for early rising and I assumed I would be the first person at work. But when I got to the office, someone opened the door, broom in hand. It was Jim Forman, SNCC Executive Secretary. He had been sweeping the floor.

Toward the end of the summer Ralph Featherstone showed up in Jackson. Ralph had begun the summer in Holly Springs, then volunteered for McComb, the second most dangerous place in Mississippi. Now he wanted to go to the most dangerous place, Philadelphia, where Schwerner, Chaney and Goodman had been killed. His idea was that it was too dangerous to have a Freedom School in a fixed site, so we would refit a vehicle as a Freedom Schoolmobile, and drive from place to place, always ready to flee if the bad guys made an appearance. Before we abandoned this plan as impractical, there were a couple of nights when Ralph needed a place to sleep. He had a terrible cold. So he slept in my bed and I on the floor. A few years later, when I was teaching at Yale, Ralph died under mysterious circumstances when a bomb exploded in a car.

Meantime, white students in the North sought to determine how they should relate to SNCC's romantic and dangerous activities in the South. The almost-entirely-white network of student groups that evolved into SDS began as picket lines outside Woolworth's and other stores in the North that practiced segregation at Southern locations. Some of the most dramatic and significant expressions of the Northern student movement in the first half of the 1960s were actually activities in support of SNCC. Thus the Free Speech movement at Berkeley in 1964-1965 originated as an effort to distribute literature and collect money for SNCC on the University of California campus.

Two strategic perspectives developed within SDS. One orientation, championed by Alan Haber and later by Greg Calvert, held that the natural place for students to organize was on campus, and that it would be artificial and in the end, destructive, for students to act as if they were poor, or black, or working-class, when in fact they were not. The other strategy, whose principal spokesperson was Tom Hayden, called for SNCC-like organizing in Northern ghettoes with the aim of creating an interracial movement of the poor. The embodiment of this scenario was the Economic Research and Action Project (ERAP) in cities like Newark, Cleveland, and Chicago.

By 1965-1966 ERAP had faltered, except in situations where SDS women were able to establish a bond with mothers "on welfare" based in part on gender. The movement against the Vietnam war, and after a few years, against United States imperialism all over the world, sucked up the energies of SDS activists, and engendered new variations of the contradictions of the early 1960s.

WHITE SKIN PRIVILEGE AND OFFING THE PIG

Creating a movement of students and non-students, in which each group played an important and relatively equal role, should not have been so difficult. There were models at hand in recent European history.

The Russian Revolution of 1905 is usually thought to have begun with a workers' march to the Winter Palace of the Czar in January 1905, on which soldiers opened fire. In fact there had been agitation throughout the previous year by intellectuals and other professional people, and by students. In the fall of 1904 there was a meeting in the tiny St. Petersburg apartment of Father Gapon, who was trying to organize among the city's working class. There had just been an incident in which some students were killed. According to the memoir of one who was present at the meeting, the workers said to each other, "We can't let the students go out there alone!" They asked Gapon to draft the manifesto to the Czar, which, several weeks later, they tried to present on Bloody Sunday.

Likewise the Hungarian Revolution of 1956 began with students, who, after all, are in a time of life and in external circumstances that encourage a concern with ideas. For weeks classes at the universities of Budapest could not be held as students engaged in a continuous teach-in. Disturbances were underway in Poland, and Hungarian students decided to march to a location in downtown Budapest where there was a statue of a Pole who had supported Hungarian democracy in the 1800s. As they did so they encountered workers on their way home after the day shift in the city's factories. Joining forces, they marched on downtown government offices, and began a revolution.

In the United States in the 1960s, what might have seemed an inevitable coalition of a student movement with the poor and oppressed off campus, occurred only in the South. Northern students opposed the Vietnam war in the belief that working-class "hardhats" supported it. We know now that although the trade union leadership supported the war and the Democratic Party presidents (Kennedy and Johnson) who waged it, rank-and-file sentiment among workers was as hostile to the war as was the case among students. The sense of isolation experienced by students was aggravated by the fact that SDS was almost entirely white whereas the young men drafted and killed in Vietnam were disproportionately black. Overwhelmed by guilt stemming from their "white skin privilege," white students and ex-students in the second half of the 1960s came to feel that they were not entitled to criticize revolutionaries in Cuba or Vietnam, black militants in the United States, or indeed, the unaccountable leadership of their own clandestine organizations.

What they must do, dedicated activists like Cathy Wilkerson came to feel, was ceaselessly to escalate their own militancy in the hope that others would follow. Might not white working-class youth be attracted to the streetfighting style of a revolutionary cadre of former SDSers? The answer turned out to be, No. Nor were would-be African American revolutionaries successful in building a mass movement. Their story, poignantly narrated by Mumia Abu Jamal in his book *We Want Freedom*, also became a tale of government murder, internal infighting, and in the end, organizational chaos. Remnants of SNCC went down with the Panthers.

As of the early 1970s, the vast, courageous, spontaneous, creative movement of the 1960s in the United States had crashed and burned. A new approach was required. Hysterical hostility to the foot soldiers of the authorities, as in the slogan "Off the pig!" was proven unproductive. Somehow the Movement had to find its way from guilt to accompaniment.

People Different from Oneself

THE LAST LINE *of Charles Mann's book* 1491, *aimed at ances-tors of Europeans, is fascinating: "Is it too much to speculate that beneath the swirling tattoos, asymmetrically trimmed hair, and bedizened robes, you would recognize someone much closer to yourself, at least in certain respects, than your own ancestors?" I would like to ask you a question underlying all discussion of what it might mean to believe "my country is the world." How should one relate to persons quite different from oneself? I suppose I am not going to surprise you if I would tell you that the so-called "whiteness theory," of the "race traitor" variety, is still well received and widespread among American anarchists.*

From prekindergarten through graduation from high school, I believe I had two African American classmates. One was the son of Walter White, president of the National Association for the Advancement of Colored People. The other later became Secretary of the United States Army. In other words, even in those far-off days, they were prototypes of the Colin Powells and Condoleezza Rices of our own day: African Americans who "made it" in the middle- and upper-class white world.

I only came to know a significant number of African Americans when Howard Zinn recruited me to teach at Spelman College. I cannot remember which came first, but one year I began the American history survey course with the Pilgrims and was asked: "Why don't you teach me about my people?" and another year I began with the slave ships, and the question was: "Why are you teaching me a special history for African Americans?"

Then came the summer of 1964 in Mississippi. It is a little difficult to describe, but with African Americans who knew me in that setting I still experience something that must be akin to the fellow feeling of mountain climbers who have made a dangerous ascent together.

WHITENESS THEORY AND OVERCOMING RACISM

"Whiteness theory" I take to be an amalgam of two propositions: (1) whether a person is considered "white" or "black" is a cultural not a biological fact (thus, for example, immigrants initially characterized as "black Irish" came to be considered "white" after they demonstrated sufficient hostility toward African Americans); (2) hostility to black workers is an essential aspect of the making of the white working class in the United States and nothing can be done about it.

As a methodology this seems to me roughly equivalent to predicting the weather by looking up at the sky. The so-called theory is an extension of the most self-evident observed phenomena.

While teaching at Spelman College and at Yale University, I tried to ask more analytical and searching questions such as:

Why didn't African American slaves in the United States revolt in larger numbers?

What is the origin of racism in the United States?

Why didn't the American Revolution abolish slavery?

Why did Reconstruction after the Civil War fail?

At Spelman I teased students with the first of these questions. What's the matter with you? I queried. How come no Haiti in the United States?

After permitting the students to squirm and feel guilty for an appropriate period, I would ask: Might it have something to do with numbers? That is: How many blacks and how many whites were there in Haiti in 1790, just before the uprising? Answer: Roughly 9 or 10 blacks for every white. And in the American South? Answer: Only in South Carolina and Mississippi were there as many blacks as whites. And so? Answer: In the United States, slaves like Frederick Douglass who in Haiti would have led an insurrection, made an altogether rational decision and instead fled to the North. When the Civil War came, even larger numbers of slaves fled into the lines of the Union Army.

As to the origin of racism I forced students to confront Shakespeare's play "Othello." Whiteness theory would suggest that Anglo Americans have always been racist, and simply brought their racism with them from England to the New World. Then how do you explain the play that was produced in London at almost the same moment that the first permanent English colony (Jamestown, founded in 1607) came into existence in Virginia?

"Othello," a story about a black man ("the Moor") married to a white woman, contains plenty of racism. It is voiced by Iago, the play's villain. He taunts Desdemona's father with a crude reference to Othello and Desdemona making "the beast with two backs," and with the suggestion that now, even now, Othello the black ram was "tupping" Brabanto's white ewe.

But this ugliness is simply swept away by the most beautiful love poetry in the English language. Othello soliloquizes:

> Had it pleas'd heaven
> To try me with affliction, had he rain'd
> All kinds of sores, and shames,
>   on my bare head,
> Steep'd me in poverty to the very lips,
> Given to captivity me and my utmost hopes,
> I should have found in some part of my soul
> A drop of patience....
> But there, where I have garner'd up my heart,
> The fountain from the which my current runs
> Or else dries up; to be discarded thence!...

So if Englishmen could imagine such a love between a black person and a white at the time they began to settle the thirteen colonies, whence came slavery and racism?

I suggested the answer: from a fall in the price of tobacco. That economic event, in the mid-1600s, made it imperative for Virginia tobacco planters to find a cheaper source of labor. They found it in Africa and in making African American slavery last forever.

Until about 1660, black and white laborers in Virginia were treated in roughly the same way as indentured servants. They feasted together, ran away together, and intermarried. By 1700, however, the enslaved status of black laborers had been made perpetual, social interaction between black and white workers was forbidden, and racism as an ideology had become imbedded. Ideology, I thought then and think now, followed economics.

But if ideology follows economics, then if economic circumstances change, ideology may change and racism loose its iron grip. "Whiteness" theory appears uninterested in such transformation. "Whiteness" theory is content to say, Look what racist slobs so many white workers show themselves to be!

That attitude makes it possible for the theorists of "whiteness" to remain college professors. Since the white working class is hopeless, why bother to be anything other than an Ivy League professor with leather patches on the elbows of one's tweed jacket?

But the white working class is not hopeless! After the Civil War, African American freedmen demanded 40 acres and a mule. I collected some of the things historians have said about their platform in a booklet entitled *Reconstruction*. As I opened this volume, published in 1967, to look at once again after many years, I found that I had tucked into its pages a xeroxed copy of the "Memorial of the Laboring Men of the United States in Convention Assembled, in the City of Washington, Dec. 6, 1869," Senate Miscellaneous Document No. 8, 41st Congress, 2nd Session. Therein a gathering obviously made up of both white and black workingmen argued the case for the freedmen's program.

According to the memorial, in 1869 the average wage of an African American agricultural laborer in the South was $60 per year. "Out of this small sum he is required to clothe himself and purchase necessary articles for subsistence, for, as a general thing, the only allowance that he receives from his employer consists of one peck of corn or meal per week."

The National Bureau of Statistics, the memorial went on, has shown that during 1869 the United States exported cotton valued at $168,000,000. After all appropriate deductions the rate of profit for employers on capital invested was about 50 per cent, "while the laborers who produced it have not only been left penniless, but are nearly $2,000,000 in debt." Resistance by organized effort is impossible, said the memorial, "for the earnings of the laborer leave him no surplus, and when he ceases to labor he begins to starve."

"Your memorialists," this petition continued, "pray that the surveyed public lands in the southern States may be subdivided into tracts of forty (40) acres each, and that any freedman who shall settle on one of such subdivisions, and cultivate the same for the space of one year, shall receive a patent for the same." The number of acres of public land in Alabama, Arkansas, Florida, Louisiana and Mississippi totaled more than 46,000,000 acres. This was more than enough to give 40 acres to each of the estimated 200,000 southern freedmen. The signers of the petition were equally divided between residents of the North and South.

This effort failed. So have all later efforts by means of which whites and blacks together sought to help all poor Americans obtain a decent average livelihood, such as the Southern Tenant Farmers Union of the 1930s. The point is to keep trying, rather than giving up the effort on the basis of a spurious theory that white workers are irrevocably committed to "whiteness."

ACCOMPANIMENT IS NOT DEFERENCE

Just as I accuse persons enamored of "whiteness" theory of surrendering any effort to overcome the racial separation of the poor, so I am criticized for espousing a theory of "accompaniment" that, so it is said, defers to whatever poor people believe and are demanding at the moment, without criticism or independent evaluation.

I understand that such deference is possible. I know a member of a far Left group who says that a grievance representative should always subscribe to whatever the grievant represents to be true. The best antidote to that attitude I know is a story told by my friend, the late John Barbero. John represented a fellow steelworker who was accused of hiding out in a remote area of the mill during the night shift and getting drunk on warm beer. Just before they went into the arbitration hearing at the end of the grievance process, John asked his "client": "One last time. You weren't drinking warm beer in the back that night?" The man replied: "That beer wasn't warm!"

The issue of whether to believe the person one accompanies also arises in the context of work with prisoners. Over more than a decade my wife and I have represented maximum security prisoners seeking to improve their conditions of confinement, and laboriously sought to establish the truth about what happened during a major Ohio prison riot in which ten persons were killed. There are a number of persons whom I love and respect but about whose guilt or innocence I am still unsure.

On a deeper level, the idea that "accompaniment" means uncritical endorsement of the poor and oppressed persons who are accompanied, is simply not what Archbishop Oscar Romero meant by the term. He explained his ideas in four pastoral letters issued in the years 1977-1979.

In the *Third Pastoral Letter* of August 1978, in particular, Romero dealt with the question of how Christians should relate to "popular organizations." He encouraged Christians to form "base communities." He directed pastors and lay ministers to take care that such communities "are not confused with other organizations and, above all, are not manipulated by them." Thus, in the language of radical politics, Romero mandated that organizations of the poor that the church helps to form must not become mere "front" groups for the programs of the Left.

Romero went on to say that the church "identifies with the poor when they demand their legitimate rights." He added:

> This solidarity with just aims is not restricted to particular organizations. Whether they call themselves Christians or not,…if the aim of the struggle is just, the church will support it…. In the same way it will denounce, with bold impartiality, all injustice in any organization, wherever it is found.

Critically important, Romero urged Christians who belong to any organization with just social, political, and economic aims "to profess their faith openly." I have experienced this myself. At the time of Gulf War I, Alice and I were deeply involved with steel mill retirees who were struggling to preserve the pensions and health benefits that had been promised to them (surely a just aim). At the same time the Workers' Solidarity Club of Youngstown resolved to picket every day against the war in downtown Youngstown. I did so faithfully, believing that this might make it impossible for the Lynds to stay in town. To my surprise, both retirees who favored the war and those who opposed it seemed to feel that this was what one could expect from Staughton. It did not interfere at all with our practical work.

In the *Third Pastoral Letter*, Romero also addressed the question of violence. He said that Christians, "even if we are a voice in the wilderness," must go on repeating, "no to violence, yes to peace." He carefully discussed a number of different kinds of violence, including "legitimate self-defense," but insisted that terrorism "provokes useless and unjustifiable bloodshed, abandons society to explosive tensions beyond the control of reason, and disparages in principle any form of dialogue as a possible means of solving social conflicts." The church, he adds in his Fourth Pastoral Letter, condemns violence that "intentionally victimizes innocent persons."

In this fourth and last Pastoral Letter, written less than a year before his death, Romero uses the term "accompanying." He asks the faithful "to accompany Christians in their political options, without the church thereby losing its identity and Christians their faith." He says that the preferential option for the poor does not mean "blind partiality in favor of the masses." Indeed:

> In the name of the preferential option for the
> poor there can never be justified the machismo,
> the alcoholism, the failure in family responsi-
> bility, the exploitation of one poor person by
> another, the antagonism among neighbors, and
> the so many other sins that [are] concurrent
> roots of this country's crisis and violence.

I submit that the foregoing is hardly a doctrine of unthinking subservience to the momentary beliefs or instructions of the poor.

I challenge those who offer this critique of "accompaniment" to explain, in detail, how they go about relating to the poor and oppressed. I suspect that they do not have such relationships at all. That makes it easy to be pure: without engagement with the world, one need only endlessly reiterate one's own abstract identity.

"Accompaniment" is simply the idea of walking side by side with another on a common journey. The idea is that when a university-trained person undertakes to walk beside someone rich in experience but lacking formal skills, each contributes something vital to the process. "Accompaniment" thus understood presupposes, not uncritical deference, but equality.

Examples of Interracial Solidarity

CAN YOU GIVE *some more historical examples of interracial solidarity of the poor? Where can we find them in American history? In addition to the abolitionist movement, two other instances come to mind. The first one is the Bacon rebellion. The second one is mentioned by Peter Linebaugh and Marcus Rediker in their wonderful book* The Many-Headed Hydra, *and that is the famous New York Slave Insurrection, or The Great New York Conspiracy of 1741.*

INTERRACIAL COOPERATION AMONG THE POOR

I must tell you that I distrust narratives about this subject matter based only on documents. Such sources may suffice to establish facts of an external, quantitative nature, but I don't consider them reliable in a matter so subtle and quicksilver as race relations.

For example, Bacon's Rebellion in seventeenth century Virginia was led by plantation owners in the Western part of the colony. There is no doubt that African American slaves took part. But except for having common enemies, what if anything did the different groups of rebels share? One common sentiment appears to have been hatred of Native Americans who stood in the way of expansion westward.

So I have formed my views on the basis of personal experiences (as in the Mississippi vignettes related previously) or on the basis of oral history narratives in which I had face-to-face communication with at least one person in the encounter. Examples are:

> ❧ In *Rank and File*, edited by my wife Alice and myself, George Sullivan's account of what happened when he arrived at an air base in Great Britain after the military decreed racial integration in the aftermath of World War II. George had grown up in a southern Illinois household saturated with racism, like that described in the opening pages of David Roediger's *Wages of Whiteness*. Arriving at an Air Force base in Great Britain, he was assigned to a barracks in which every one else was African American. When George cut his hand in the kitchen a black colleague volunteered to sew on his sergeant's stripes. "He sat and sewed those stripes on my uniform while we got to know each other."

> ❧ Also in *Rank and File*, Sylvia Woods' memory of how a white Communist in the shop where she worked demanded equal access for blacks to better-paying jobs. Even the white guy from Tennessee who hated black people went to a union party "and danced with a black woman. He was elected steward and you just couldn't say anything [derogatory] to a black person. So, I have seen people change."

> ❧ As partially described in my book *Lucasville*, the relationship between Keith Lamar a.k.a. Bomani Shakur (African American) and Jason Robb (Caucasian leader of the Aryan

Brotherhood), two of the "Lucasville Five" sentenced to death for their alleged roles in a 1993 prison rebellion. White and black prisoners, confronted with a common oppressor, in our experience display a similar attitude. Of course we are different, they say. You wouldn't want to put a person who loves "soul" music in the same cell as a man who digs "country"! But when it comes to making common cause to deal with prison administrators, yes, of course, we need to do that, and both blacks and whites must have a voice. I sat across from, laughed with, and queried these two, through the transparent partition that always separates us at the Ohio State Penitentiary, as recently as yesterday morning.

On this basis I have come to some definite conclusions.

I think people can overcome differences in race, ethnicity, religion, and for that matter, anything else, on the basis of shared experience. Usually it is a common experience of oppression that brings people together. I believe that it happens among soldiers. (Think of all the World War II movies in which a Jew from New York, a Polish steelworker from the Midwest, and an African American make common cause.) I know that it happens among prisoners.

The three black men and two Caucasians sentenced to death after this rebellion have maintained their solidarity for almost fifteen years. The question, of course, is: When soldiers or prisoners come back to ordinary civilian life, "on the street" rather than behind bars or in foxholes, what then?

Anabaptism and Movements of the 1950s and 1960s

EARLIER IN OUR *conversations you referred to the political importance of Liberation Theology. You also mentioned an interest in Buddhist metaphysics. Yet, you are a Quaker. In your essay,* Liberation Theology for Quakers, *you and Alice made suggestions about a possible dialogue between the two traditions. You were also, for a brief period of time, part of the Bruderhof society. One of the things we share is a passion or fascination with Anabaptism, and the movement of radical reformation that exclaimed those timeless words: "kein vorsteer" and "omnia sunt comunia." It is interesting to note that one of the bestsellers of new movement fiction is the novel "Q," written by the Wu Ming collective, which tells the story of a sixteenth century Anabaptist in a world turned upside down. What is the role of radical reformation in the development of the American revolutionary tradition? What is the connection between the Civil Rights movements of the 1950s and 1960s, and Anabaptists of the sixteenth century, both feeling themselves to be "blessed communities"?*

This question presents the very large conundrum of how radical Protestantism (Quakers, Brethren, Mennonites, Hutterites, and the like) and then radical Catholicism (culminating in liberation theology) have affected the American revolutionary tradition, and the civil rights movement.

I say "conundrum" because so much about these connections is still unknown. Think of a garden or forest in which, when one digs down, there is a tangled, complicated root system invisible from the surface of the earth. The historical connections implicated by this question are similar. Why was Tom Paine able to communicate so well with North American colonists almost from the moment of his arrival in Pennsylvania? What made antislavery a burning existential concern in nineteenth century America when, except for Quakers, it had been a secondary matter of policy at the time of the Revolution? How is it that the Student Nonviolent Coordinating Committee (SNCC) practiced consensus decisionmaking? Why did Students for a Democratic Society (SDS) fasten on the concept of "participatory democracy"? How did the Movement of the Sixties come into being and for what reasons did it collapse?

I am not going to pretend to be able to answer any of these questions. I am very critical of any one who offers easy answers to them. I would rather they remain mysteries than that they be subjected to casual, or heavy-handed and dogmatic interpretation from any direction.

I should like to offer the following analogy. The radical Reformation rebelled against an institutionalized Christianity that was centralized, dogmatic, corrupt, forgetful of its roots, and overly prepared to make peace with the secular society in which it was imbedded. Late nineteenth century anarchism rebelled against a Social Democratic institutionalization of socialism that was centralized, dogmatic, corrupt, forgetful of its Utopian roots, and overly prepared to make peace with an encircling capitalist society.

The candid historian has to remember that the early Christianity to which reformers have sought to return was itself contradictory and imperfect. Scholars like John Dominic Crossan seek to untangle portions of the New Testament that may have preserved the actions and words of Jesus from portions that were not "history remembered" but "prophecy historicized" (meaning, that's how it must have been because that is what was prophesied). The communities of the radical Reformation, in the sixteenth and seventeenth centuries and today (the Bruderhof, the Western Hutterites of Canada and the United States), tend to be patriarchal and authoritarian. Leaders forget about rotation in office and remain in positions of authority year after year. Differences emerge between a group of insiders who live high off the hog, and other strata who might have been hired as wage labor or simply enjoy less of the good things of life. Repeatedly, too, little communities absorbed by the economic and inter-personal challenges of survival, drift away from the more fundamental mandate of the New Testament: to feed the hungry, welcome the stranger, visit the imprisoned, and in the larger society as well as in small-scale prefigurations make all things new.

There are particular traps for the unwary in liberation theology, as well. Gradually, as in the pastoral letters of Archbishop Romero, the idea emerged that the radical out-sider should "accompany" the poor and oppressed as someone different but equal. However, what then happens when the worker or peasant who is accompanied picks up a gun?

On the other hand, it is all too easy to relapse into cynicism and to forget the magical moments when solutions emerged that no one person had foreseen, when protago-nists acted with simple dignity and clarity, when all things economic were shared, when decisions were truly made by consensus no matter how late the meeting, when the circle of participants held together.

The project of achieving the Good Society, of bringing in the Kingdom of God, of realizing in practice that Other World that is possible, has both subjective and objective com-ponents. For myself, as for liberation theologians, Marxism provides the needed objective analysis. But Marxism is inadequate as a guide to practice, to personal decisions. For that one must turn to the efforts over the centuries to live the good life here and now exemplified by small religious communities.

I say this with conviction because I have experienced it. When my wife and I lived at the Macedonia Cooperative Community, I would get up at 5 a.m. to do the morning milking, and stumble out into the dark and cold with my wool hat pulled above one ear so as to hear the cow bells. At length the cows roused themselves and I trailed after them toward the cow barn. At these times, as the sun began to emerge over the line of hills that surrounded our mountain valley, I felt that everything I could see as the morning flooded in was part of a good way of life that my wife and I were building up together with our companions. The memory stayed with me when, later on, Alice and I felt obliged once again to journey into the hard, cruel, outside capitalist world, and tried to bring change about on a larger scale.

I am not the only one to have felt the need for such support and subjective inspiration. Tom Paine is perhaps the single greatest revolutionary we can recall in the English-speaking world on both sides of the Atlantic. He died in New York City in 1809. In his Will he wrote:

> I know not if the Society of people called Quakers, admit a person to be buried in their burying ground, who does not belong to their Society, but if they do, or will admit me, I would prefer being buried there; my father belonged to that profession, and I was partly brought up in it.

Native Americans and Colonists Who Lived Together

A NEW BOOK *by the same band of anti-globalist novelists is called* Manituana. *It is "a story from the wrong side of history," that begins in the Mohawk valley in 1775, at the dawn of the American revolution, "when everything was still possible," with Native Americans and colonists living together for generations.*

Usually, in academic books on American history, we encounter two opposing narratives: one of the legacy of civilizing, and the other of the legacy of conquest. What about the "wrong side" of early American history, far less documented and explored, following the journeys of the "many-headed hydra," a history that offers examples of mutual aid and solidarity between the natives and the colonists? It wasn't a rare occasion that colonists would "go to Croatan," that is, join the native Americans in the Hobbesian "wilderness." For instance, Richard White in his seminal work The Middle Ground *mentions the story of a deserted fortress with a writing on the wall saying "we are all savages."*

I do not have the detailed knowledge to answer this question in a comprehensive way but I will offer three paths into the forest.

There appeared in the *New York Times* a month or two ago an Op Ed piece based on narratives of females captured by Native Americans in eighteenth century New England. It says two fascinating things. First, the women sometimes liked what they found and chose to stay with the Indians rather than to be "set free" and returned to white society. Second, subsequent editions of the initial narratives by these women were revised in the direction of making it seem that they had been oppressed and brutalized while living among the indigenous.

As you know I wrote my Master's Essay on tenants in the Hudson Valley during the Revolution. Thomas Humphrey has written a follow-up study entitled *Land and Liberty: Hudson Valley Riots in the Age of Revolution* (De Kalb: Northern Illinois University Press, 2004). He brings out the fact that the tenants, mostly persons from New England of British descent, and Native Americans, shared the conviction that the owners of large manors had stolen the land. See e.g. pp. 47-48: Stockbridge Indians "sought to secure their claims to most of their traditional land by encouraging whites to settle some of it…. [T]hey wanted to work with insurgents to dismantle the great estates."

You may recall that I once mentioned a novel that described a Quaker meeting in colonial America held in darkness so that white, Native American, and African American participants would not be disoriented by one another's skin color. I have found the book: Jan de Hartog, *The Peaceable Kingdom* (Greenwich, Conn.: Fawcett Books, 1971). I have no idea what he used for sources but it is well worth reading. However, as a fellow truth seeker I must also ask you to read another historical novel, LeGrand Cannon, Jr., *Look to the Mountain*. This wonderful novel about revolutionary New Hampshire ("the mountain" is Mt. Chocorua, which Howard Zinn, his two children and I climbed together) depicts all too accurately the fact that for the ordinary colonial frontiersman Indians were nothing other than hated beings who threatened their families. Whit Livingston treks to the Connecticut River to fight the British because he fears they will bring their Indian allies to central New Hampshire and massacre his wife and children.

Consensus Decisionmaking

LET ME ASK *you about another mystery. In* Strategy and Program *you say that "[w]hy consensus prevailed in early meetings of the movement (including SNCC meetings in the almost underground settings of the Southern movement) is something of an historical mystery." As you know, I am a big proponent of consensus, and I am very critical of the arguments against consensus as a "privilege" of "middle-class activists." I remember a story about a contemporary strike in France. Somebody suggested that something is " worth taking the vote on." Somebody retorted: "Oh no, no vote. We have to come to a decision together." What do you think of consensus as a decisionmaking procedure (and I would argue that it is much more then that)? And is there any truth to the story, very popular among the activists, that consensus was introduced to the Quakers by the Native Americans—perhaps at one of those meetings "held in darkness"?—and then transmitted to the leftist radicals?*

I have experienced consensus in at least six contexts.

The least illuminating has been the experience of consensus in a Quaker meeting. The British historian Christopher Hill believed that the early Quakers were poor farmers and artisans, and that consensus derived from a medieval village's decisions about the single pattern of cultivation possible on the village land. But today, Quaker consensus tends to middle-class pettifoggery.

At the Macedonia Cooperative Community all decisions were by consensus. We never voted. Meetings continued into the small hours and a particular beloved member was well known for saying at, perhaps, 1 a.m.: "It doesn't feel right. It doesn't ring true." Then we would start all over again. But like Hill's medieval Quakers, we were driven by a need to get on with a common livelihood. No one forgot that the morning milkers (of whom I was one) had to get up at 5 a.m. We recognized that one person might have perceived something that we all needed to address.

As your question suggests, civil rights workers in SNCC practiced consensus. I used to be exasperated by white radicals in the North who would say that "real revolutionaries" made decisions in a hierarchical, military way. SNCC workers faced far more danger than these Northern blowhards. Precisely for that reason, decisions were by consensus: no one felt comfortable deciding when and how another person should risk his or her life. As SNCC spokesperson Stokely Carmichael once said, "We never proclaimed that the organization had to proceed by consensus rather than majority vote…. It just happened that way…because it had to…because the issues are deadly serious." Carmichael, *Ready for Revolution*, p. 300. By contrast, Cathy Wilkerson in her *Flying Close to the Sun* tells us that membership in the Weather organization was frustrating because decisions made in secret came down from on high, one never knew the rationale for decisions nor did one have the opportunity to question and discuss them.

The Workers' Solidarity Club of Youngstown went a step further. There were no officers, only a chairperson for each meeting. There were no dues, only voluntary contributions. Rather than feeling a need to come to a unanimous decision, individual members would say, "I'm going to do so-and-so (such as take firewood to a picket line). Would any one like to come with me?" It worked for twenty years. No one felt pushed to do something he or she did not want to do.

Alice reminds me of decisionmaking by a group of Visiting Nurses. When trying to decide whether or not to form an independent union, I suggested, Why don't we take a straw vote? They voted unanimously to form a union. When management decided to lay off the Licensed Practical Nurses, one of whom was white and two of whom were black with many years of service and families that depended on their income, the nurses with least seniority were asked to go into another room and decide whether they would be willing to risk layoff if management rejected the union's request that all the nurses take rotating layoffs. The nurses with least seniority agreed. However, when the issue was whether or not to participate in a program sponsored by management and the vote was split nearly half and half, it was decided that the union would not take a position but would allow members to act as individuals.

I have been part of a consensus decision by approximately fifteen prisoners in a supermax penitentiary. Each man was locked in a separate cell with a solid steel door. Participants could hear each other and then "vote" by putting a forearm out the food slot in the door of the cell. We discussed how to respond to a proposal by the State. I called for a Yes or No vote. One man voted both Yes and No, and appeared to be the only No vote. When I gently questioned him, an anonymous voice commented on the fact that the voter had been brought to the penitentiary after being hit on the head with a metal spatula. "That's what happens when you are hit on the head with a spatula!" his friend cackled. The entire cell block collapsed in laughter. We had achieved consensus.

Palestine and Israel

A FEW HOURS *ago I received information about the proclamation of the so-called independence of Kosovo. I am very much against this imposed mono-ethnic independence. One of the worst plagues of the Balkans, immediately next to foreign interventionism, is nationalism. I am convinced that it is the responsibility of the new anarchist Left to be faithful to a true politics from below, to the Utopian political imagination, and to go beyond seemingly unavoidable ethnic and statist solutions. These are very complicated problems and contradictory situations that defy ready-made models, instant formulas, and ideological simplifications. You told me once that one of the rare issues on which you changed your mind almost completely is that of Israel and Palestine. In 1994, together with Alice and Sam Bahour, you edited and published* Homeland, an Oral History of Palestine and Palestinians. *Can you tell me more about this transformation, this evolution of your thoughts on the Palestinian question, and the process of making of this book?*

A CONCLUSION

I am going to begin with a conclusion. Every one knows

that the central problem in Palestine is Israeli occupation of the West Bank (the rectangular area bounded on the West by Jerusalem, on the North by Lebanon, on the East by the Jordan River, and on the South by the Sinai desert). If it were simply a matter of ending the occupation by withdrawing Israeli troops, that would be one thing. But in fact upwards of 250,000 Israelis now live in illegal settlements within the West Bank. There are not enough settlers to force the Palestinians to leave, but the settlers are sufficiently numerous to make a "two state solution" impossible.

So what is to be done?

I submit that there is no logical answer to this question. Or rather, there is a logical answer, namely, a single bi-national secular state in all of Palestine, but the fact that Israelis would be a little less than half the population in such a state makes it seem frightening and politically impossible to them. Bishop Tutu and others point out that in South Africa, whites make up a much smaller percentage of the population in bi-national South Africa than Jews would be in a bi-national Palestine. Israelis still say No.

So what is to be done?

Here I wish to introduce what might be considered a distinctively anarchist perspective. In anarchist theory there is always a dual power in the sense that beneath the surface of official society there is a network of institutions created from below. A number of persons seem to suggest that in a situation like that faced by the Palestinians, one has to give up the goal of creating a state of any kind in the foreseeable future, and instead, maintain an alternative society in quasi-underground, unofficial institutions like the extended family.

Sam Bahour, who lives in Ramallah and co-edited a volume of interviews with Alice and myself, says: "Palestinians are not very good at winning, but they are good at not losing."

In the draft resistance movement of the 1960s we used to

say: "If you don't have a headquarters, then there is nothing for some Marxist grouplet to take over and there is nothing for the police to destroy."

In historic Afghanistan, according to Sarah Chayes in her book *The Punishment of Virtue*, Afghans have always operated with both a Plan A and a Plan B. Plan A applies when the surrounding aggressive nations—Russia, the British Empire, India, Pakistan, the United States—occasionally give Afghanistan an interlude in which it can govern itself as a single national community. Plan B becomes necessary when one or another of the neighboring powers invades and appears to take power. Afghans, according to Ms. Chayes, then revert to what she calls "*yaghestan*."

For centuries, courtly Persian monarchs flung this epithet at the rock-strewn land that

> lay at the far fringes of their empire. The early Muslim conquerors broke their teeth on the place for decades and never really reduced it. By "yaghestan," the Persians meant a land of the rebellious, of the incorrigibly ungovernable.

According to Ms. Chayes, "reverting to yaghestan served again and again as a fallback position for a people who, every once in a while, did grudgingly gather under one banner into something like a nation.... [When that] national government came under attack, Afghans were quick to dissolve it, and run like water between the fingers of their would-be conquerors."

I believe Palestinians now find themselves obliged to maintain "yaghestan." It will be a long time before they can hope to take part in governing the bi-national state that the situation requires. But, in the meantime, they can live dignified, even heroic lives of collective resistance and small-scale self-government while waiting for their Jewish neighbors to come to their senses.

A CROOKED JOURNEY

Now let me describe the unusual path by which I came, finally, to this conclusion.

From pre-kindergarten through twelfth grade, I attended private schools of the Ethical Culture Society in New York City. The Ethical Culture Society originated in the late nineteenth century when it sought to create schools for working-class Jews. By the time I came along in the 1930s, the schools were still overwhelmingly Jewish but the students were mostly upper middle class.

The orientation of the Ethical Culture schools was expressed in words written over the platform of the school auditorium on West 64th Street: "The Place Where Men Meet To Seek The Highest Is Holy Ground." I graduated from sixth grade on that platform. I received my diploma from a leader of the Society, John Lovejoy Elliot. He was associated with a "settlement house" on the Lower West Side of Manhattan. It was said of Mr. Elliot, as it was said of Eugene Debs, that whenever he went for a walk in the neighborhood he came back with empty pockets. In the high school associated with the schools, on 242nd Street, there is a plaque set into the wall of one of the buildings with words from Mr. Elliot to the effect that, The only thing in life I have found worth living for, working for, and dying for is human love and friendship.

On that same platform, beneath those same words about "the highest," I was later inducted as high school student body president.

I think of the Ethical Culture creed as reform reform Judaism. There was no ritual, no belief in supernatural beings, only ethics.

It was not true of me that some of my best friends were Jewish. All my friends were Jewish.

WE'VE DONE ENOUGH DYING

One of my friends was the late Daniel Lourie. Before there

was an Israeli state there was a "Jewish entity" in Palestine, just as there is now a Palestinian entity. Danny's father was Arthur Lourie, who represented the Jewish entity in the United States.

One weekend Danny took me to a farm in Cream Ridge, New Jersey, where young people prepared to "make aliyah": to go to Israel and live in collective farms, or khibbutzim.

Sunday morning found me hoeing in the garden with a man whose face I remember as grizzled and weatherbeaten. He was probably about thirty. I considered him very old.

In my youthful socialist enthusiasm (I was about fifteen) I said to him, "So what's with this Zionism? What happened to socialist internationalism?"

My companion turned, put down his hoe, and looked at me. He said, "We've done enough dying on other people's barricades."

YOU'RE WRONG

I entered college as a believer that Jewish settlement in Palestine represented a model for a new, decentralized social-ism. Then I encountered a friend of the family of a young lady at Wellesley. I remember his name only as "Jimmy." He had spent time in the Middle East, I think at the American University in Beirut.

I burbled out my belief in Jewish settlement in Palestine as a model society, a wave of the future. Like the man with the hoe, Jimmy turned, looked at me, and said, "You're wrong."

He went on to explain that Jewish settlers had simply seized the land that they farmed from Palestinians who were already living there.

MARTIN BUBER

My next encounter with the issue of Palestine came in the 1950s when I made a trip on behalf of the Macedonia Cooperative Community. Our red pick-up truck found its way to Ann Arbor where I stayed with a prominent Quaker couple, Kenneth and Elise Boulding. It happened that Martin Buber was speaking that evening. I went to hear him.

I was already an admirer of Buber because of his book *Paths in Utopia*. There he seemed to argue that Marx and Lenin in certain writings (*The Civil War in France, State and Revolution*), the anarchist theorist Gustav Landauer, and just possibly, Israeli settlements in Palestine, might indeed represent a path to a decentralized future.

I remember a short, stocky man with a huge white beard speaking to a vast audience. I came away with the distinct impression that Buber advocated a single bi-national state in Palestine.

GULF WAR I

There my thoughts rested as I turned to other matters: civil rights in the South, Vietnam, the rank-and-file labor movement. I recall vaguely taking note of TV footage displaying conditions in Palestinian refugee camps.

When Gulf War I began, at a meeting attended by a variety of local groups opposed to the war, the chairperson was a large young man named Sam Bahour.

We got to know Sam and to plan with him various activities, such as counseling young people who might be thinking about military service. Gulf War I ended after only a few weeks, however, and so the books about Selective Service and Conscientious Objection returned to their file drawers. Instead, together with Sam and others we planned an occasion at the Arab American Community Center in Youngstown.

That year Ramadan, Passover, and Easter all fell at more or less the same time. Persons who identified with any of these three traditions were invited to an evening meal at the Center. The only ground rule was that if you spoke, you must speak about personal experience. Political speeches were not allowed.

It was an amazing evening. Our friend Jules Lobel, whose family on his father's side had lived in Israel since the eighteenth century, spoke. So did Jim Ray, a Presbyterian chaplain who had been assigned to a prison camp during the Korean war.

But the speakers who blew us all away were Arab. Sam's father Sami Bahour, for example, told of growing up in Palestine as a fervent young Muslim and, as a teenager, preaching outside the mosques. It came to seem to him that a Muslim Palestine might not address the disparity between rich and poor that distressed him. He decided to come to the United States. His assumption was that in this country one needed only a shovel, to gather up the gold that lay loose in the streets. Instead he found himself working long hours in a bakery in Youngstown, Ohio.

A friend then told Sami Bahour about a sure way to get rich in the United States. You bought a carload of junk and drove to Mississippi. Twice a year the African American sharecroppers were paid, and early the next morning you presented yourself at their doors. Not knowing whether you were a white man, they would fearfully let you in, and then buy some piece of junk in order to get rid of you. By the time your car turned the corner the watch would stop working.

At the Center that evening, in the hush of a semi-religious occasion and with dozens of friends and neighbors listening in, Sami Bahour said that a thought came to him. "You know," he said to himself. "Mississippi is a good deal like Palestine. There is only one difference: Here I am one of the oppressors." He went back to Youngstown, opened a grocery store, and assisted African Americans who wished to open grocery stores that might take away his own business.

Of course many of the stories told that night concerned life in occupied Palestine. So remarkable were they that Alice and I began to seek permission to visit persons who had spoken at the Center, as well as others to whom we were referred, and tape their recollections. Sam Bahour then suggested that we accompany him to Palestine and do further taping. We used our next two summer vacation in this way, and the result is a book, edited by Sam, Alice and myself, entitled *Homeland: Oral Histories of Palestine and Palestinians*.

JOE HILL

There is one story, however, that didn't find its way into *Homeland* and that I would like to tell here.

During our second summer visit to Palestine we went to the Golan Heights. The Golan Heights are a plateau that lies between northeast Israel and Syria. Prior to the Six Day War of 1967 the Golan Heights were part of Syria. Israel seized the Heights during the war and thereafter encouraged Israeli settlers to make their homes there.

Mosques were destroyed, and remained in that state as we drove past them. Signs along the roads in English and Hebrew (but not in Arabic) warned of danger from land mines. The only remaining Arab villagers huddle together under a very large mountain, Mt. Herman. Members of several Arab families had been caught unawares by the beginning of the Six Day War and now find themselves separated by the de facto border between Israel and Syria. Alice and I watched them speaking through megaphones to one another.

The Arabs who remain in Majdhal Shams, within the Golan Heights, appear to make a living mainly by growing apples. The apples are stored in a large cooperative cooler until it is possible to ship them. Something that caught my attention was a fragment of conversation about land titles. The Arabs could not understand the inflexibility with which Israelis view the boundaries of property. "We ourselves," they explained, "believe that from generation to generation the boundaries of a family's property may need to be adjusted, depending on the number of people in a family and their neighbors' needs, as well."

Our group—Sam, Alice, myself, and a few younger Arab Americans—were invited to a barbecue in an apple orchard.

An extremely potent Syrian white lightning, called arak, flowed freely. It was decided that each group should sing for the other, and I was nominated for the visitors. I decided to sing "Joe Hill."

I determined that before starting to sing I would explain that Joe Hill was not the typical, parochial American. He had been born in Sweden. Before he was framed and executed during World War I, he was thought to have taken part in the Mexican Revolution. He...Before I could continue, our host, who had drunk a good deal more arak than had I, held up a hand.

"You don't have to explain," he said. "Joe Hill fought with Spartacus. Joe Hill was in Chile in the 1970s, and in El Salvador and Guatemala. But right now," he concluded, "Joe Hill is a Palestinian."

SUBER AND HOLOCAUST

There is an Arabic word that denotes the capacity to survive. "*Suber*" is the name of a small cactus that can go long periods of time without water. Palestinians say of one another, "So and so is *suber*," meaning, That is one tough hombre; that is a survivor.

Jews, of course, have their own experience of Holocaust. When a choral group to which Alice and I belong visited Eastern Europe, we had the opportunity to visit Auschwitz. The Nazis, like Pol Pot in Cambodia, took photographs of those they were preparing to execute. It was unbearable to see the row after row of fresh, young faces of those who were about to die.

Between the determination of those who are suber not to abandon their homes in historic Palestine, and the fierce intention to survive of Holocaust survivors, what room is there for hope? It is particularly dismaying to see Israeli soldiers and prison personnel repeating in their treatment of Palestinians many of the very things that were done to European Jews. There can be little doubt that it was the Israeli (as well as the South African) practice of indefinitely detaining suspected opponents, without criminal charges, that served as a model for the United States when it abandoned 800 years of habeas corpus jurisprudence so as to create Abu Ghraib and Guantanamo.

Still, so far as I am concerned, the place where men meet to seek the highest remains holy ground. It is inconceivable that the Jewish people will permanently turn away from what their own prophets have taught the world for an even longer time. Welcome the stranger; succor the widow; visit the prisoner; feed the hungry: these are teachings that humankind has learned from the prophets of the Old Testament and from another Jew, Jesus of Nazareth, in Matthew 25. We shall overcome.

Anti-War Movements in the 1960s and in the New Millennium

I RECENTLY READ *a book that you published in 1966 with Tom Hayden,* The Other Side. *Can you tell me more about the time when you were "aiding and abetting" the enemy, about your visit to Vietnam? What is the difference between internationalism then and now? What is the difference between American anti-war movements then and now?*

THEN AND NOW

I was very much involved in the movement against the Vietnam war for two years, from early 1965 until Spring 1967. Thereafter I felt that the movement had grown to a point that I was not required to keep it going.

My involvement in the movement against the Iraq wars has been less. During Iraq War I, I picketed every noon in downtown Youngstown. In the five years of Iraq War II my contributions have been: (1) to put forward the idea of objection to a particular war based on the Nuremburg doctrine of war crimes, (2) to help to pass at the American Historical Association a resolution against the war, as we had failed to do in 1969.

I think there are two major ways in which the setting or context of protest against war has changed in the past fifty years.

1. In Iraq, there does not appear to be a single state or state-in-process-of-becoming arrayed against the United States occupation.

When I was growing up or in early adulthood there was always some national entity, seeking to resist the United States or its policies, that protesters could support.

Thus in the Spanish Civil War of 1935-1937 the anti-war movement sought to protect the democratically elected government.

In World War II, except for a handful of pacifists most Leftists in the United States supported our "Soviet ally."

In Vietnam, of course we condemned the puppet government in Saigon. But the National Liberation Front drew into itself all currents of opposition to the United States occupation, except perhaps the Buddhists. This led to an important division in the anti-war movement. One wing called for "Victory to the NLF." This slogan was the more plausible because President Eisenhower admitted in his memoirs that in a democratic election in Vietnam, Ho Chi Minh would have won. Tom Hayden, with whom I traveled to North Vietnam in December 1965, leaned toward support for and alliance with the NLF.

The other wing of the anti-war movement called for the immediate withdrawal of United States troops but had reservations about the "other side," and did not offer it uncritical support. This was my position.

In 1966 I was invited to become part of the Bertrand

Russell War Crimes Tribunal. I assumed I would accept. But I found myself asking, "Wouldn't the Tribunal be more credible if it received evidence of war crimes by any party to the Vietnam conflict?" I said that the "crimes" of the National Liberation Front, if such there proved to be, would be as dust in the balance when compared to the use of saturation bombing, cluster bombs, napalm, Agent Orange, and "tiger cages" by the United States and the Saigon governments. I asked, "Suppose the evidence is that the NLF tortured unarmed prisoners?" My youthful interlocutor answered, "Anything is justified that will drive the imperialist aggressor into the sea." "But," I went on, "a 'crime' is something that is wrong no matter who does it." I declined the invitation.

During my exchanges with the Tribunal, Dave Dellinger, following in my footsteps, made a trip to North Vietnam. When he got back he said that they had asked him whether Martin Luther King might join the Tribunal. He had replied, Probably not (it was a year later when Dr. King came out against the war), but if so "Staughton and I will do it." He was entirely justified in saying this because for about five years we had never disagreed about anything. I explained to Dave my decision not to join the Tribunal. He said that he agreed with me but he was so concerned about the use of cluster bombs by the United States that he would say, Yes. Although each of us respected the position of the other it turned out to be something of a parting of the ways with Dave.

After the Vietnamese victory in 1975, *WIN* magazine put out a special issue on the end of the war. I said, Now we will have to protest things done by the Vietnamese. Alice and I signed one of the early protests against the Vietnamese "re-education" camps.

In Iraq, no unified movement or government-in-process-of-becoming has presented itself. I suspect that Muqtada al Sadr will eventually lead such a movement and he has consistently called on Iraqis to resist the American occupiers rather than killing each other. But for the moment he is lying low.

Nineteen sixty-five was the year of most intense political activity in my life. Early that year I was still into civil rights: SNCC invited me to Selma to consult about setting up Freedom Schools. But on the plane back to New Haven, I read that United States soldiers had been killed at Pleikhu, South Vietnam, and in response the United States had begun to bomb North Vietnam. I recall feeling, Oh, so that is what I am supposed to be doing.

I chaired an anti-war meeting at Carnegie Hall in New York City. In April, I chaired the first march on Washington against the war. In August, I was arrested along with Dave Dellinger and Bob Moses as several hundred protesters sought to declare peace with the people of Vietnam on the steps of the Capitol. And in December, I went to Hanoi.

It is difficult to find words for the sense of urgency those of us in the anti-war movement felt that year. Almost every month, it seemed, President Lyndon Johnson would send tens of thousands more troops to Vietnam. One reason for demonstrating in August was that we feared that by the time college campuses re-opened, so many American soldiers would be in Vietnam that protest would not be permitted.

An indication of what I mean by "sense of urgency" is the action of Norman Morrison. A Quaker, he had been searching for means to express his outrage. Early in November, he read an article in *I.F. Stone's Weekly* that described the bombing of a South Vietnamese village, leaving many civilians, including many children, dead. That same day Norman took his infant daughter Emily and drove to the Pentagon. Stationing himself below Secretary McNamara's office window, he placed Emily to one side, poured kerosene over himself and set himself on fire.

In the spring of 1965, I attended a teach-in at Berkeley in which I called for a civil disobedience movement so massive that the "kitchen cabinet" of confidants, on whom President

Johnson relied in making strategy decisions about the war, would be forced to resign. And indeed, within two years Secretary of Defense McNamara, Secretary of State Rusk, National Security Adviser Bundy, and the President himself, had all left the government.

Nineteen sixty-six was the year a draft resistance movement came into being. That summer about a dozen young men, most of whom had been in Mississippi, met at our New Haven apartment and made plans to go to the SDS national convention and seek support for a program of induction refusal.

This brings me to the second major difference between the anti-war movement of the 1960s and the anti-war movement today.

2. In the 1960s young men were subject to conscription whereas today, there is a volunteer army.

Being subject to "the draft" put the war squarely in the middle of every young man's personal life. For a time, students with lower grades were subject to conscription while students with better grades were deferred. "We Won't Go" became the natural organizing principle for the anti-war movement.

Later, soldiers in Vietnam became the center of insurgency, and the movement in the States supported them as best we could with "coffee houses" near military bases, and the like.

In the era of wars in the Gulf the heroes of military resistance have been young men who volunteered for military service, served in Iraq, and were so horrified by what they saw that they refused to re-deploy. Such were Sergeants Camilo Mejía and Kevin Benderman.

A variant on the theme is the experience of Lieutenant Ehren Watada who volunteered to go to Afghanistan but refused to serve in Iraq on the ground that the United States had launched a preemptive war, or war of aggression, in Iraq that was a "war crime" as such crimes had been defined in the Nuremburg Tribunal.

This new circumstance of young men in military service requires us to do some new thinking.

I believe the Nuremburg Tribunal is a critically important but also a two-sided event. On the one hand, it was obscene that representatives of a nation that had just dropped atomic bombs on Hiroshima and Nagasaki should have presumed to sit in judgment on those who initiated the Holocaust. On the other hand, it was a great and continuing gift to humanity that the Nuremburg Tribunal defined war crimes that would henceforth apply to all persons, of whatever country: war crimes such as the mistreatment of prisoners; crimes against humanity; or crimes against the peace, crimes of aggressive war.

The importance of "war crimes" as defined at Nuremburg is that henceforth you should not have to be a pacifist, opposed to all wars, in order to refuse to serve in a particular war where war crimes are being committed. This is the transition that laws and military regulations need to make so that the Mejías, the Bendermans, the Watadas, and others similarly situated, can be excused from further military service.

I have tried to contribute to this transition by writing friend of the court briefs for Benderman and Watada.

That's why, with whatever embers remain in the fire within me and whatever fuel is left in the tank, I continue to do everything I can in opposition to United States imperialist wars.

Self-Sacrifice

I AM NOT *sure if you are familiar with the poem by Paul Goodman by the name "Ballad of the Pentagon":*

Staughton Lynd he said
to the Secretary of War,
"If on my little son
this can of gasoline I pour,

can you light a match to him?
Do you dare?"
The master of the Pentagon
said nothing but sat there.

"Then how do you command
your soldiers to rain
blazing gasoline
on little yellow children?"

This happened in America
in 1965
that people talked about
burning children alive.

Was this the same day when Norman Morrison committed suicide? Do you know what the reaction was of the "master of the Pentagon" to his suicide? When you went to Vietnam, did people there know of Norman Morrison and his sacrifice?

THE MCNAMARA MEETING

I spoke to Secretary McNamara as part of an anti-war delegation during the spring or summer of 1965.

As with so many of my memories, what remains is an image of McNamara, his hair slicked straight back, sitting at the end of an oval conference table.

Paul Goodman's poem helps us retrieve part of the conversation. My son Lee, born in May 1958, was seven years old. Apparently I asked the Secretary of Defense, If I were to pour a can of gasoline over my son, could you set a match to it? According to Goodman, McNamara "said nothing."

This conversation took place during the first part of 1965, whereas Norman's death came in early November. Goodman seems to think Morrison was present at the meeting with McNamara but Morrison's widow and I agree that he was not.

Thus there is no reason to think that what I said directly influenced Norman Morrison. All of us in the anti-war movement were acutely aware of napalm, the jellied gasoline that sets a human body alight. A photograph widely used in the movement showed a child with part of her face scarred and distorted by napalm, and another, even better known, picture showed a naked child running down a road toward the viewer. Moreover, there had been several instances of self-immolation by Vietnamese Buddhist monks. The idea was in the air.

THE EFFECT ON MCNAMARA

Biographers concur that Norman Morrison's death affected Secretary McNamara intensely. No one knows whether Morrison chose to immolate himself within sight of the Secretary's office, but McNamara witnessed Morrison's burning body from his office window. "Years later McNamara was barely able to talk about what had happened," writes biographer Deborah Shapley.

Moreover, it was apparently at roughly the time of Norman's suicide—the end of 1965—that the Secretary of Defense began deeply to doubt the wisdom of the war he now calls a terrible mistake. In a memoir, Norman Morrison's widow Anne Welsh has carefully collected the evidence.

First, in his own memoir, *In Retrospect: The Tragedy and Lessons of Vietnam*, Robert McNamara indicates that from his standpoint anti-war protest began the day Norman Morrison killed himself. He says that prior to November 2, 1965, "anti-war protest had been sporadic and limited...and had not compelled attention." At "twilight that day, a young Quaker named Norman R. Morrison...burned himself to death within forty feet of my Pentagon window." The former Secretary of Defense adds these extraordinary words:

> Morrison's death was a tragedy not only for his family but also for me and the country. It was an outcry against the killing that was destroying the lives of so many Vietnamese and American youth....

> I reacted to the horror of his action by bottling up my emotions and avoided talking about them with anyone—even with my family.... And I believed I understood and shared some of his thoughts.

Second, journalist Paul Hendrickson in his 1996 book, *The Living and the Dead: Robert McNamara and Five Lives of a Lost War*, quotes McNamara as saying that Morrison "may have been correct if by such actions he could bring to bear the attention he sought." Hendrickson also calls attention to McNamara's testimony at the Westmoreland versus CBS trial in the 1980s. Asked when he reached the conclusion that the war could not be won militarily, McNamara replied, "I believe I may have reached it as early as the latter part of 1965." Within a month of Norman's death, Hendrickson writes, now-declassified documents show that McNamara was "urging the president in memos and in White House meetings and in private conversations to consider a bombing pause."

Finally, according to Anne Welsh, Chester L. Cooper in his book *The Lost Crusade* states that observers of McNamara noticed "a discernible change in mood in late 1965. It was not so much a transition from 'hawk' to 'dove' [but] from overflowing confidence to grave doubts."

THE EFFECT ON THE VIETNAMESE

It is well-known that Norman Morrison's action had an enormous impact on the Vietnamese. Hayden, Aptheker and I made our trip to Hanoi less than two months after Norman's death and were in a position to observe that impact.

At a factory we saw a poster captioned, "The flames of Morrison will never die." The members of a village we visited sent "their best wishes to Mrs. Anne Morrison." The Vietnamese poet laureate had written a poem entitled "Emily," the name of the child Norman set to one side before his death. The attorney general of Vietnam compared the poem to an old story in which "unity comes from shared suffering."

More than thirty years later when Anne Welsh visited North Vietnam, many persons told her where they had been at the moment they learned of Norman's action, just as Americans remember where they were when they learned of John Kennedy's assassination. Simply, Norman's death caused Vietnamese to believe that there was at least one person in the United States who understood what they were experiencing.

THE EFFECT ON WAR RESISTERS IN THE UNITED STATES

Brian Willson is a man who attended the same high school in Chautauqua, New York from which Norman Morrison graduated. Later Brian volunteered for Air Force duty in Vietnam. Brian describes how the librarian at the Air Force base in Vietnam where Brian was stationed noticed the unusual assortment of books that Willson was checking out of the library, and invited him to dinner. After the meal the family sang songs, Brian writes, "one of which…they translated into English especially for me." The song was about Norman's death. Brian Willson suddenly realized that this was the same Norman Morrison who he remembered from high school, and was "the first Eagle Scout I ever knew." Overcome, Brian Willson broke into tears. Eighteen years later he would sit down on the track of a railroad train carrying munitions to a port for shipment to anti-insurgent government forces in Central America, resulting in the loss of both his legs.

THREE KINDS OF SELF-SACRIFICE

If the facts set out above may be accepted as true, they present an extremely important issue. It is both an ethical issue and an issue of effectiveness.

In recent world history, there have been individuals prepared not just to risk their lives but with certainty give up their lives for the sake of a better world. Their self-sacrifice has been of three different kinds: (1) The actions of suicide bombers, often directed wholly against civilians; (2) The attempt to assassinate individual political or military leaders, almost always resulting (whether or not successful in killing the targeted officeholder) in the death of the assassin; (3) Nonviolent self-destruction as exemplified by Norman Morrison (as well as by Alice Herz, whose self-immolation preceded his, and Roger LaPorte who acted similarly soon after).

At the risk of giving great offense and stirring controversy, I assess these three kinds of action as follows:

1. Acts of violence that indiscriminately kill innocent civilians are always and everywhere wrong. They are ethically indefensible. They are also demonstrably ineffective: in the case of Palestine, for example, they have confused and dissipated what would otherwise have been overwhelming world condemnation of the Israeli occupation.

2. At least in the late nineteenth and early twentieth centuries, individual assassination was the characteristic anarchist "propaganda of the deed." Setting aside all ethical questions, I invite readers to compare its effectiveness in any historical situation known to them with the results of Norman Morrison's action. Suppose that instead of killing himself, Norman had attempted to kill Secretary McNamara? Is there any conceivable possibility that that could have done

as much to end the horror of Vietnam as Norman's self-sacrifice accomplished?

3. I trust readers will not understand me to advocate any form of killing, whether of others or self. My point is that for the individual willing to lay down his life for his brother, see John 15:13, Norman Morrison's nonviolent manner of doing so is incomparably the best. Indeed, I believe it would greatly benefit worldwide anarchism in its praiseworthy advocacy of direct action were it also to insist on the additional ingredient that that action should be, whenever possible, nonviolent, and to recognize in Norman Morrison a prophet of a better way.

Central American Solidarity

YOU MET BRIAN WILLSON *in Youngstown, and you helped him in writing the book that was published under the title* On Third World Legs. *This whole experience brings us to yet another region, and yet another internationalist chapter of your life, to Central and Latin America. What was the Central American solidarity work like? Was there anything in this internationalist episode that you find important to impart?*

My wife Alice and I made five trips to Nicaragua between 1985 and 1990. We used two- or three-week summer vacations from our work at Legal Services in Youngstown, Ohio.

Our initial trip was prompted by two things. On the evening news show of public TV, we saw an interview with a young woman who said she was a Quaker (as are we). She planned to go to Nicaragua with a delegation sponsored by

Witness for Peace that would try to interpose itself between the contras, invading Nicaragua from Honduras, and the Sandinista villages in that remote part of the country.

At about the same time, there was an editorial in *The New York Times*. It said that when the Frente Sandinista de Liberación Nacional (FSLN) came to power, a number of armed supporters of the former Somoza government came into the hands of the victorious Sandinistas. One of the three founders of the FSLN and a member of the FSLN executive committee was a man named Tomas Borge. Borge found himself face to face with a man who had tortured him when Borge was imprisoned. "Now I will have my revenge," Borge is said to have told his prisoner. "I'm going to let you go." According to the *Times*, the Sandinistas released all their prisoners except those who could be proved to have committed specific crimes.

On that first trip to Nicaragua we traveled with an interreligious group. We were accompanied by Seth Rosenthal, son of our friend Pat Rosenthal, who spoke Spanish. Perhaps the most remarkable moment of that first trip came in a restaurant in Puerto Cabezas, on the eastern, Pacific coast of the country. There were Miskito Indians who lived near the Honduran border in that part of the country. The Sandinista government had forcibly moved them away from the international border. We discussed this in a conversation that went from Miskito to Spanish, then (by way of Seth) from Spanish to English, then from English to Spanish to Miskito again.

Leftists in the United States have often romanticized a revolutionary society under siege by the United States. It was so for many years in the case of the Soviet Union. In the early 1960s revolutionary Cuba presented the same challenge. Now here we were in yet another revolutionary effort, and we were determined not to be deceived by official propaganda.

Yet we were deceived. Not until the Sandinistas fell from power in the election of 1990 did the extent to which things were run from the top down become clear. For example, only then did we learn (thanks especially to the writing of Margaret Randall) that the leader of the women's organization AMNLAE was chosen not by the women themselves, but by the largely male FSLN executive committee.

At the same time, on that trip and afterwards there were extraordinary experiences that introduced us to Latin American "liberation theology" and deepened our understanding of what Gustavo Gutierrez calls "the preferential option for the poor."

We stayed in a Nicaraguan household four times. On three occasions, that household was the family of Rosa Solis in Barrio Riguero, Managua. We knew next to no Spanish. The Solis family knew even less English. (There is a photograph of the two of us and several members of the family in *Living Inside Our Hope*.)

THE PREFERENTIAL OPTION FOR THE POOR

On two trips to Nicaragua we visited hamlets in the far North. This was the area harassed by the contras to which Witness for Peace had hoped to travel.

Along the side of the road to Ojoche (pronounced "oh-ho-che"), one saw crosses where contras had ambushed and killed other travelers. That evening, as we walked back to the home where we were to sleep, we were accompanied by the village "*responsable*" with an AK-47.

There was an organic beauty to household furnishings in Ojoche that we saw nowhere else in Nicaragua. Polished tree branches, white stucco walls and contrasting red brick surfaces, reminded Alice and myself of our efforts at the Macedonia Cooperative Community to make our surroundings beautiful despite great poverty.

Ojoche, at the time we visited, was trying to create a series of cooperatives: for pottery, for the making of honey, for baking bread.

Then two years later we spent a week in the nearby

village of El Bonete (pronounced "baw-neh-teh"). Many of the poorest families in Ojoche had been given land by the central government provided they moved to El Bonete and organized it in cooperatives. The land had been abandoned by a rich landowner who had left for Miami.

El Bonete was the poorest community we have ever seen. Alice judges the level of poverty partly by the condition of the dogs and cats. In El Bonete they were walking skeletons. The children had running sores. When it was discovered that Alice was a seamstress, she was pressed into service and got the village sewing machine running again. But it took a search of the whole village to produce a button. (The button that was found was from a United States military uniform, presumably going back to the 1920s). It had hardly rained in a year and the residents of El Bonete were beginning to sell off their cattle.

Father Joe Mulligan arranged for us to stay with two nuns, members of the Little Sisters of Jesus. Nellie's father had been a railroad engineer in Argentina. Carmencita came from a *campesino* family in El Salvador.

The Sisters' home was like any other in the village, except that there was a small *capilla* (chapel) built against one side of the house. Within the little chapel, one sat on a rush mat on the floor or on cement blocks. The altar was a tree stump. Against one wall was a fabric embroidered by Carmencita with Romero's famous words: "Unless a seed drops into the ground and die, it cannot bring forth fruit." Every day the Sisters, Alice, and I would gather in the *capilla*.

We sang freedom songs for them. They taught us a song from that part of Nicaragua: "When a group of brothers gathers at the altar, God's smile is there. Lord, we come today to give you praise for so much good that you have given us." "*Tanta bondad*" (so much good) did not seem especially obvious to Alice and myself but it was to Nellie and Carmencita.

Another song was from the Salvadoran equivalent to

Nicaragua's Peasants' Mass. The last portion of the Mass, or *despedida* (the dismissal), declares: "When the poor come to believe in the poor, Then we will be able to sing of liberty. When the poor come to believe in the poor, We will construct fraternity."

I felt that in that little house I had finally discovered, and touched with my own hands, the preferential option for the poor. At midday it was so hot that one could only rest indoors. Above the bed where I took my siesta there was a bookshelf. The books on that bookshelf were, on the one hand, the homilies of Archbishop Romero, and on the other hand, the works of Che Guevara. There were three copies of *Where There Is No Doctor*.

MEXICO AND MARTHA

We also made three trips to Mexico and have visited Guatemala, where Martha, our younger daughter, now lives.

My single strongest memory of Mexico City is of the home in which the Russian revolutionary Leon Trotsky lived the last years of his life, and was murdered. Like many Latin American homes the house is really a compound, with buildings set around a central yard. Trotsky and his friends erected crude gun turrets at the four corners of the compound, because the first attempt on his life was by means of an armed assault. Then he was killed when a young man gained entrance to Trotsky's study, ostensibly to show him a manuscript and, as Trotsky bent over his desk to read it, put an axe in his skull.

Not far south of the capital is a workers' education center which Alice and I attended twice and which we made it possible for several Youngstown co-workers to attend. Three of our friends who made the journey were African American. All were visibly affected by a society that was less racist than the United States, but also, where poverty was greater and where the poor nonetheless shared whatever they had.

Finally, we visited the Zapatista stronghold of Chiapas with Martha and her Chilean friend, Roberto.

Guatemala has been the least attractive of the Central American places we have visited. I think this is because of the terrible violence of the early 1980s. I compare what one finds there now to a forest after a great fire. Small green shoots of life are poking up through the blackened surface of the forest floor. But it will take time.

Martha, however, is deeply engaged. She is completely fluent in Spanish and has married a Guatemalan-American. She works for an organization called Maya Traditions, which assists women's weaving cooperatives.

I feel that Martha has been able to take a further step in her father's desire to be a citizen of the world.

Do We Need Rights?

I WAS HAVING *an interesting conversation in a social center in London a few months ago. It was a heated discussion with fellow anarchists and fellow Peoples Global Action members who were demanding that we should stop using terms like "rights," imposed on us and sanctioned by the State. I think that your experience as a lawyer and activist, as well as a theorist who followed E. P. Thompson's line of thinking about law as being a somewhat more complicated affair than just an irksome bourgeois imposition, could be immensely instructive for the new anarchists. Let us talk about critical legal theory—the first, at least according to my knowledge, intelligent attempt to understand law from this perspective—and your contribution to what I see as a much more serious model of understanding the law. Do we need "rights?"*

Should new anarchists see law and rights as intrinsically corrupt concepts?

I have confronted these questions several times in my life. Forgive me if I repeat myself.

First, when I was an undergraduate at Harvard, one evening I found myself in a booth at a tavern called Jim Cronin's with the university Communist Party (all four or five of them). They baited me with the question, "Did I think there were ethical norms that applied throughout history?" Of course I was supposed to say, "Each period of class rule (slavery, feudalism, capitalism, socialism) produces different rules of behavior; there are no timeless or universal ethical norms."

I answered "incorrectly," knowing perfectly well what I was doing. I said, "Yes, I think that there are ethical norms that apply throughout history."

Second, in the spring of 1966, I declined to join the War Crimes Tribunal being organized by Bertrand Russell.

Third, toward the end of the 1960s an atmosphere of "anything by our side goes" came to predominate on the American Left. Black Panthers and others called police officers "pigs." I am the only person known to me who publicly opposed this practice.

Even those individualistic rights most obviously akin to the economic claims of capitalist entrepreneurs should not be casually dismissed, I argued. Consider habeas corpus: the idea that the state cannot simply seize a person and conceal him or her from public view, but can be required to produce the prisoner in open court and to explain with what crime he or she is charged. That right goes back to Magna Carta in 1215. It was expanded and made more specific and enforceable during the English Revolution of the seventeenth century. "Free Born" John Lilburne, spokesperson for the movement known as "the Levelers," was repeatedly brought before Star Chamber to defend himself, without a lawyer, without a presumption of innocence. In one of his pamphlets he speaks of being thrown once more into "my old familiar lodgings in the Tower [of London]." People who would casually dismiss or do away with the rights for which heroes like John Lilburne struggled lack a sense of history, and a proper humility toward those who went before us on the path.

Do I mean to suggest that justice is even-handed, or that the poor have an equal chance with the rich in a court of law? Of course not. But where do we go with this insight? That we can do anything we want, and because we are pure and righteous, we should never be punished? That our assassinations or suicide bombings are justified because it is we who do them, whereas our opponents, should they carry out precisely the same acts, deserve whatever repression can be mustered against them?

I have a hard time with theorizing that does not appear to arise from practical activity or lead to action, or indeed, that seems to discourage action and to consider action useless.

I don't think I am intellectually inept. Yet I confess that much of what is written about "post-Marxism," or "Fordism," or "deconstruction," or "the multitude," or "critical legal studies," or "whiteness," and that I have tried to read, seems to me, simply, both unintelligible and useless.

What is the explanation for this universe of extremely abstract discourse? I yearn to ask of each such writer: What are you doing? With what ordinary people do you discuss your ideas before you publish them? What difference does it make, in the world outside your windows and away from your word processor, whether you say A or B? For whom do you consider yourself a model or exemplar? Exactly how, in light of what you have written, do you see your theoretical work leading to another world? Or would it be more accurate to suggest that the practical effect of what you write is to rationalize your comfortable position doing full-time theorizing in a college or university?

Here I shall discuss an example of such theorizing, Critical Legal Studies.

CRITICAL LEGAL STUDIES

In the United States, critical legal studies originated with the writings of so-called "legal realists" such as Karl Llewellyn in the 1930s. It was revived in the 1970s and 1980s by persons on the Left such as my friend Karl Klare.

Legal realism amounted to a crude debunking of abstract legal discourse. It was suggested that verbal conflict about the First Amendment, or due process, or cruel and unusual punishment, did not really concern these worthy ideals. Legal practitioners picked up whatever brick it was useful to throw in a particular circumstance. The abstractions used by competing lawyers were simply weapons with which each sought to enhance the likelihood of victory on behalf of a client.

As an historian who has also been a practicing lawyer for more than thirty years I consider this analysis dramatically misplaced. Where lawyers repeatedly betray their supposed devotion to uncovering truth is primarily in their treatment of facts, rather than in their use of legal abstractions. They conceal facts that they know which might be helpful to the other side. They deliberately mischaracterize facts in a way that seems helpful to their clients.

In attacking legal discourse as such, critical legal theorists throw out the baby with the bath. There sticks in my mind the experience of a Harvard professor named Martha Minow. Minow was on her way to a court encounter in which she was to argue on behalf of a female client. It suddenly occurred to her: How can I give up abstractions such as equal rights? What weapons are left to me if I consider such concepts mere rationalizations for more pragmatic interests?

I have written an article entitled "Communal Rights," published in the *Texas Law Review*. There I defended in particular legal concepts such as Section 7 of the Wagner Act, or National Labor Relations Act, pronouncing the right of workers to engage in concerted activity for mutual aid or protection such as picketing, striking, or forming a union. I argued that we would wish such a right to exist in any imaginable good society, so that workers might most effectively defend themselves against the oppressions of whoever their new rulers turned out to be.

To be sure, any legal activity perforce runs the danger of encouraging a certain fetishism. Lawyers whose livelihood depends on the money they make from clients have a self-interest in exaggerating their own importance. In so doing they are likely to use long words and to cite the names of cases with which their clients are, of course, unfamiliar.

A contrasting approach will emphasize that, at best, whatever lawyers can accomplish in a court room is likely to be more effective if accompanied by the direct action of the clients themselves. Lawyer and client should aspire to work together, as two hands engaged in a single project. Above all the lawyer will emphasize the likely dispositive significance of facts, and the client's inevitably greater knowledge of the facts when compared to whatever knowledge the lawyer may have.

I challenge Critical Legal Theorists to say: How will your critique of all legal discourse and activity assist the 10,000 Palestinians indefinitely detained in Israeli jails without criminal charges? What is your plan for bringing an end to indefinite confinement at Guantanamo?

I think I can best convey what I am talking about by some examples drawn from my own activity.

First, though, I want once again to emphasize the centrality of a right relationship between working-class protagonist and professional associate. On the one hand, the professional—whether journalist, minister, doctor, lawyer, teacher, or whatever—must feel a profound respect for the insights and perspective of his or her collaborator. On the other hand, as Archbishop Romero stressed in his pastoral letters about "accompaniment," there can be no place for a false deference whereby the associate romanticizes and exempts from criticism the experience of the activist.

I think an action defined as a "crime" remains a crime no matter who commits that action.

I think political murder is just as wrong when undertaken by the persons who sought to kill Tsar Alexander and President McKinley, as when undertaken by those who assassinated the Kennedy brothers, Malcolm, and Dr. King.

I think the "other world" that we hope is possible will ban capital punishment under all circumstances. What must at all costs be repudiated is any easy acceptance of "our" violence, any desire for revenge, any disregard of rights for our adversaries that we would insist on for ourselves were it we who were in jeopardy.

I challenge anarchists to explain to me what they believe is accomplished when participants in anti-globalization efforts deliberately initiate violence, when they set out to provoke the authorities into acts of repression.

I ask whether any of those engaged in such "propaganda of the deed" can rebut the approach of Nelson Mandela. He was in charge of the "spear of Africa," the guerrilla wing of the African National Congress. Yet he consistently brought down his weight on the side of destroying property (electric generating facilities, for example) but not, could it be avoided, human beings.

What do my anarchist friends think of the Truth and Reconciliation Commission over which Bishop Tutu presided after the African National Congress came to power? Would you be willing to forgive those who have tortured and killed your friends and relatives, provided they described their actions in the presence of surviving relatives and sought to make amends?

Do you believe in the execution of hostages? Lenin authorized it. The FMLN in El Salvador did it. What about the execution of prisoners without trial? The Spanish anarchists engaged in it. I submit that such actions are always and everywhere wrong.

War, Peace and Nonviolence

HOW WAS YOUR *outlook on war, peace and violence formed? I would like to ask you in specific about one book and one film that we talked about a lot:* Bread and Wine, *by Ignazio Silone, and "Grand Illusion," a film made by Jean Renoir.*

My outlook on war and peace was formed as a child and adolescent. Mary Bohan, my Irish nurse, taught me "The Minstrel Boy," with the verse (as I remember it):

> The Minstrel fell but the foe man's chains,
> Could not bring that proud soul under.
> The Harp he loved never spoke again,
> For he tore its strings asunder.
> And said, "No hand shall sully thee,
> Thou soul of love and bravery.
> Thy songs were made for the pure and free,
> They shall never sound in slavery!"

One evening, presumably after Mary sang this song to me once again, I asked her to call my parents wherever they were and tell them I was never going to be a soldier.

Another strong influence was my mother.

My mother was student body president at Wellesley College when World War I ended in November 1918. She said that students, in a spontaneous celebration, marched into the chapel singing a popular song of the day, "Good morning, Mr. Zip, zip, zip."

My mother and her friends considered this frivolous. They organized a second occasion characterized by Rudyard Kipling's poem, "Processional": "The captains and the kings depart…. Lest we forget, lest we forget."

I also remember my mother's reaction to a Soviet documentary that our family watched during World War II. In general our household was very sympathetic to the Soviet war effort. I can remember pouring over maps in the newspaper showing little black arrows for the Nazi armies and little white arrows for the Soviet.

However, this particular documentary depicted German soldiers with ridicule. Their feet wrapped in enormous clumps of rags, the Germans awkwardly surrendered as derisive music was played. My mother was furious! "You never ridicule a defeated adversary," she insisted.

GRAND ILLUSION

The strongest single influence on my notions about war and peace was a French movie of the 1930s entitled "Grand Illusion." Our family watched it. I watched it again with my college roommates, and for a time we conversed in quotations from the flick. I now have a copy, given to us by a college friend who later joined the Society of Brothers, or Bruderhof.

The film was made by Jean Renoir, a son or grandson of the French impressionist painter. The leading characters are Marechal, a French auto mechanic, played by Jean Gabin; a German aristocrat, Rauffenstein, played by Eric von Stroheim; and a French aristocrat, de Boeldieu, played by Pierre Fresnay. Fresnay played the lead in another French movie that greatly influenced me about the life of the French saint, Vincent de Paul.

Briefly, Marechal and de Boeldieu are in a French war plane during World War I that is shot down by Rauffenstein. Later, after Rauffenstein is badly injured and can no longer pilot a plane, he becomes the commandant of a prison in which Marechal and de Boeldieu are confined. The prison is a castle, I believe the so-called Wartburg in western Germany.

De Boeldieu devises a plan of escape. The plan calls for him to create a diversion by playing a flute while Marechal and a middle-class Jew named Rosenthal escape by way of a homemade rope dropped outside the walls. Marechal protests. De Boeldieu responds: "I know your preferences. Besides, it would amuse me." Marechal struggles to find words of thanks. "You're so formal," he finally says, as he helps de Boeldieu wash the white gloves that the latter plans to wear. De Boeldieu replies with a little smile: "I am formal with my mother and with my wife."

The plan works. The pair disappear down the rope. De Boeldieu is finally cornered by Rauffenstein high in the cliffs that are a part of the fortress. They speak in English. "You understand, if you don't come back, I'll have to shoot," the commandant calls out. De Boeldieu responds: "Nice of you, Rauffenstein, but it's impossible!" Rauffenstein fires. The shot proves fatal. As de Boeldieu lies dying (in the commandant's apartment), Rauffenstein apologizes for his clumsiness. "No, no," his friend says. "It was dark. I was running. And you know," he adds, "for members of our class mine is the best way to go. You will go on dragging out a useless existence." After de Boeldieu's death, Rauffenstein cuts his geranium, "the only flower in the fortress."

Meantime, Marechal and Rosenthal make their way toward the Swiss border. But Rosenthal has badly twisted his ankle and goes more and more slowly. Finally Marechal says he will go on alone. Both men profess to be overjoyed by this decision. Marechal adds: "Besides, I never liked your kind." Rosenthal responds: "It's a little late for that." Marechal walks off singing a song about a little boat that recurs throughout the movie. Rosenthal, sitting on a rock, calls out: "I'm so happy you're leaving I too can sing!" He also begins to sing about the little boat. Once he is sure Marechal cannot see him, he breaks into tears.

Then comes what is for me the most gripping moment of the movie. The movie frame shows Rosenthal on his rock, weeping. Then something comes into the frame from one side. It is…the edge of Marechal's beatup overcoat. Marechal takes his friend under the arm and helps him to his feet. They go on together.

As dusk falls, traveling more and more slowly, they near a farm house. They agree that they must stop. They'll bed down in the barn beside the farm house, and take their chances. As they settle into the straw they hear the noise of someone opening the door. Marechal leaps to his feet and picks up a huge club. "Don't move!" he hisses to Rosenthal.

The barn door opens. In comes a cow, followed by a woman with a lantern. She starts. Rosenthal, who speaks some German, says: "*Mein Fuss ist kaput. Ich kann nicht weiter*" (My foot is done for. I can't go on). The woman says, "*Kriegsgefaengnisse?*" (prisoners of war?). Marechal and Rosenthal don't answer. Well, the woman says: "*Ich bin ganz allein hier. Komm ins Hause*" (I'm all alone here. Come into the house).

They follow her warily. She heats a pan of hot water in which to soak Rosenthal's foot. As she does so, there is a sound of singing. It is German soldiers! There is a rap on the shutter. The woman, Else, opens it. A bespectacled junior officer asks: "How far is it to Hildesheim?" Else says: "Twelve kilometers." "Twelve kilometers!" the soldier exclaims. "I'd rather stay here with you." She closes the shutter. The soldiers move off. She has not betrayed her guests.

Else shows them the house. There are pictures on the wall of various males. They are her husband and brothers. She calls out the names of the battles where each died, commenting: "Our greatest victories."

Marechal and Rosenthal stay with Else and her little daughter, Lotte, through much of the winter while Rosenthal's foot heals. But finally, they must go and, as they explain, rejoin their units. Else weeps. "I have been alone too long. This long waiting!" Marechal promises to come back for her after the war.

Soon after Marechal and Rosenthal stand in snow under fir branches. "You're sure this is the border?" Marechal asks. "It doesn't look different from any other place." Rosenthal assures him, yes, this is the German-Swiss border.

In case something should happen as they make their way across an open field to what they think is Switzerland, they embrace and say good-bye. "So long, dirty Jew," Marechal exclaims. One of them remarks, "Maybe this will be the last war." The other responds, "What an illusion!"

A German ski patrol arrives a moment too late as the two plod across the frontier in the deep snow. One of the soldiers raises his rifle to shoot. "Stop," says his companion. "They are in Switzerland."

BREAD AND WINE

Now this is the center, the heart, the beginning and the end. Everything is here: Marxism, Christianity, direct action, liberation theology, accompaniment…. My oldest friend (now deceased) Danny Newman, son of a rabbi, held up a paperback copy in the subway on our way home from school and asked if I had read it. Have you read it? (Be sure to read the original mid-1930s text.) Some of my favorite scenes are near the beginning.

Don Benedetto is an elderly priest and was Pietro Spina's schoolmaster. Don Benedetto's sister, who also serves as his housekeeper, arranges a birthday party. Only a few of the ex-students come. All have to a greater or lesser extent compromised with the fascist regime. They look at old photographs. They ask Don Benedetto, Who was your favorite student? He responds, What have you heard of Pietro Spina? The younger men know that Spina is a Marxist revolutionary (Silone was in fact on the executive committee of the Third International) who has recently returned to Italy. One of the students says, Am I my brother's keeper?

"The old man was standing near the fireplace, and the reply made him go pale. He almost staggered. He walked slowly over towards Concettino, took his head between his trembling hands, looked him in the eyes, and said, quietly, almost in tears: 'My poor boy, is this the pass to which you have come? You don't know how terrible are the words you have just spoken, the most terrible words in Genesis, and Genesis is a terrible book'." (pp. 19-20)

Another former student at the party is a doctor, Nunzio Sacca. Don Benedetto asks him what he knows of Spina. Sacca narrates his schoolmate's revolutionary wanderings. "I have also heard from a relative of his that he is suffering from lung trouble." Don Benedetto comments: "Foxes have holes, and the birds of the air have nests; but the son of man hath not where to lay his head. He goes on living according to the pure dreams of his adolescence, and the Christian countries hunt him like a wild beast."

One morning soon after there is a knock on Sacca's door. A peasant stands there, and tells the doctor that there is a sick man who needs his help. The doctor gets in the carriage. He says, "We know each other. Who is the patient?" The peasant replies evasively. He recalls hearing the doctor make a speech years ago in which he advocated liberty. The doctor asks again who the patient is. The peasant tells of how he went to southern France to work on the building of a big tunnel. There was a man who used to meet him when he left work, and the two of them would talk. And you know, he goes on, that man came to my house last night. He was feverish. In great alarm the doctor says, Are you taking me to see Pietro Spina? The peasant replies that when the catechism speaks of the works of mercy it doesn't say that we should first inquire about a person's political ideas. He explains that in the countryside it is the custom that if a strange animal comes to your doorstep, you first take it in and then wait for the owner to appear. "How much more so should one receive a human being." (pp. 23-27)

MATTHEW 25

You need to understand that while growing up I learned absolutely nothing about Christianity, despite the fact that my father went to Union Theological Seminary and my mother was an intense believer until she reached college. So concepts such as "the works of mercy" were to me phrases from a foreign language, encountered for the very first time in *Bread and Wine*.

Later, I undertook to do research for a scholar at the University of Chicago named Helen Mims. I found myself reading a so-called "mystery play" of the medieval City of York. In it I encountered the story of the Last Judgment, in which Jesus/God sends some persons to Hell and seats others at his side for everlasting depending on whether "when I was in prison, you visited; when I was hungry, you fed me," and so on. Both the sheep and the goats reply, But we never saw you before in our lives! Oh yes you have, they are told. Inasmuch as you did it (or did not do it) to the least of these, you did it unto me.

It took me a couple of weeks to realize that this scene had not been created by the medieval City of York, but came from Matthew 25 in the New Testament. This little story became the center of my life. Inasmuch as one does or does not feed the hungry, care for the sick, welcome the stranger, visit those in prison, one does or does not participate in the Divine. A personal God seems to me childish anthropomorphism. But Matthew 25 is the core of everything.

AIN'T I A WOMAN?

In a famous incident of the nineteenth century antislavery movement, Sojourner Truth, an African-American woman and escaped slave, stood before an audience in the North and asked, "Ain't I a woman?" In effect she challenged any man among her listeners to show that he had given as much as she had given to the movement for a better world.

Her question is one that I have asked myself. I have the biological equipment of a male. I have played a "manly" role in life as captain of the high school baseball team, student body president, backcountry camper and canoer, father and grandfather. During the first quarter century of our marriage, my wife Alice contributed more than I to our family income:

I lived "by the sweat of my *Frau*." However, I did what I could and in the next thirty years of our marriage, I was able to earn more.

Nevertheless, I have often reflected that my take on life is overwhelmingly female. I cannot imagine killing another human being. When a notice from my draft board arrived in the 1950s, I concluded that I wasn't going to kill anyone, but also, that I should share the same dangers as young men of my age who did not know that one could seek to be a Conscientious Objector: accordingly, I asked my draft board to permit me to be a noncombatant member of the Army Medical Corps. (The casualty rate for Army medics was higher than for infantrymen, so I considered that I could rebut the charge of cowardice.) After my draft board agreed, I declined to take weapons training and spent most of Basic Training washing dishes and huge pots in the unit kitchen.

When I walk into a room I believe I instinctively seek ways to bring all present into a circle of mutual understanding. I have painstakingly sought to resume communication with individuals who have been antagonists in particular situations, and find in my late seventies that I have few personal enemies. No doubt in part because of my relatively protected and privileged path in life, I cannot remember telling a lie.

The world has sometimes seemed to me to be divided into gardeners and builders. Gardeners try to grow things. They understand that in any growing season there will be some successes and some failures. They try not to impose a preconceived blueprint on reality. I am a gardener.

One form of gardening is to seek what we in Youngstown came to call "brownfield" rather than "greenfield" development. Brownfield development begins with what already exists and tries to preserve what is good at the same time that what is bad is squarely addressed. Thus on the Lower East Side of New York City in the late 1950s, I helped to inaugurate the "Cooper Square Alternative Plan." The city wanted to bulldoze the city blocks between Cooper Union and Houston Street, scatter existing residents to the four winds, and replace the old tenements with high rise buildings at gentrified rents. With the aid of two city planners (whom I recruited on a visit to City Hall), the residents devised a plan that would permit the existing residents to remain at the same time that physical structures were replaced or rehabilitated. Believe it or not, after forty years of struggle the residents won.

Similarly in Youngstown and Pittsburgh, I worked with those who tried to rebuild steel mills on existing sites, retaining the workforce and the infrastructure already in being. We lost that struggle.

Finally, as I have made clear elsewhere in these conversations, I no longer wish to be part of "taking state power" but rather aspire to nurture self-governing local entities, linked in horizontal networks of decisionmaking and action.

Am I wrong to imagine the foregoing to be attitudes characteristic of women?

HELEN MERRELL LYND AND MARY CUSHING NILES

My mother, Helen Merrell Lynd, and my wife's mother, Mary Cushing Niles, came of age during and just after World War I. Both were strong, intellectual women. Each worked with her husband as an equal partner. In my mother's case, this was the collaboration that produced the sociological classic, *Middletown*.

Alice's mother was the first woman admitted to Johns Hopkins University (but only in the night school!), where she majored in economics, while simultaneously pursuing a degree in music at the Peabody Conservatory of Music.

One can glimpse the essential character of the marriages of these women in the stories of how they met their husbands-to-be. Harry Niles and Mary Cushing Howard met at a dance in Baltimore. When Harry returned home that night he was asked whom he had met and what they had talked about. He said that he had met Mary Cushing and they had talked about women's suffrage. (That was in the spring of 1917.)

My father met my mother on a trail in the White Mountains of New Hampshire. He had been to the top of Mt. Washington and stayed at the Lakes of the Clouds hut nearby. As he tramped out along the Dolly Copp Road, his undershirt hanging from the back of his pack to dry, he met Deacon Edward Merrell and two of his daughters. They had stayed at the Lakes of the Clouds hut shortly before my father.

There was conversation, and somehow it turned to Thorstein Veblen's *Theory of the Leisure Class*. My father was so taken by the two young women that he climbed back up Mt. Washington to look at the guest book at the Lakes of the Clouds and thus discover the names of those he had met at the base of the mountain. Of course, he had the problem of discerning which of the two young women was the one who had read Veblen. Apparently he guessed right.

MORE ON HELEN LYND

My mother Helen Lynd died from the aftermath of a stroke. When she first experienced the stroke, she lost the ability to speak. Then, somehow, words came again. According to her hospital roommate, the first word that she spoke was: "love."

Mother always said, with emphasis, that she was "not a women's libber." But I think what this meant (as I recall her explaining it) was that when she went into the dining room at Sarah Lawrence College, which she had helped to found and where she taught, she considered it equally legitimate to sit down with a man as with a woman.

But the fact is, Helen Lynd exemplified what Carol Gilligan has described as women's "other voice." She tended to view ideas in the contexts in which they had arisen, and to which they might be applied, rather than as abstractions. Whereas my father was inclined to denounce people from a distance, my mother's practice, at least if someone she knew personally was involved, was to pick up the phone.

I believe that Helen Lynd considered that, in the last analysis, social change comes through individuals. A person thinks or acts in a new way; others gather around that breakthrough; soon a new institution confronts the powers-that-be. One might speak of a Mendelian theory of social evolution. Any notion that a mere change in environment—war, unemployment, disintegration of the nuclear family, whatever—automatically results in social change is rejected. Giraffes do not grow longer necks in order to reach bananas. Rather, somewhere in the social scheme of things there occur mutations, individual mutations, and then everything else follows. So this was the problem: How do those changes occur in individuals that lead on, in time, to large social transformations? This question pursued Helen Lynd for more than half a century, from the 1920s to her death in 1982.

Where does my mother's book *On Shame and the Search for Identity* fit in? I suggest that there she sought to explicate the detailed process by means of which, she came to think, there could occur the kind of personality mutation that she believed would in the long run lead to a better world.

If I may attempt a paraphrase, I think she was saying: To go forward into the new is to make oneself vulnerable. But that which is exposed in experiences of shame is not only our ridiculous nakedness, our pathetic inability, our disconcerting errors. It is the lineaments of our particular soul and self; it is our pride; it is our glory. He or she who hopes to make a contribution to the better world, to the new day, must be willing to endure what Erik Erikson called repeated experiences of adolescence and to persist despite many failures.

This is a deeply Christian view of things, recalling the suffering servant who was despised and rejected of men before, in the long sweep of history, at least in some sense triumphing in the end. It is also a profoundly Hegelian attitude, because it envisions the possibility of a dramatic dialectical reversal, what Hegel called an *Aufhebung*.

I think that when my mother glimpsed the connection between, on the one hand, the humiliation of what she called the shame experience, and on the other hand, the discovery of identity, it must have seemed to her like perceiving the structure of DNA. Somehow, I believe it seemed to her, she had laid hold of the intimate mechanism by means of which an individual can change so fundamentally as to be able to bring something new into the world.

MEN HAVE HAD THEIR CHANCE

My wife Alice and I have a recurring dialogue. I say, "Men have had their chance. They have blown it. Now it should be women's turn." Alice rejoins, "What about Golda Meir? What about Margaret Thatcher?"

Nevertheless I think it is a fact that, overall, women tend to be associated with grassroots, nonviolent initiatives for change. Think of the women's "committees" in the Palestinian first *intifada*. Think of the role of Ella Baker in encouraging organizers for the Student Nonviolent Coordinating Committee to proceed by way of face-to-face contact, one local community at a time. Think of the women's "auxiliaries" in strikes that, on closer examination, turn out to be the glue that holds the movement together.

I think a millennium or two in which women took the lead would be helpful to all concerned.

Humanitarian Imperialism and Nonviolent Civil Disobedience

I ALREADY MENTIONED *Kosovo. Students recently rebelled in the streets of Venezuela. I read that they were "helped" by special trainers in nonviolent civil disobedience, some of them from my country, members of the movement that used to be called Otpor! Thousands of comfortable middle-class San Franciscans are protesting against the violence in Tibet, while screaming at local Chinese workers. Things one reads on Darfur are beyond belief. There seems to be no war and no catastrophe that western humanists cannot make worse. How do you relate, in this context, to the relationship between humanitarian imperialism and nonviolent civil disobedience?*

These questions are inter-related: people turn to "humanitarian imperialism" when nonviolence appears to have failed. I will try to sort them out a little.

HUMANITARIAN IMPERIALISM

My very bright sixteen-year-old granddaughter has just written a school essay on Burma. She writes: "Immediate international action is needed to save the weakening protest movement in Burma," and "the international community must act now"; the sanctions imposed after the previous protest movement of 1988 was crushed were "obviously unrealistic"; the people of Burma are "waiting to see what the world will do."

Such sentiments are also voiced in support of intervention in Darfur, as they previously would have justified international action in Rwanda.

Andrej, you know more than I about the last major instance when so-called humanitarian intervention actually occurred, in southeastern Europe. Alas, the "international community" and "the world" as they presently exist are for the most part made up of nation states with capitalist economies, with their own narrow self-interests. I have the following impressions: (1) The United States and NATO members in Europe had no interest in preserving the multi-ethnic Yugoslavia created under Tito; (2) The capitalist nations of the world wished to destroy the last vestiges of public ownership in Serbia and open up the area to foreign private investment; (3) Bombing was chosen as a means of intervention so as to preserve the lives of NATO soldiers without regard for the civilians and ancient bridges of target areas.

The instance of what might be viewed as humanitarian imperialism that most challenges me is the Civil War in the United States, 1861-1865. But before turning to that event I want to make some preliminary points about terrorist violence.

MARXIST AND ANARCHIST TERRORISM: AN HISTORICAL DEAD END

Notwithstanding their many differences, historically Marxism and anarchism have shared a predilection for terrorist violence.

I am anxious not to be misunderstood. In both Marxist and anarchist traditions there have been benign, compassionate persons who literally sought not to hurt a fly. Prince Kropotkin, the communist anarchist, was such a man. Among Marxists, Rosa Luxemburg, when imprisoned for her opposition to World War I, took care when permitted little walks outside her cell not to crush the structures built by ants near her path. After her release from prison in the fall of 1918, Luxemburg's first public act was to call for the abolition of capital punishment. Eugene Debs, also imprisoned for a speech condemning World War I, made such an impression on fellow prisoners in the Atlanta penitentiary that when Debs was set free, the warden briefly released the entire prisoner body from their cells so that they could wave good-bye to him.

Nonetheless, it is just a fact that most Marxists and most anarchists have considered violence the necessary midwife of a new society. By "terrorist violence" I mean violence directed at civilians as well as combatants, the execution of prisoners without individual due process, and the like.

Marxists practiced terrorist violence in the mass execution

of hostages during the Civil War that followed the Bolshevik revolution and in the Purge Trials of the 1930s. It will not do to lay such actions solely at the feet of Stalin. Lenin personally ordered the mass execution of hostages during the Civil War.

Anarchists practiced terrorist violence in assassinations and assassination attempts directed at the Russian Czar, United States president William McKinley, and the chief executive officer of United States Steel, among others. These actions were rationalized as "propaganda of the deed." On occasion they were accompanied by exhortations to make use of the worker's best friend, dynamite.

Sometimes Marxists practiced individual assassination, as in the murder of Trotsky, and sometimes anarchists engaged in mass terrorism, as in the summary execution of groups of prisoners during the Spanish Civil War. Both movements expressed consistent disdain for pacifists.

During the 1960s interest in what can fairly be termed terrorist violence revived in the United States. I can vividly recall an SDS leader toward the end of the decade casually referring in a speech to "icing" and "offing," that is, murdering, political opponents. In her book *Flying Close to the Sun*, former Weatherperson (and my personal friend) Cathy Wilkerson tells how she and others in SDS fell under the spell. The African psychologist Frantz Fanon had presented terrorist violence as a cleansing psychological experience that could help members of oppressed communities experience empowerment. Filled with anger at the apparently unending horror in Vietnam, circles of Weatherpersons sought to create homemade bombs. There was an explosion in early 1970 at a town house in New York City owned by Cathy's parents in which two men, one her lover and another a close friend, as well as a female comrade, were killed.

The plan, never carried out, had been to set off bombs at an officers' recreational event in Fort Dix. With hard-won candor Cathy writes: "Only years later did I realize that it was only because our actions failed, because we had sacrificed some of our own, that our anger could be heard. Had our original plans been successful, any acknowledgment of our outrage against the war would have been overshadowed by others' outrage at us...."

Revolutionaries all over the world who have used violent means have struggled to discern what kinds of violence are appropriate and under what circumstances. I have the impression that there was a difference in this regard between guerrillas in El Salvador and Nicaragua. There were individual assassinations in both countries. Hostages were taken in both countries but to the best of my knowledge, only killed in El Salvador. Only in El Salvador, likewise, were bombs planted in roads that would kill the first persons to come by, whether friend or foe.

The bottom line is that, in my opinion, terrorist violence has been a catastrophic failure whether practiced by Marxists or anarchists. In Palestine, the suicide bombing of Israeli citizens has thrown away the worldwide sympathy that might otherwise have flowed to the victims of occupation. Indeed, "failure" is an inadequate word. I remember two Soviet visitors to Spelman College when I was teaching there. We discussed Stalin's misdeeds which our visitors characterized as *ŏsheebke¢* "mistakes." Thumbing through my Russian-English dictionary I sought the word for "sin."

THE AMERICAN CIVIL WAR

The American Civil War destroyed slavery in the United States at the cost of more than half a million lives. The war began in 1861. The Emancipation Proclamation issued in 1863. In 1865 came the end of the war and Lincoln's assassination.

The strongest nonviolent movement in United States history had sought to end slavery during the period 1820-1860. William Lloyd Garrison was perhaps its principal spokesperson. Characterizing the United States Constitution as "a covenant with death and an agreement with hell" he advocated secession by the free states of the North. More moderate abolitionists deluged Congress with petitions.

After passage of the Fugitive Slave Act in 1850, Northern abolitionists began to advocate and use violence to protect fugitive slaves. Frederick Douglass, an escaped slave and the most prominent African American in the anti-slavery movement, split with Garrison and declared that any means necessary to end slavery were justified. When the war came, both Garrison and Douglass supported the Union armies, and successfully urged the enlistment of African Americans and the uncompensated abolition of slavery as a war measure. A century later the memory of Sherman's march to the sea and other aspects of "humanitarian imperialism" still inspired the resentment and resistance of Southern whites.

Could slavery have been ended in any other way? Was this humanitarian intervention justified?

I do not know the answer.

NONVIOLENT CIVIL DISOBEDIENCE

In the face of all the above, can one speak of nonviolent civil disobedience as anything other than a middle-class parlor game?

First of all, I submit that nonviolent civil disobedience has brought about change at least as fundamental as change engineered by violence. The transformation of South Africa has already been mentioned. Add to that the collapse of Communist regimes throughout Eastern Europe, prompted not by violent insurrection but by masses of people in the streets, carrying candles. A resident of Brno, Czechoslovakia described to my wife and myself the series of demonstrations that brought about the change in that city: each evening, the crowd of demonstrators in the central square grew larger and the police fewer, until finally there were no police at all. Indeed I think it not impossible what when future humanity looks back on the twentieth century, even the Holocaust,

Hiroshima and Nagasaki will appear in retrospect somewhat as the Thirty Years' War in seventeenth century Europe does today, a time of unimaginable dreadfulness; and what will stand out in retrospect as most important is the discovery and initial practice of massive nonviolent civil disobedience. Gandhi and Dr. King, not Hitler and Robert Oppenheimer, may be the lives most studied. School children may be asked to master the details of Gandhi's March to the Sea and the strike of garbage workers in Memphis, as well as World War I and Auschwitz.

It would be silly to suppose that anyone can "prove" this suggested perspective to be correct. It is a little like nonviolence itself. One can only suggest it, flesh out its details in imagination, and then seek to exemplify it.

My wife Alice and I have edited a collection of texts entitled *Nonviolence in America: A Documentary History*, published by Orbis Books in 1995 and now in its sixth printing. I refer the reader to that compendium and here touch on the contributions to the nonviolent tradition of three persons: Henry David Thoreau, David Dellinger, and Barbara Deming.

Thoreau's contribution lay principally in clarifying the idea of civil disobedience, not nonviolence. Thoreau, it should be recalled, delivered a speech in his home town of Concord, Massachusetts entitled "In Defense of Captain John Brown." Thoreau's message was that each one of us can begin, here and now, to do what is right and refuse to do what we know to be wrong. Anywhere in the world that young men and women act on the precept, "Someday they'll have a war and nobody will come," they act in a manner proposed by Thoreau.

There are overtones of Christianity in Thoreau that are often overlooked. The New Testament says that the person who would save his life, must first be prepared to lose it (Matthew 16:25; Mark 8:35; Luke 9:24). In his essay on civil disobedience, Thoreau breathtakingly applies this same thought to the United States as a nation. There are, he writes, cases "in which a people, as well as an individual, must do justice, cost what it may…. This people must cease to hold slaves, and to make war on Mexico, though it cost them their existence as a people." In the same essay he anticipates Archbishop Romero's teaching concerning "accompaniment" of the poor and oppressed. "Under a government which imprisons any unjustly, the true place for a just man is also a prison…. It is there that the fugitive slave, and the Mexican prisoner on parole, and the Indian come to plead the wrongs of his race, should find them."

In my experience the most important practitioners and theorists of nonviolence in the United States, after Thoreau, have been David Dellinger and Barbara Deming. I had the privilege of knowing David and Barbara personally. They were fellow members of the editorial board of *Liberation* magazine. My family also lived for a time with the Dellingers in a commune in New Jersey.

David has written an autobiography entitled From *Yale to Jail*. He was imprisoned twice for refusing to cooperate in any way with military service during World War II. It is an extraordinary saga. (Once, while David was hunger striking, the warden told him that his wife was dying and her dying wish was that David would give up his fast before her death. David decided this was a lie. It was.) The single most significant episode tells what happened when another conscientious objector, a 20-year-old young man named Bill Lovett, came to David for help because "three prisoners…had selected him as the object of their sexual desires." Dellinger decided that he would stand guard in front of Lovett's cell that night.

> As soon as lights were out and the guard had disappeared, a bankrobber friend with a key sprung me from my cell and I went down to Bill's cell…. I had hardly gotten to Bill's cell when four, not three, prisoners arrived…. I began by engaging them in conversation.

(In the Nashville, Tennessee demonstrations against seg-regated restaurants, Reverend James Lawson did exactly the same thing: confronted with hostile hecklers, he started to talk with them.)

> Acting as casually as I could with my back to Bill's door, I said nothing about him but talked about the prison, asking them questions about their "raps" (charges and sentences), work crews, time spent in the Hole, knowledge of other prisons, etc. At last, I mentioned the long hunger strike Bill and I had been on and how we had been force-fed through a tube that was shoved through our noses and down into our throats.

David went on to say of his friend Bill, "He's brave, but he's still a kid." The would-be assailants responded that David was protecting Bill because Bill was his boy. David said, No.

The talk went on. "Soon it was clear that, hit-and-miss, I had reached something inside my companions that was establishing a bond of common experience and shared feel-ings." But the men did not leave, and finally David took the leap of saying that he knew why they were there, and: "I decided to come down here and do my best to prevent it…. I was going to tell whoever it was that they would have to stick a shiv into me before they could stick it into Bill."

Three of the group faded away, leaving Steele, a man with cold and indeed steely eyes and voice, and a terrible reputation.

"Motherfucker," Steele finally said. "You'd let someone stick a shiv into you to save him. Holy motherfuckin' Christ!" Soon after that, Dellinger concludes, "we left together [and] from then on, we were all friends, and none of them ever bothered Bill."

David Dellinger concludes that once inside his cell, "with the door closed, I began shaking all over, sobbing uncontrollably." When he got out of prison he was unable to tell the story. "But after more than four decades of silence, twice in recent years I tried to tell it…. But both times I choked up and couldn't continue. I am crying now."

With equal courage and clarity, Deming undertook in an essay on "Revolution and Equilibrium" to respond to the gurus of the movement of the late 1960s, especially Frantz Fanon, and Carl Oglesby in his book *Containment and Change*. (Barbara's essay may be hard to find. There are lengthy excerpts in *Nonviolence in America*, pp. 405-427.) My wife and I have always prized especially her exposition of "the two hands." Those involved in nonviolent rebellion, she writes, simultaneously obstruct the adversary in pursuing business as usual and make it impossible for the adversary to "strike back without thought and with all his strength. They have as it were two hands upon him—the one calming him, making him ask questions, as the other makes him move." Deming says that if nonviolence is pursued there will be casualties, but fewer persons will be killed, and fewer innocent persons will be killed, than on the path of violence.

In the end it will not suffice to quote texts to each other. We influence one another through our lives.

CONCLUSION

These days all conversations seem to come back to the Zapatistas. What would they have to say about humanistic imperialism and revolutionary nonviolence?

All over Mexico one can purchase miniature representations of Zapatista combatants just under four inches high. They are masked. They hold little pieces of wood, representing guns. What is their message?

As I indicated earlier, the evidence from the Zapatistas' initial "Declaration" in January 1994 is that for a very short time they thought their uprising would develop along traditional Marxist lines. They would advance on the national capital. They would appeal to the workers and peasants in the Mexican Army not to shoot them down. They would seize state power.

Then everything changed and for more than a dozen years the Zapatista strategy has been more or less as follows: From time to time, as in the march on the zocalo and the "other campaign" of 2006, the Zapatistas go forth from their villages, traveling throughout Mexico, talking with other grassroots groups, even addressing the national legislature. They have also brought law suits in an unsuccessful effort to legitimate their indigenous system of justice. For the most part, however, the Zapatistas stay in those villages of Chiapas where they are a majority and in small ways, with inadequate resources, build a new society within the shell of the old.

It is a fundamentally nonviolent strategy. There have been instances where they are classically nonviolent: in one case, when government soldiers sought to build a road into their jungle retreat, Zapatista women blocked the road each day, and the government eventually abandoned the project. But there are government soldiers and military bases all over Chiapas, and the Zapatistas make it very clear that if attacked, they will defend themselves with arms.

This is not my personal belief. I am a pacifist. In the early 1950s, when I applied for noncombatant (1-A-O) status within the United States military, I explained to FBI agents who came to inquire that if there were ever to be a social-ist revolution in the United States I would seek to play a nonviolent role in it. (That was the last time I talked to FBI agents who did not have a warrant. One learns.)

But if the worldwide movement for another world in the twenty-first century is to be a fundamentally nonvio-lent movement, yet prepared to defend itself with arms if attacked, I think that will be a big step forward from classical Marxism and anarchism.

In general:

It has all turned out rather differently than I supposed it would!

When I was a teenager in the years just after World War II, I expected that the United States would be a socialist society by the time I was thirty.

That idea was not as silly as it may seem in retrospect. Most Left economists predicted that when military spending declined after the war, the economy would return to Depression conditions and discontent would mushroom.

On the other hand, I remember saying to a group of my father's graduate students gathered in our family living room that it seemed to me change was most likely to come from colonies and neo-colonies, not from the advanced capitalist world. That expectation was accurate.

Now, as I come toward the end of my journey, I am encouraged by the many manifestations of the new Movement. I hope that the vision Andrej Grubacic and I have sought to sketch in these pages will seem helpful, especially to younger people on whom the future depends.

For myself, finding my way beyond what I have called "Burnham's dilemma," imagining a transition that will not culminate in a single apocalyptic moment but rather express itself in unending creation of self-acting entities that are horizontally linked, is a source of quiet joy.

My strongest wish for the new Movement is that individuals will find it more and more possible to reconcile, to find common ground, to prefigure another world in the way we relate to each other. That process is the inwardness of nonviolence. What is essential is the wanting and the seeking.

Books and Articles Mentioned In or Relevant to the Text

DENIS O'HEARN

Denis is the author of *Nothing but an Unfinished Song: Bobby Sands, the Irish Hunger Striker who Ignited a Generation* (New York: Nation Books, 2006).

ZAPATISMO

Teresa Ortiz' collection of oral histories is *Never Again a World Without Us: Voices of Mayan Women in Chiapas, Mexico* (Washington D.C.: Epica, 2001). The quoted phrase from the First Declaration from the Lacandón jungle is in John Womack, Jr., *Rebellion in Chiapas: An Historical Reader* (New York: The New Press, 1999), p. 249. Womack's summary of the military success and failure of the EZLN offensive is at p. 43. Additional quotations from the proceedings of Zapatista conferences and declarations by Zapatista leaders are from Womack's collection and from *Shadows of Tender Fury: The Letters and Communiques of Subcomandante Marcos and the Zapatista Army of National Liberation*, ed. Frank Bardacke et al. (New York: Monthly Review Press, 1995), and *Our Word is Our Weapon: Selected Writings [by] Subcomandante Marcos*, ed. Juana Ponce de León (New York: Seven Stories Press, 2001).

THE HAYMARKET ANARCHISTS

The most recent treatment of the "Haymarket anarchists" is James Green, *Death in the Haymarket: A Story of Chicago, the*

First Labor Movement and the Bombing That Divided Gilded Age America (New York: Pantheon Books, 2006).

THE WOBBLIES

One may make the acquaintance of the Industrial Workers of the World (the IWW) through its monthly newspaper, the *Industrial Worker*, P.O. Box 13476, Philadelphia, PA 19101. A recent study of interracial unionism among waterfront workers organized by the IWW is Peter Cole, *Wobblies on the Waterfront: Interracial Unionism in Progressive-Era Philadelphia* (Urbana and Chicago: University of Illinois Press, 2007). The similarity of IWW labor organizing and the local unionism of the early 1930s is explored in Staughton Lynd ed., *"We Are All Leaders": The Alternative Unionism of the Early 1930s* (Urbana and Chicago: University of Illinois Press, 1996), pp. 4-7.

THE SPANISH CIVIL WAR

Self-organization during the Spanish Civil War is discussed in the second portion of Noam Chomsky's 1969 essay "Objectivity and Liberal Scholarship," available in *Chomsky on Anarchism* (Edinburgh and Oakland: AK Press, 2005), pp. 40-74.

LUXEMBURG, WEIL AND E.P. THOMPSON

Daniel Singer, mentioned in the question to which this section of the text responds, wrote *Prelude to Revolution: France in May 1968*, second edition (Cambridge, MA.: South End Press, 2002) and *Whose Millennium: Theirs or Ours?* (New York: Monthly Review Press, 1999). The most satisfactory collection of the writings of Rosa Luxemburg is *Rosa Luxemburg Speaks*, ed. Mary-Alice Waters (New York: Pathfinder Press, 1970), which contains her crucial essay on the 1905 Revolution entitled "The Mass Strike." Various works by Edward Thompson are cited throughout "In Memoriam: E.P. Thompson," in Staughton Lynd, *Living*

Inside Our Hope: A Steadfast Radical's Thoughts on Rebuilding the Movement (Ithaca and London: ILR Press, 1997). A useful introduction is a collection edited by his widow Dorothy Thompson, *The Essential Thompson* (New York: The New Press, 2001). Portions of *The Poverty of Theory*, mentioned in our text, will be found at pp. 445-478.

Ignazio Silone's great novel should be read in the English translation of the original Italian text: Bread and Wine (New York and London: Harper & Brothers, 1937).

NEW ANARCHISM

New Anarchism is a term that Andrej Grubacic uses to describe the most recent reinvention of the anarchist thought and practice. What distinguishes the new anarchism of today from the new anarchism of the '60s and '70s, or from the work of US-UK based authors like Murray Bookchin, Paul Goodman, Herbert Read, Colin Ward and Alex Comfort, is its pronounced global perspective. Some of the useful essays on new anarchism include David Graeber's "New Anarchists" in *A Movement of Movements: is Another World Really Possible?*, ed. Tom Mertes (London: Verso, 2004); Andrej Grubacic, "Towards Another Anarchism" in *World Social Forum: Challenging Empires*, ed. Jai Sen and Peter Waterman (Montreal: Black Rose Books, 2007). A good introductory essay by David Graeber and Andrej Grubacic, "Anarchism or the Revolutionary Movement of the 21st Century," is available on line at http://www.zmag.org/znet/viewArticle/9258. See also Leonard Williams, "The New Anarchists," paper presented at the annual meeting of the American Political Science Association, Philadelphia, PA, Aug. 31, 2006, online, pdf, 2008-05-07 http://www.allacademic.com/meta/p152623_index.html.

THE WORKING CLASS

Cathy Wilkerson, *Flying Close to the Sun: My Life and Times as a Weatherman* (New York: Seven Stories Press,

2007), is a penetrating account of the attempt by some SDS organizers to ally with working-class youth. The oral histories of a number of rank-and-file workers, including John Barbero and Ed Mann, are collected in *Rank and File: Personal Histories by Working-Class Organizers*, ed. Alice and Staughton Lynd, third edition (New York: Monthly Review Press, 1988). Writings by the two most acute analysts of the modern labor movement in the United States are gathered in Martin Glaberman, *Punching Out & Other Writings*, ed. and introduced by Staughton Lynd (Chicago: Charles H. Kerr, 2002), and Stan Weir, *Singlejack Solidarity*, ed. and with an afterword by George Lipsitz (Minneapolis: University of Minnesota Press, 2004).

DIRECT ACTION AND ACCOMPANIMENT

Charles Payne, *I've Got the Light of Freedom: The Organizing Tradition and the Mississippi Freedom Struggle* (Berkeley: University of California Press, 1995), offers a point of entry to appreciation of the Student Nonviolent Coordinating Committee (SNCC). Also highly recommended are Wesley C. Hogan, *Many Minds, One Heart: SNCC's Dream for a New America* (Chapel Hill: University of North Carolina Press, 2007), and two accounts by protagonists: *Deep in Our Hearts: Nine White Women in the Freedom Movement* (Athens and London: University of Georgia Press, 2000), and *Ready for Revolution: The Life and Struggles of Stokely Carmichael* (Kwame Ture), ed. Michael Thelwell (New York: Scribner, 2003).

The words ascribed to Adam Michnik come from Jonathan Schell, "Reflections [:] A Better Today," *The New Yorker*, Feb. 3, 1986, p. 60. Myles Horton's autobiography is *The Long Haul: An Autobiography* (New York: Doubleday, 1990). Horton's conversations with Paolo Freire are in *We Make the Road By Walking: Conversations on Education and Social Change* (Philadelphia: Temple University Press, 1990). Staughton Lynd's granddaughter Hilary Rybeck Lynd wrote the quoted paper about Burma for a high school class in Lebanon, New Hampshire in fall 2007.

RADICAL INTELLECTUALS

The exchange between Staughton Lynd and Jesse Lemisch described in Andrej Grubacic's question can be found in "Voices from the Past: Intellectuals, the University, and the Movement," *Journal of American History*, v. 76, no. 2 (September 1989), pp. 479-486.

BURNHAM'S DILEMMA

Burnham's argument is set forth in *The Managerial Revolution: What is Happening in the World* (New York: John Day, 1941). On E. P. Thompson's views about the transition to socialism, see Staughton Lynd, "Edward Thompson's Warrens: On the Transition to Socialism and its Relation to Current Left Mobilizations," in *Labour/Le Travail*, v. 50 (Fall 2002), pp. 175-186.

ACCOMPANIMENT

Robert Lynd's summer in Elk Basin is described in Staughton Lynd, *Living Inside Our Hope*, pp. 22-25. Romero's pastoral letters can be found in Archbishop Oscar Romero, *Voice of the Voiceless: The Four Pastoral Letters and Other Statements* (Maryknoll, New York: Orbis Books, 1985).

INTELLECTUALS AND ACCOMPANIMENT

The soliloquy by Othello quoted in the text occurs in Act IV, Scene II. The citation to *Brandenburg v. Ohio* is 395 U.S. 444 (1969). Howard Zinn tells about climbing a New Hampshire mountain with Staughton Lynd in *You Can't Be Neutral on a Moving Train: A Personal History of Our Times* (Boston: Beacon Press, 1994), p. 181.

DUAL POWER

The three books mentioned are Hannah Arendt, *On Revolution*

(New York: Viking Press, 1963); Leon Trotsky, *History of the Russian Revolution*, three volumes (Ann Arbor: University of Michigan Press, 1961); and John Reed, *Ten Days That Shook the World* (New York: Modern Library, 1935).

PARTICIPATORY ECONOMICS

Many of its advocates call participatory economics "parecon" for short, and it is an anarchist-inspired vision of doing economics differently than under capitalism and authoritarian socialism. Participatory economics elevates certain values, such as solidarity, equity, diversity, self-management, and efficiency, to central organizing principles, and then proposes a set of institutions that can foster those values while accomplishing economic functions. Parecon has workers and consumers councils where workers and consumers employ diverse modes of discussion, debate, and democratic determination to attain true self-management. In parecon, there are no corporate owners and managers deciding outcomes from the top down. Parecon has "balanced job complexes" in which each worker does a fair combination of empowering and rote labor, and has a system of remuneration for effort and sacrifice. Parecon also does away with markets and utilizes instead "participatory planning" of workers' and consumers' councils cooperatively negotiating inputs and outputs for all firms and actors in accord with true and full social costs and benefits of economic activities. The most important works on participatory economics include Michael Albert, *Parecon: Life After Capitalism* (London: Verso, 2004); Michael Albert, *Remembering Tomorrow: from SDS to Life After Capitalism* (New York: Seven Stories Press, 2007); *Real Utopia: Participatory Society for the 21st Century*, ed. Chris Spannos (Oakland: AK Press, 2008).

OLD AND NEW MOVEMENTS, SEEDS OF SOLIDARITY, REBUILDING OUR MOVEMENT

C. Wright Mills, *The Power Elite* (New York: New York

University Press, 2003), fundamentally influenced early SDS, and André Gorz, *Strategy for Labor* (Boston: Beacon Press, 1967), contributed to the search for a "new working class" in the mid-1960s.

The experience of Illinois coal miners in the 1920s and 1930s is narrated in Carl Oblinger, *Divided Kingdom: Work, Community and the Mining Wars in the Central Illinois Coal Fields During the Great Depression*, second edition (Springfield, Illinois State Historical Society, 2004). Camilo Mejia has set out his experience as a war resister in *Road from ar Ramadi: The Private Rebellion of Staff Sergeant Camilo Mejia, An Iraq War Memoir* (Chicago: Haymarket Books, 2007). As to prisoners, and their potential to overcome racial division and act together, two accounts are Staughton Lynd, *Lucasville: The Untold Story of a Prison Uprising* (Philadelphia: Temple University Press, 2004), and Jamie Bissonette, *When the Prisoners Ran Walpole: A True Story in the Movement for Prison Abolition* (Cambridge, Mass.: South End Press, 2008).

ANARCHISM AND VISION

Anarchist theorists mentioned in Grubacic's question are Gustav Landauer, Paul Goodman, Colin Ward and Murray Bookchin. Gustav Landauer (1870-1919) was one of the leading theorists on anarchism in Germany in the end of the nineteenth and the beginning of the twentieth centuries. His teachings have been kept alive by his disciples Erich Mühsam (1878-1934) and Martin Buber (1878- 1965). Readers should be acquainted with Buber's anarchist masterpiece *Paths in Utopia* (Syracuse: Syracuse University Press, 1996). Paul Goodman (1911-1972) was one of the most important—and much neglected—American anarchists. His anarchist works include *Drawing the Line: Political Essays*, ed. Taylor Stoehr (New York: Free Life Editions, 1977); *New Reformation: Notes of a Neolithic Conservative* (New York: Random House, 1970); *Decentralizing Power: Paul Goodman's Social Criticism*, ed. Taylor Stoehr (Montreal:

Black Rose Books, 1994); *Format and Anxiety: Paul Goodman Critiques the Media*, ed. Taylor Stoehr (Brooklyn, NY: Autonomedia, 1995); *Growing Up Absurd: Problems of Youth in the Organized System* (New York: Random House, 1960; London: Victor Gollancz, 1961); *Utopian Essays and Practical Proposals* (New York: Random House, 1962); *The Community of Scholars* (New York: Random House, 1962); and *Compulsory Mis-education* (New York: Horizon Press, 1964). Murray Bookchin (1921-2006) was an American anarchist and philosopher, founder of the social ecology movement, and libertarian municipalism—a left libertarian vision of a future society. His most important anarchist works include *Post-Scarcity Anarchism* (Oakland: AK Press, 2004); *The Spanish Anarchists: The Heroic Years* (Oakland: AK Press, 1997); *The Ecology of Freedom: The Emergence and Dissolution of Hierarchy* (Oakland: AK Press, 2005); and *Urbanization Without Cities* (Montreal: Black Rose Books, 1991). Colin Ward (1924-) was an editor of the British anarchist newspaper *Freedom* from 1947 to 1960, and the founder and editor of the monthly journal Anarchy from 1961 to 1970. His many works include *Anarchism: A Very Short Introduction* (New York: Oxford University Press, 2004); *Talking Schools* (London: Freedom Press, 1995); *Housing: An Anarchist Approach* (London: Freedom Press, 1976); and *Anarchy in Action* (New York: Harper & Row, 1973).

AMERICAN RADICAL HISTORIANS

Thomas Humphrey's comment about the "box on the side of the page" comes from his "Leases and Revolution in New York's Hudson Valley," an unpublished paper prepared for a conference on "Class and Class Struggles in the Atlantic World" (Sept. 2003). David Brion Davis's review of Peter Linebaugh and Marcus Rediker, *The Many-Headed Hydra: Sailors, Slaves, Commoners, and the Hidden History of the Revolutionary Atlantic* (Boston: Beacon Press, 2000), appeared in *The New York Review of Books*, July 5, 2001.

The books on slavery mentioned in the text include Marcus Rediker, *The Slave Ship: A Human History* (New York: Viking Penguin, 2007), and Simon Schama, *Rough Crossings: Britain, the Slaves and the American Revolution* (New York: HarperCollins, 2006). In "English Abolition: The Movie," *The New York Review of Books*, June 14, 2007, Adam Hochschild suggests that the centrality of Wilberforce in the film "Amazing Grace" results from the fact that the principal financier of the movie, Philip Anschutz, is a major backer of the Christian right and has "long sought to make a film about Wilberforce," who "thought gambling almost as sinful as slavery" and is a cult figure among American fundamentalists.

The open letter to John Sweeney appeared in "The Rise of the House of Labor," *In These Times*, Dec. 25, 1995. Barbara Ehrenreich's comment on Andrew Stern is quoted in Steve Early, review of John Sweeney, *America Needs a Raise*, and Andrew Stern, *A Country That Works*, in *Working USA*, v. 10, no. 1 (Mar. 2007).

Jim Pope's findings on the self-organization of miners is set forth in James Gray Pope, "The Western Pennsylvania Coal Strike of 1933, Part I: Lawmaking from Below and the Revival of the United Mine Workers," *Labor History*, v. 44, no. 1 (2003), pp. 15-48.

ECONOMIC INTEREST AND IDEOLOGY, SONS OF LIBERTY
In *Class Conflict, Slavery and the United States Constitution: Ten Essays* (Indianapolis and New York: Bobbs-Merrill, 1967), Staughton Lynd recounts in more detail his research on farm tenants and artisans summarized in the text. James C. Scott's analysis of the ideology of the oppressed appears in *Weapons of the Weak: Everyday Forms of Peasant Resistance* (New Haven and London: Yale University Press, 1985).

HISTORY BY PARTICIPANTS IN THE STRUGGLE
Wesley Hogan kindly provided transcripts of minutes of

the SNCC staff meetings in June and November 1964. The minutes are to be found in the SNCC papers at the King Center in Atlanta, microfilm reel 3, frames 975-992, and reel 11, frames 935-959.

MILITANT INVESTIGATION

Militant investigation, or militant research, aims at producing knowledge useful for militant or activist ends. As a practice of intellectual production, militant investigation does not accept a distinction between active researcher and passive research subjects. Activists using this approach make use of a range of types of inquiry that resemble social and oral history, ethnography, journalism. This term was made known by the Italian Marxist tradition, where it is also known as co-research, or class composition analysis. The recent interest in militant investigation is best captured in *Constituent Imagination: Militant Investigation, Collective Theorization*, ed. David Graeber, Stephen Shukaitis and Erika Biddle (Oakland: AK Press, 2007).

HISTORY AS ACCOMPANIMENT

The quoted comment about "dessert" is from Mid-Atlantic Radical Historians Organization (MARHO), *Visions of History: Interviews with E. P. Thompson [and others]* (New York: Pantheon Books, 1976), p. 154. Mumia Abu Jamal's history of the Black Panther Party is *We Want Freedom: A Life in the Black Panther Party* (Cambridge, MA.: South End Press, 2004). Staughton Lynd tells about his work with steelworkers in *The Fight Against Shutdowns: Youngstown's Steel Mill Closings* (San Pedro, CA: Singlejack Books, 1983). His work with prisoners is presented in the previously-cited *Lucasville: The Untold Story of a Prison Uprising* (Philadelphia: Temple University Press, 2004). He has also co-authored a play about the Lucasville disturbance that was produced in seven Ohio cities in April 2007.

PEOPLES' GLOBAL ACTION AND "COUNTER-SUMMITS"

Peoples' Global Action (PGA) is the most important net-work of the global movement of movements. PGA was officially born in the North, in Geneva 1998, but, like the whole movement of movements, it's a curious meeting of Northern activists with peasants struggling in the Global South. It was born out of an exceptional meeting. Among the participants who endorsed its "manifesto" were the Canadian Postal Workers, Earth First!, European and Korean activists, Maori, U'wa and Ogoni people. No one is empowered to act as a PGA spokesperson. No one can represent PGA. This network has no spokespeople, no "experts," no professional theoreticians. It is not well known that the very idea of de-centralized Global Days of Action ("counter-summits") was an invention of direct-action activists around Peoples' Global Action. These, PGA-inspired demonstrations, from Seattle onwards, provided a context within which we redeveloped creative forms of direct action, like street parties, blockages, occupations, anti-capitalist carnivals and so on. The idea of decentralization led to the establishment of other networks such as Indymedia. The official web site of the organization can be found at www.agp.org.

THE GLOBAL MOVEMENT OF MOVEMENTS

Among many books devoted to this topic, a few works are of an outstanding quality: David Graeber, *Direct Action: An Ethnography* (Oakland: AK Press, 2008); *World Social Forum: Challenging Empires*, ed. Jai Sen and Peter Waterman (Montreal: Black Rose Books, 2007); Boaventura de Sousa Santos, *The Rise of the Global Left: World Social Forum and Beyond* (London: Zed Books, 2006); *We are Everywhere: The Irresistible Rise of Global Anticapitalism*, ed. Notes from Nowhere (London: Verso, 2004).

ANABAPTISM AND MOVEMENTS OF THE 1950S AND 1960S

John Dominic Crossan presents Jesus of Nazareth as a

rebel against the Roman Empire in *The Historical Jesus: The Life of a Mediterranean Jewish Peasant* (San Francisco: HarperSanFrancisco, 1991). In *Excavating Jesus: Beneath the Stones, Behind the Texts*, written together with archaeologist Jonathan L. Reed (San Francisco: HarperSanFrancisco, 2001), Crossan offers archaeological evidence for the proposition that Nazareth in Jesus' lifetime was experiencing a commercialization not unlike present-day globalization, with the result that peasants and artisans were falling into debt and losing their means of livelihood. *The Birth of Christianity: Discovering What Happened in the Years Immediately After the Execution of Jesus* (San Francisco: HarperSanFrancisco, 1998), argues that early Christians, like contemporary radicals, developed somewhat different ways of life, on the one hand in isolated Utopian communities and on the other hand in the world.

WU MING, ANABAPTISTS AND NATIVE AMERICANS

The authors of the novels *Q* and *Manitunia*, mentioned in Andrej Grubacic's question, are Wu Ming and Luther Blisset. In 1994, hundreds of European artists, activists and pranksters adopted and shared the same identity. They worked together to tell the world a great story, create a legend, give birth to a new kind of folk hero. In January 2000, a fifth person joined the four authors of *Q* and a new band of authors was born, Wu Ming. "Wu Ming," or "anonymous," is a Chinese word, and the name of the band is meant both as a tribute to dissidents and as a refusal of the celebrity-making machine which turns the author into a star.

CONSENSUS DECISIONMAKING

In *Society and Puritanism in Pre-revolutionary England* (London: Secker and Warburg, 1964), at pp. 493-494, Christopher Hill suggested that "only one form of cultivation was possible at one time in the common fields," and this fact underlay the Quaker sense of the meeting that "carried over into the modern world something of the desire for unanimity which meant so much to the medieval communities."

PALESTINE AND ISRAEL

The interviews collected by Staughton Lynd, Alice Lynd and Sam Bahour in Youngstown, Ohio and in Palestine were published in their *Homeland: Oral Histories of Palestine and Palestinians* (New York: Olive Branch Press, 1994). Sarah Cheyes describes "yaghestan," as quoted, on p. 68 of her *The Punishment of Virtue: Inside Afghanistan after the Taliban* (New York: The Penguin Press, 2006), and then carries this theme through the remainder of her extraordinary book.

ANTI-WAR MOVEMENTS IN THE 1960S AND IN THE NEW MILLENNIUM, SELF-SACRIFICE

The reader who wishes to know more about Norman Morrison's self-immolation, and its effect on Secretary McNamara, the Vietnamese, and Brian Willson, should begin with Anne Morrison Welsh, *Held in the Light: The Sacrifice of Norman Morrison and His Family's Search for Meaning* (Maryknoll, New York: Orbis Books, 2008). Paul Goodman's poem appears in his *Collected Poems*, ed. Taylor Stoehr (New York: Random House, 1973), pp. 180-181, and is excerpted with permission. Norman Morrison was strongly advised by the Quaker meeting which employed him that he should not take part in the August 1965 Assembly of Unrepresented People; see Anne Morrison Welsh, "Norman Morrison: Deed of Death, Deed of Life," in *Friends and the Vietnam War* (Wallingford, PA.: Pendle Hill, 1998), p. 128. Deborah Shapley reports Secretary McNamara's state of mind after he witnessed Morrison's suicide in *Promise and Power: The Life and Times of Robert McNamara* (Boston: Little, Brown and Company, 1993), pp. 353-355. As for the impact of Morrison's action on the Vietnamese, see, in addition to Ms. Welsh's memoir, Staughton Lynd and Tom Hayden, *The Other Side* (New York: New American Library,

1966), pp. 60, 62, 69-70, 74, 80, 83; and on Brian Willson, S. Brian Willson, *On Third World Legs*, with an Introduction by Staughton Lynd (Chicago: Charles H. Kerr, 1992), pp. 19-20.

CENTRAL AMERICAN SOLIDARITY
The writings of Margaret Randall that are particularly relevant are *Walking to the Edge: Essays of Resistance* (Boston: South End Press, 1991); *Gathering Rage: The Failure of 20th Century Revolutions to Develop a Feminist Agenda* (New York: Monthly Review Press, 1992); and *Sandino's Daughters Revisited: Feminism in Nicaragua* (New Brunswick, N.J.: Rutgers University Press, 1994).

DO WE NEED RIGHTS?
Staughton Lynd's article "Communal Rights" is reprinted in *Living Inside Our Hope*, pp. 89-110.

WAR, PEACE AND NONVIOLENCE
Carol Gilligan, *In a Different Voice: Psychological Theory and Women's Development* (Cambridge, Mass. and London: Harvard University Press, 1982), and Helen Merrell Lynd, *On Shame and the Search for Identity* (New York: Harcourt, Brace and Company, 1982) explicate the two points of view—or the two aspects of a single feminist point of view—identified in the text.

NONVIOLENT CIVIL DISOBEDIENCE
The incident involving Bill Lovett is told in David Dellinger, *From Yale to Jail: The Life Story of a Moral Dissenter* (New York: Pantheon Books, 1993), pp. 132-137.

Index

About the Authors

STAUGHTON LYND taught American history at Spelman College and Yale University. He was director of Freedom Schools in the 1964 Mississippi Freedom Summer. An early leader of the movement against the Vietnam war, he was blacklisted and unable to continue as an academic. He then became a lawyer, and in this capacity has assisted rank-and-file workers and prisoners for the past thirty years. He has written, edited, or co-edited with his wife Alice Lynd more than a dozen books.

ANDREJ GRUBACIC is a dissident from the Balkans. A radical historian and sociologist, he is the author of *Don't Mourn, Balkanize: Essays after Yugoslavia, The Globaliztion of Refusal,* and the forthcoming *Hidden History of American Democracy,* and edited *From Here to There: The Staughton Lynd Reader.* A fellow traveler of Zapatista-inspired direct action movements, in particular Peoples' Global Action, and a co-founder of Global Balkans Network and Balkan *Z Magazine,* he is associate professor and department chair in Cultural Anthropology and Social Transformation at California Institute of Integral Studies.

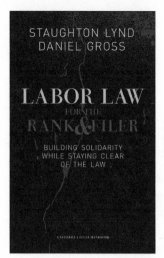

PM Press was founded in 2007 as an independent publisher with offices in the US and UK, and a veteran staff boasting a wealth of experience in print and online publishing. We produce and distribute short as well as large run projects, timely texts, and out of print classics.

We seek to create radical and stimulating fiction and non-fiction books, pamphlets, t-shirts, visual and audio materials to entertain, educate and inspire you. We aim to distribute these through every available channel with every available technology—whether that means you are seeing anarchist classics at our bookfair stalls; reading our latest vegan cookbook at the café over (your third) microbrew; downloading geeky fiction e-books; or digging new music and timely videos from our website.

PM Press is always on the lookout for talented and skilled volunteers, artists, activists and writers to work with. If you have a great idea for a project or can contribute in some way, please get in touch.

PM Press . PO Box 23912 . Oakland CA 94623
www.pmpress.org